"From the opening lines of 'The Sadhana of Mahamudra,' the practitioner is plunged into a sacred world at once devastatingly brilliant and profoundly human. The reverberation that arises from the combined energies of the natural world, our longing and devotion to become free, and the obstacles of fear, complacence, and neurotic habit patterns that keep us bound and suffering, breaks us open into an experience of vivid presence and openness through which the awakening heart of love shines naturally and fully. Especially in these challenging times, as I work to bring the Buddhist teachings to others, I feel how much we need the formulations of devotion, trust, faith, and sanity that the sadhana evokes with such richness and depth. I am so excited that this collection of commentaries and teachings on 'The Sadhana of Mahamudra,' edited by Carolyn Gimian, is entering the world at this particular time when its messages are so deeply necessary and healing."
—ELIZABETH MONSON, author of *Tales of a Mad Yogi*

"'The Sadhana of Mahamudra' provides the source code for a powerful, meaningful, and vibrant life on earth. This text has had a profound impact on the arc of my life and work in the world. It radiates the essence of the core practices of Tibetan Buddhism, embodying this wisdom tradition as it enters the stream of life in the West, transforming our culture and society."
—DAVID NICHTERN, senior teacher in the lineage of Chögyam Trungpa Rinpoche, founder of Dharma Moon

"These brilliant and profound tantric teachings fearlessly proclaim all-pervasive wisdom. They invite us to step beyond aggression and the warfare of materialism. Through our reading study and practice, we join the vast celebration of wakefulness."
—GAYLON FERGUSON, author of *Welcoming Beginner's Mind*

"I first came to know 'The Sadhana of Mahamudra' some twenty years ago. A collection of students dedicated to this amazing offering from Chögyam Trungpa Rinpoche generously decided to share this great treasure of our times with me. To this day, it continues to move me on profound levels. This amazing guide, *The Sadhana of Mahamudra: Teachings on Devotion and Crazy Wisdom*, will no doubt inspire both longtime students and new seekers to connect with this sacred gift."
—OWSLEY BROWN III, chair of Festival of Faiths

T0370106

The Sadhana of Mahamudra

Teachings on Devotion and Crazy Wisdom

Chögyam Trungpa

FOREWORDS BY
Diana J. Mukpo and Samuel Bercholz

SHAMBHALA

Shambhala Publications, Inc.
2129 13th Street
Boulder, Colorado 80302
www.shambhala.com

Cover art: "Hum" by Chögyam Trungpa
Cover design: Daniel Urban-Brown

9 8 7 6 5 4 3 2 1

Printed in the United States of America

Shambhala Publications makes every effort to print on acid-free, recycled paper.
Shambhala Publications is distributed worldwide by Penguin Random House, Inc.,
and its subsidiaries.

LIBRARY OF CONGRESS CATALOGING-IN-PUBLICATION DATA
Names: Trungpa, Chögyam, 1939–1987 author.
Title: The Sadhana of Mahamudra: teachings on devotion and crazy wisdom / Chögyam Trungpa.
Description: Boulder: Shambhala Publications, 2025. | Includes bibliographical references and
index.
Identifiers: LCCN 2024013668 | ISBN 9781645473787 (trade paperback)
Subjects: LCSH: Mahāmudrā (Tantric rite) | Meditation—Buddhism. | Tantric Buddhism—
Doctrines. | Padma Sambhava, approximately 717–approximately 762.
Classification: LCC BQ8921.M35 T725 2025 | DDC 294.3/4435—dc23/eng/20240706
LC record available at https://lccn.loc.gov/2024013668

CONTENTS

FOREWORD

In the modern world, religion often has a bad reputation because of all the damage that has been done in the name of religious faith. When people have a fanatical allegiance to religion, it can lead to very destructive action. If our religious motivations are based on fear, looking for an external savior, or eliminating our personal problems, then religion can become an agent of spiritual materialism. If we don't take responsibility for our own lives and instead give in to fear and blame, that can cause tremendous damage in the world.

The Vidyadhara, Chögyam Trungpa Rinpoche, presented the pure teachings of the buddhadharma. That approach and the basic approach of Buddhism altogether is based on discovering realization within oneself rather than looking for it outside. That understanding allows us to care for ourselves and to experience sanity in a simple, straightforward way. With the tools that the buddhadharma provides, we also have the capacity to effect change in the world.

In 1968, when I first visited Samye Ling, which was Rinpoche's practice center in Scotland, he had only recently returned from his trip to Bhutan, where he had discovered "The Sadhana of Mahamudra." He brought the text back with him, newly translated into English. I remember that the translated text was crudely mimeographed on colored sheets of paper.

The next time I saw him, again at Samye Ling, he was recovering from a car accident that had left him crippled on one side. I realized that he was a completely different person than he had been before his accident. It wasn't just his physical demeanor that had changed. Before the accident, he had been so youthful, pure, and light. Now he was more heavy and solid, he seemed much older, and he had an unfathomable quality that I hadn't experienced before. He was transformed. In the past, I had noticed how he radiated loving kindness. Now, although his kindness was still apparent, there was a wrathful quality.

Undoubtedly, receiving "The Sadhana of Mahamudra" as a terma was connected with this powerful time in Rinpoche's life when his manifestation and his teaching style changed and blossomed. This was also a time filled with difficulties and obstacles.

Part of the power of Trungpa Rinpoche was that he himself fully manifested the principles that he taught. He never took a shortcut for himself. He experienced a great deal of personal pain and suffering. He always took responsibility for himself and never allowed himself—or his students—a break. That adherence to genuineness was a powerful weapon for cutting self-deception, one that he gave to all his students. "The Sadhana of Mahamudra" is one of the most powerful practices we have because of how it directly addresses human issues and problems of human life.

I'm delighted that the teachings that Rinpoche gave on this practice are now being published in this new edition. I hope that the practice of the sadhana will continue for decades and generations to come—and that it will help liberate us and enable us to help solve the terrible problems we have created for ourselves in this world.

Diana J. Mukpo
May 2, 2024

FOREWORD

The first time I encountered "The Sadhana of Mahamudra" was in 1971 at the San Francisco Dharmadhatu, the first urban center that Chögyam Trungpa created in America. He was visiting San Francisco, and during a group session on the full-moon night of his visit, he handed out copies of a crudely mimeographed text called "The Sadhana of Mahamudra." He asked everyone who was there to chant this. I remember thinking that it was very "foreign," to me. I had no idea what a *sadhana* was and very little idea of what *mahamudra* was. It had many names of people in it that I had never heard of, and it involved a lot of mumbling, which was ostensibly reciting mantras. It was completely different from anything I had ever done before. At that time, in these very early days, we were told that we should only do the sadhana as a group practice on the full moon.

That became a regular practice for me and many other people. I was already a publisher in those days, having published the North American edition of Trungpa Rinpoche's book *Meditation in Action*. He was very interested in meeting his publisher when he first came to America. We had established a company called Shambhala Publications, and Rinpoche was very interested in how an American publisher had come up with that name, which was already widely known in Asia as a mythical utopia, one could say.

By the time I encountered "The Sadhana of Mahamudra" for the first time, I was already his student, and we were starting to talk together about new publishing projects and many other things. As I became familiar with the sadhana and began to realize its inherent power, I thought to myself, *It's ridiculous that we're squinting to make out the words of this text from a very badly reproduced copy of a copy of the original English translation.* So I was inspired to typeset the sadhana in hot metal and have it produced as a letterpress edition. I also commissioned artwork from Glen Eddy, who was a very talented painter of Tibetan thangkas. He created a number of wonderful drawings to accompany the text of the sadhana.

We decided to make the dimensions of the new version of the sadhana similar to a traditional Tibetan *pecha*, or text. I worked with Wesley Tanner on this project. He had a letterpress shop in Berkeley called ARIF Press. We printed something like 1,500 copies of the sadhana and distributed them to all the meditation centers that Chögyam Trungpa had established in North America. People used this edition for a number of years, until the copies were pretty much gone. They kept disappearing from the centers. Practitioners would take them home and fail to return them! So then, a new edition was published around 1988 in a different format by the Nalanda Translation Committee, and that's still available today.

The Shambhala Publications edition of *The Sadhana of Mahamudra* includes the complete text of the sadhana, along with all the teachings that Trungpa Rinpoche gave on the meaning and significance of this text. This is the first time that the text has been made available to a general audience without any restrictions placed on it. So, it's come a long way from being practiced solely in a group on the full moon to now being available to the public. Culturally, the situation is quite different from what it was in the early 1970s. Tibetan Buddhism has become much more a part of the culture. There are many practice texts, or sadhanas, that are easily available. We feel that the time has come for this material to be more publicly known and practiced, without the restrictions of that time—when no one had a clue of what this precious text might be or what it might mean.

I've been practicing "The Sadhana of Mahamudra" for more than fifty years now, and I find it actually more profound than ever, especially given the continuing degeneration of the planet through pollution, climate change, and all those environmental issues, as well as physical, psychological, and spiritual materialism being ever more rampant.

I still introduce the sadhana as it was introduced to me. I just say: "It's the full moon. Let's practice this sadhana. Just sit down and follow along." I'm part of a loosely organized sangha that meets every month or so, and the last time we met, I presented "The Sadhana of Mahamudra" to the group. Out of twenty-five people or so, only four or five of the people there had ever heard of this practice. Nevertheless, they found it extremely powerful and moving. As time goes on, I find the sadhana is ever more poignant and valuable in working with the issues of our time. It's a way of working with the difficulties of this life and also a way to view and clarify our own minds.

"The Sadhana of Mahamudra" is a true treasure of the mind of Chögyam Trungpa Rinpoche, who was a seminal figure in bringing the practice lineage to the West. As I have said before, the Vidyadhara Chögyam Trungpa Rinpoche was the Guru Rinpoche of the West.

He was a living emanation for our time of all the lineage figures who appear in the sadhana: principally the Karmapas and Guru Rinpoche. What is presented in the sadhana is not just philosophy. It is Trungpa Rinpoche communicating his wakefulness, or enlightenment.

Having played an early role in the publication of "The Sadhana of Mahamudra" for the close disciples of Trungpa Rinpoche, I am so pleased that Shambhala Publications can now present this text and the extraordinary teachings associated with it to the broad audience of those who follow the path of the Buddha.

Samuel Bercholz
May 27, 2024

INTRODUCTION

———

"The Sadhana of Mahamudra" was born in extraordinary circumstances: during a retreat in a cave in Bhutan called Taktsang, a place where the great yogi and teacher Padmasambhava practiced in the eighth century. When Chögyam Trungpa Rinpoche traveled there in 1968, accompanied by one of his Western students, he was at an impasse. In 1959, he had engineered a daring escape from his Tibetan homeland and made a new home in a vastly different world in India. In just a few short years, when he moved to Great Britain, he found himself in a completely new milieu yet again. By 1968 he had been in the West long enough to have an appreciation for its ways. He found himself deeply inspired to bring the profound practice and insight he had inherited into an entirely new culture that would benefit from what he had to offer. And yet he was stuck.

He had been trained since the age of five in a rigorous system of study and meditative practice, one intended as a direct path to the Buddha's realization. Those methods of training had existed nearly unchanged since the twelfth century.[1] He longed to share that training and understanding but couldn't quite see how to communicate it in his new environment. The buddhadharma was a foreign plaything in his new home, often intellectualized or romanticized. When he fled Tibet, he left behind the teachers who had trained him since he was a child, the monasteries he was responsible for, and a society in which his role was clear. In Britain he studied comparative religion, philosophy, politics, and economics at Oxford University, as well as flower arranging and calligraphy with local teachers, and he eventually started a small meditation center in the Scottish countryside. Wearing monk's robes in this adopted homeland, he often felt he was treated like a piece of Asian statuary, uprooted from its sacred context and set on display in the British Museum. Few other Tibetan teachers offered support, at the time feeling that Westerners were sweet but uncivilized and not capable of training in genuine dharma—at least at present. Deep in his heart, he felt it must be otherwise. What to do?

In later years, Trungpa Rinpoche counseled students faced with daunting circumstances not to drive themselves into "the high wall of insanity,"[2] desperately trying to will and think themselves out of a corner. Instead, he advised, allow the uncertainty of those pivotal moments to unfold completely and rely on one's meditative discipline to keep oneself on the ground, just as the Buddha famously touched the earth directly prior to his enlightenment. As he describes in both the first talk and last talk in this book, while on retreat in the cave at Taktsang, Trungpa Rinpoche let the uncertainty build and build. And a breakthrough occurred.

With great clarity, he saw that the obstacle to a flowering of the Buddha's teaching and practice in the modern world was not simply the lack of good cross-cultural communication. It was materialism. Not the focus on material wealth alone, but a subtler, deeper form of apparent comfort: spiritual materialism. He coined this term to describe the desire for a spiritual path that led you to *become* something, to attain a state of which you could be proud, instead of a path that unmasked your self-deception. The conviction dawned that if people could only see and cut through spiritual materialism, they would find the genuine spiritual path; it would be fulfilling in a way that made attainments uninteresting and unnecessary. He left the retreat intent on finding students willing to make this journey with him.

One of the provisions he offered students for that journey was "The Sadhana of Mahamudra," the very text he had discovered in the retreat. Before too long, he established the tradition of having the sadhana practiced on the new- and full-moon evenings every month in the centers he founded. In those early days and to this day, it was offered to people at all levels of experience with meditation, from the very newest to the most experienced. As the Nalanda Translation Committee has written:

> In offering a sadhana in English to anyone coming through our doors, the Vidyadhara gave beginning students a taste of the tantric way of engaging the world: the fearless view that all aspects of mind are workable and that whatever we experience is sacred world—a single circle beyond confusion. This practice also served as the primary statement for the Vajradhatu/Shambhala[3] way of engaging the dharma. It proclaims that genuine dharma

becomes possible only when physical, psychological, and spiritual materialism are cut through.[4]

While a sadhana can be read as a document ("like a newspaper," Trungpa Rinpoche once said) to glean its meaning and its messages, it is not a document per se. It is a ritual meant to be enacted. In practicing "The Sadhana of Mahamudra," we reenact the realization that gave birth to it. We inhabit Trungpa Rinpoche's worldview. The vivid imagistic language of the sadhana (e.g., "the thick, black fog of materialism") has raw power that requires little commentary. We get a feeling for it when we first recite it, and ever after. We take a leap, a leap to a place we already are, as Trungpa Rinpoche indicated. Practicing the sadhana with little preparation, therefore, can work quite well. The sights, sounds, and feelings wash through and over us and convey a feeling of connectedness and self-liberation.

At a certain point, though, the sadhana cries out for deeper investigation. So much of its language is deeply encoded. It comes out of a rich context that we are being invited into. For example, what does it mean for us to say out loud, "My whole being is Dorje Trolö" or "the experience of joy becomes devotion"?

Precisely because the practice of the sadhana can take on deeper meaning as we become more familiar with its context, Trungpa Rinpoche presented two seminars in 1975 to explain the literal meaning of unfamiliar terms and unpack the deeper meanings that lay within. Taken together, these two seminars (bolstered by an excellent glossary in this volume) form the basis for a commentary on the practice. Following long tradition, we read and study the commentary to derive more richness from the practice itself. It lives and breathes, changing each time we enact it, yet staying fundamentally, adamantinely, the same.

In these ten talks, Trungpa Rinpoche lays the groundwork we need to gain a deeper appreciation of the sadhana. At the same time, he uses the sadhana commentary as a vehicle for delivering key messages about how to be a good student, and in particular how to be a good student within the tantric tradition—at whatever level you choose to engage it. Therefore, many of the talks center on the theme of devotion and how we relate to the teacher, the spiritual friend, and the guru. In essence, the sadhana *is* an act of devotion. As a result, it's critical for us to refine our understanding of what devotion is and is not.

To begin with, Trungpa Rinpoche establishes in no uncertain terms that the guru is not a hero to be worshipped or a parental figure to be impressed. Devotion is not an act of theater we produce, hiding our nasty bits behind the backstage curtain. In the talk on surrendering from the second seminar (chapter 9), Trungpa Rinpoche ties devotion into the act of offering. Following a strongly devotional section in the sadhana when we call out to the teachers of the lineage ("I still aspire to see your face") and then identify with their realization ("It is wonderful to arrive in your domain"), we offer everything we have of every kind ("Food, wealth, companionship, fame, and sensual attachments"). He makes clear that offering is essential and total. We have to "give the giver." The essence of spiritual materialism is to make an offering of our impressive spiritual prowess, hoping to be confirmed by the teacher. In the surrendering chapter, we learn that the point of offering is to be emptied out, to reveal every corner of our world in all its neurotic glory. Only then are we ready to receive real teachings, because ego is being undercut.

"No one is home" and therefore the teachings have room to take up residence in our hearts and minds. Devotion is not a business deal where we negotiate payment for the goods. It's a literal surrender, whereby we allow the guru to ransack our treasury, taking what we hold most dear. We let it happen because we've never experienced a way of being as profound as we find embodied in the gurus of the lineage. As the subtitle of the sadhana indicates, they are an "ocean of siddhas," beings who exhibit the kind of power that is hard to ignore.

In one of the most vivid and potent talks (chapter 7), Trungpa Rinpoche says the world we offer up to the siddhas is a charnel ground, a place where birth and death occur all the time simultaneously: "the chaos that takes place in our neurosis is the only home ground that we can build our mandala on." And by *our* mandala, he means the mandala of the siddhas, because we *are* them, and like them we "fearlessly enjoy the mahamudra and attain the experience of maha ati"—referring to the two great Indo-Tibetan meditation traditions embodied in the sadhana, about which we'll learn more below.

In this charnel-ground talk, he provides commentary on the section of the sadhana that describes the ground on which the siddhas will have their palace: "that great graveyard in which lie buried the complexities of samsara and nirvana . . . the universal ground of everything . . . the basis of freedom and also the basis of confusion." If we are to fully embody the realization of the siddhas, we first have to be honest with ourselves and stop looking for something else, somewhere else, an alternative reality that is a "better, higher, more loving, less aggressive place." The search for a holy place set apart is once again the quest of spiritual materialism, a fool's errand. Realization will arise only within the mess we find ourselves in.

In the iconography of the sadhana, atop this foundation of ruthless honesty sits a huge rock mountain. In the commentary, Trungpa Rinpoche lets us know that this rock represents faith—not faith in something outer, but rather faith that what we see is what we get. It is, he says, "seeing things as they are—whatever they might be—precisely, directly, and without any hesitation." This is the foundation on which genuine practice is built, and this faith that obliterates wishful thinking is represented as solid rock. On top of this rock sits a triangle, which "radiates the blazing red light of inner warmth and compassion." The triangle is a standard tantric symbol that represents a cervix that constantly gives birth.

What it gives birth to is openness: "giving, opening, extending yourself completely to the situation, to what is available around you, being fantastically exposed." In spiritual materialism, we escape reality by creating our own territory. We give birth to further territory that has our label on it, and therefore we become more closed off. By contrast, in the sacred mandala invoked in the sadhana, our ground is our commitment not to attempt escape. From that emerges a rock of faith in seeing things as they are. On top of that is a birth canal that continually breeds openness and exposure to whatever presents itself. This is a path, a process of development over time, but in the sadhana it's represented as a physical reality that exists all at once.

On the foundation of honesty, faith, and openness, the main figures of the sadhana will take their seat. We offer them everything ("filling the whole universe") and we ask of them the ultimate ("that confusion may dawn as wisdom"). The central figure is a combination of two great lineage figures, one from the maha ati lineage of the Nyingma (Padmasambhava in his wrathful manifestation as Dorje Trolö) and one from the mahamudra lineage of the Kagyü (Karma Pakshi, the second Karmapa). In the head, throat, and heart centers within Padmasambhava/Karma Pakshi are three more of the Karmapas, the leaders of the Kagyü lineage. Chögyam Trungpa Rinpoche was trained by people from each of these lineages and by people who intermingled these lineages.

In describing the essence of the sadhana, he tells us that these two traditions together make a very powerful and desirable combination, and it would be wiser to feel them embodied harmoniously within oneself rather than to see them as opposing schools of thought. They make beautiful music together. Maha ati, he says, represents *space*, and mahamudra, *energy*. He describes the combining of these two in a variety of other intriguing ways. When these two traditions are joined and seen as one, it brings together

insight and emotion (since insight needs to become more emotional, and emotion needs to become more insightful)
brains and heart
power and discipline
wretchedness (fully appreciating our neurosis) and glory (fully appreciating that we are enlightened as we are)
the gradual path toward enlightenment and the sudden path of realization on the spot
control and relaxation
playboys and pilots
devotion and crazy wisdom

And there's the rub. Devotion—giving even the giver, losing our home—combines with crazy wisdom. That's the cocktail at the heart of "The Sadhana of Mahamudra."

But what is this crazy wisdom? At one point, he says it is "wisdom gone wild"; at another point, he says it's "craziness gone wise." It's pointless to try to pin Trungpa Rinpoche down to a final definitive description; his is the finger pointing at the moon. It is for us to experience it directly. But he gives good hints.

When wisdom goes to its farthest extent, he says, it manifests as an uncompromising form of compassion that does not concern itself in any way with how the compassioner will be perceived. It's a light that shines on whatever it encounters without discrimination, without hesitation, cowardice, paranoia, or fear. "Whatever is needed will be done," he says. Whatever and whoever needs to be worked with will be helped. The crazy-wisdom person gives up on no person and no situation. Everything is seen in terms of its "primordial wakeful quality." Because the crazy-wisdom person sees people as awake, they are treated as awake—whether they like it or not. From the perspective of confused mind, this is far from genteel behavior: it's crazy and it threatens ego. From the perspective of enlightened mind, though, it is the wisdom with which we are born let loose, the purity beyond clean and unclean, and the ultimate expression of buddhahood.

Practicing "The Sadhana of Mahamudra" is like flipping a switch that connects us to a live current, a power supplied by practitioners stretching back more than twenty generations. The power we can feel as we practice this ritual emerges from the intimate experience of a student—Chögyam Trungpa Rinpoche—who devoutly followed the instructions of his teachers and became a teacher himself, yet never lost the spirit of a humble student. As we intone the words of the sadhana, he and the teachers before him seem to be whispering in our ears. They pass on more than technical instructions and doctrines. They pass on the very means for us to experience realization—not by following a one-size-fits-all formula, but by experiencing it for ourselves firsthand in the slime and muck of our own neurosis.

I have been studying these talks off and on going back to 1978, when I first listened to the series on audiotape. Every time I return, I am not disappointed. The topics in here are subtle and profound, but the fact that they are tied to a practice you can do repeatedly makes them practical. Crazy wisdom, which could be obscure and highfalutin and weird, has a very earthy quality instead. If you're returning to this territory, welcome back. You will not be disappointed. If you're entering here for the first time, I envy you. It's a place you can happily return to for the rest of your life. May your emotion become more insightful and your insight more emotional. May your wretchedness come together with your glory. May compassionate energy arise without pretense and a roaring flame of blessings shoot into the sky.

Barry Campbell Boyce
Halifax, Nova Scotia
April 2024

Editor's Introduction

Born in a remote area of Tibet in 1940, Chögyam Trungpa was destined to travel to the West, where he would have a monumental influence on the development of Buddhism in North America and, in fact, throughout the world. He was recognized during infancy as an incarnation of the holder of an important lineage of Tibetan teachers and was taken to Surmang Dütsi Tel Monastery where he was enthroned as the eleventh Trungpa. There, over the course of many years, he received an arduous and thorough training, becoming fully educated in the ancient Buddhist traditions of practice and study. Although during this formative period it was not yet clear what the future might hold, there were many signs that Chögyam Trungpa's life might take him into foreign territory.

As a child, he had occasional dreams of a world with airplanes and motor cars, but he did not know precisely what he was envisioning. Later, while still in Tibet, Trungpa Rinpoche was intrigued by the images decorating cookie tins he was given from England, which showed pictures of the Houses of Parliament and Buckingham Palace. When he saw his first portrait of the king of England on one of them, he was absolutely fascinated, especially by the king's crown, which appeared to him to have double dorjes, familiar Tibetan symbols, on it. Intrigued and inspired by these and other images from the West, he talked with his main teacher, Jamgön Kongtrül, about his impressions. Jamgön Kongtrül told him, "If you left this particular part of the world, you might be playing with the energies of the universe." He added, "Be careful. But, at the same time, if you are too careful, we might lose our teachings and the power of the teachings."[1]

Until the age of nineteen, Trungpa Rinpoche continued his training in Tibet, completing his advanced studies of the buddhadharma while serving as the abbot of his monastery. In 1959, he was forced to leave Tibet when the Chinese took control of the country and placed a ransom on his head. His xxii — EDITOR'S INTRODUCTION

escape involved a ten-month trek over the Himalayas, during which he narrowly avoided capture and finally reached India on the verge of starvation. He used a form of Tibetan divination to help him make decisions about the route. His was one of the longest and most arduous of the journeys made by Tibetans fleeing to India. He carried with him very few personal or religious belongings. However, he was proud that he could bring something much more precious with him, the wisdom of his lineage. He writes:

> In any situation, there is always some dignity, some goldlike element. Tibet is a lost country, at this point. The Chinese occupied my country, and they are torturing my people. It is quite horrific.... We Tibetans were unable to avoid that situation. Nonetheless, the Tibetan wisdom has escaped. It has been brought out of Tibet. It has something to say, something to offer. It gives us dignity as Tibetans.[2]

In India, he embraced new experiences and perspectives, many of which prepared him for a future life in the West. He learned a fair amount of rudimentary English there and became interested in Western poetry and Japanese calligraphy. Only a few years later, in 1962, he acquired a scholarship to study at Oxford University and set sail for England and another strange new world.

Overall, these were challenging times for Chögyam Trungpa. He made an extremely poignant and difficult journey as an immigrant, first to India, then to England, and finally to North America. He truly experienced and understood the disruption and pain of leaving behind one's original upbringing and culture. At the same time, he saw a path forward for himself and other Tibetans, one that would involve genuine communication and immersion in the new worlds they encountered in the West.

In England, although he could see the potential to connect more deeply with Western people and their culture, he was not fully able to achieve this goal. He was caught between his upbringing as a devout monk, a way of life that was a familiar part of his upbringing—the past—contrasted with the potentials of secular modern life, which included elements of both freedom and extreme materialism. And there were other limiting factors: He was conquering the English language through night classes, seminars, and tutorials he took in Oxford. Yet he also found that no matter how much he might be willing to assimilate a new culture and language, he was not to be truly accepted by the English. Many wanted him to manifest as a saintly but exotic presence for them while not truly understanding or valuing the depth of who he was or the profound relevance of the wisdom he held and was prepared to share.

In the early years in England, while still wearing robes most of the time and outwardly presenting as a dedicated monastic, he ventured out when he could in lay clothing, alone or with trusted compatriots, to explore life around him. This included clandestine encounters and affairs, going to the pub to have a forbidden pint, learning to drive and adventuring around the countryside—and generally crossing a lot of boundaries that presented themselves to him.

Chögyam Trungpa was an iconoclast even during this early period, and his teachings will always have that effect—of challenging the status quo, the norms, the given territory of spirituality and how it operates. He was, to use the parlance of our times, a disrupter. When we look at the current situation that we are facing in our own time, this early period of his life in the West may inform our own challenges. What are the boundaries that we must cross?

For Trungpa Rinpoche, one such border crossing occurred in 1968 when he returned to Asia after more than five years in England. That year, at the invitation of the queen of Bhutan,[3] Trungpa Rinpoche journeyed to Bhutan. He traveled to Taktsang Cave in Bhutan to do a retreat and found there, in the recesses of his mind, a kind of bible or handbook for conquering spiritual materialism. Metaphorically speaking, he opened a huge fissure in the mountain that comes from destroying the *rudra*, or the fortress, of ego, reaching into the emptiness to pull a formerly nonexistent gem, "The Sadhana of Mahamudra," into our world.

"The Sadhana of Mahamudra" had a tremendous impact on Trungpa Rinpoche's development as a teacher and on the whole thrust of his teaching in the West. In a sense, the most articulate presentation of spiritual materialism and the most profound understanding of how to vanquish it are presented in this *sadhana*, or practice text. In this, as well as other areas of his teaching, Trungpa Rinpoche first had the main realization, full and complete within itself, received almost in an instant. He then spent years sharing that understanding with others. This approach is, in fact, quite orthodox. The Buddha first became enlightened; only some weeks later did he begin to teach. Similarly, Chögyam Trungpa discovered the heart teachings of his lineage—an expression of the ecumenical tradition of Rimé—in Taktsang in 1968. He spent the next two decades sharing that realization with others. What he found in Bhutan helped to provide him with the tools of bravery and the strength to cut through his own hesitation and reticence, engaging fully with the Western world to connect with the thousands who presented themselves as ripe for these teachings.

These teachings in "The Sadhana of Mahamudra" on overcoming spiritual materialism and invoking crazy wisdom laid the ground for Trungpa Rinpoche's later emphasis on creating an enlightened society. One of the books that inspired him in 1968 during his retreat at Taktsang was Erich Fromm's *The Sane Society*. Underlying the creation of such an awake society is the necessity of overcoming the crippling neurosis and confusion generated by the materialistic outlook. We can be grateful that Chögyam Trungpa made this powerful journey from contemplating a sane society in Bhutan to proclaiming teachings on enlightened society in North America a decade later.

Chögyam Trungpa arrived in America in 1970. *Cutting Through Spiritual Materialism*, his first major book based on teachings given in America, was published in 1973 and resonated with the spiritual seekers of the time. It was a bestseller in the seventies and eighties, and it continues to be one of his most respected and widely read books. There is no better accompaniment to *Cutting Through*—to learn to practice or actualize its view—than engaging with "The Sadhana of Mahamudra." In the sadhana, Chögyam Trungpa shares with us the view, practice, and action that shaped his campaign to bring the genuine practice lineage to America.

Trungpa Rinpoche's teachings were always rooted in the importance of the sitting practice of meditation, breaking down conceptions and overly conceptualized thought by connecting with the simplicity and emptiness of just sitting. But he also knew the power of energy and magic. Those principles of transformation are powerfully embodied and explicated in "The Sadhana of Mahamudra" itself and in Chögyam Trungpa's talks on the sadhana, which are the core teachings presented in the present volume.

We know in our hearts, minds, and bones that we are facing a mega crisis in this era, one that frightens us, divides us, and makes us question whether we and our world are up for it. We need simplicity, we need kindness, we need to slow down and get real. But we also need bravery, we need power, we need ways to shine and influence and conquer, without aggression, while also transcending our cowardice and hesitation. Those abilities are what "The Sadhana of Mahamudra" and its attendant teachings embody.

"The Sadhana of Mahamudra" is called a *terma* teaching. In Tibet, Chögyam Trungpa had already been recognized as a *tertön*, a teacher who discovers, or reveals, terma. Terma are considered to be prophetic teachings
that the great guru Padmasambhava (and others) concealed in physical locations throughout Tibet and in the realm of mind and space. As Trungpa
Rinpoche describes in his book *Crazy Wisdom,*

> He [Padmasambhava] had various writings of his put in gold and
> silver containers like capsules and buried in certain appropriate
> places in the different parts of Tibet so that people of the future
> would rediscover them. . . A lot of [these] sacred teachings have
> been revealed. One example is *The Tibetan Book of the Dead.*
> Another approach to preserving treasures of wisdom is the style of
> the thought lineage. Teachings have been rediscovered by certain
> appropriate teachers who have had memories of them and written
> them down from memory. This is another kind of hidden treasure.[4]

"The Sadhana of Mahamudra" is such a mind terma.

One characteristic of a terma is that it is revealed, or discovered, at the
time when it will be useful. Terma teachings have an unfabricated freshness
or originality to them. They are prophetic in the sense that they are in some
way tied to a time and a set of circumstances in the present that connect to
and are drawn forth from their ancient origins.

Having said all this, I would note that this whole idea of terma is pretty
science fiction-y. Trungpa Rinpoche didn't tell anyone in the early days in
America that "The Sadhana of Mahamudra" was a terma. He talked about
writing the sadhana—not discovering it. He was well aware of the tendencies of spiritual seekers of that era, and of this one, to indulge in love and
light and to make something as weird as terma into something even weirder!
At the same time, while not yet saying that it was terma, he sometimes
pointed to the extraordinary nature of this composition. In presenting the
sadhana in a talk to his community in Boulder in 1975, he said that he had
composed the sadhana "not by intention, but by force of some kind."[5] He
also talks about this energetic aspect of receiving—or writing—the sadhana
in chapter 1:

> That was a particular point of realization, very quick, although I
> had no visions of any kind. Nothing extraordinary happened to

me at all; the headlines of this sadhana just came up in my head, flashed in my mind. The whole headline flashed in my mind.

What was happening interested me a great deal. I felt that the experience might be some kind of leverage, some kind of handle or staircase through which I might be able to relate or communicate, by means of that particular discipline and message, which is said by nobody, but which was in my head. That message was very powerful and very important for me.[6]

And in the last chapter of the book, he describes the process of writing the sadhana in this way:

During the writing of the sadhana, I didn't particularly have to think of the next line or what to say about the whole thing; everything just came through very simply and very naturally. I felt as if I had already memorized the whole thing. If you are in such a situation, you can't manufacture something, but if the inspiration comes to you, you can record it.[7]

Clearly, he is describing something beyond the normal process of writing a poem! Yet, any one of us who does any "creative" writing will, I think, recognize aspects of this process of receiving words and images from an unknown place.

It is not vital for us to resolve the nature of terma here—does it *really* come to us from the past? Who knows? More to the point: This is a teaching that appeared, wherever it arose from, to address the difficulties of the present and the future. It can be a vehicle to help us navigate problems we are facing in this world. It gives us the juice, the energy, to work with all this insanity we call modern life.

The entire text of the sadhana itself is included in this volume. This is the first time that the complete text has been made available to all readers without restrictions. It seemed warranted and in fact important to include the complete teaching here, given the urgency and the demands of the times. Hopefully, you will engage with this material with appreciation for its sacredness and a little wariness. You might begin by simply reading the text and the commentary. If you want to go further and practice the sadhana, that's a noble aspiration. Best if you can find people who already practice the sadhana and join them. Originally, Trungpa Rinpoche recommended the sadhana as a group practice. By and large, that is still how it is done.

Taken together, the text of the sadhana and the attendant commentary are a bit like an instruction manual for being shot in a rocket to the moon. By just reading this book, in a way, you never leave the ground. The text itself is earthy, direct, and beautiful. The commentary is eye-opening and profound. But be careful: there is something more at work here. Encountering this majestic practice, you might just find yourself catapulted into outer space.

One of the things that I most appreciate about Trungpa Rinpoche's commentary on the sadhana is that it is so accessible, Western, and modern in approach. He was not interested in impressing his audience with all the links that could be made to traditional, esoteric Tibetan vajrayana teachings, and this is part of what makes these talks so profound and so applicable for Western students. Devotion is a very tough sell for Westerners. Here are some of the most revealing, direct, upfront teachings on the teacher-student relationship. If we are to have a hope of developing authentic devotion, we need this understanding. What would we do without Chögyam Trungpa to demystify devotion while also not giving an inch as to its necessity for the "long game" in treading on the Buddhist path? I for one would not have a clue without this man's crazy wisdom, his generous and unwavering dedication to saying it straight and making it real. If you want to explore what the combination of devotion and crazy wisdom could lead to, I commend this book to you. Read it, be fairly warned, and decide for yourself how to engage.

More than other teachers of his time and more than many who have followed, Chögyam Trungpa Rinpoche was attuned to the conflicts that would arise in this current era. Throughout his teachings, he addresses the potential for chaos and the possibilities for resolving our deepest cultural and spiritual dilemmas. "The Sadhana of Mahamudra" is one of the most potent responses he presented. While it will not solve the world's problems, it can convey strength and bravery to seek that resolution. Let us hope that it will continue to be available for many generations.

In thinking about the audience for this volume, I realized that Trungpa Rinpoche never linked the practice of the sadhana to solitary retreats. He presented it as something that anyone could read or practice together with others in a group setting, and he clearly felt that it would benefit people of diverse backgrounds and persuasions. People of many faiths and of no faith have encountered, adopted, and practiced "The Sadhana of Mahamudra" over the decades, beginning in the earliest years after Chögyam Trungpa discovered the text in Bhutan and brought it to the West. It has always appealed to a varied audience, speaking to many who are working with the extreme difficulties of modern life. So who, really, does that leave out?

One hopes that with this new edition from Shambhala Publications will come many new readers and practitioners of the sadhana, whose minds will be turned to the dharma and whose determination to overcome spiritual materialism will fuel genuine practice and realization. We may also hope that the genuine ecumenicism of the sadhana and its fearless proclamation of wisdom free from concepts will help to increase peace and sanity in this troubled world.

Were he still alive today, in 2024—thirty-seven years after his death— Chögyam Trungpa would be eighty-four. He was truly one of the great Tibetan OGs, a pioneer who carried and transmitted the genuine understanding and practice of his ancient lineage from Tibet to the West.[8] He was one among many extraordinary Tibetan teachers who came out of Tibet during this era. A very few of them are still with us, but the teachings they gave remain as their gifts to humanity.

Trungpa Rinpoche lived in North America for the last seventeen years of his life. He taught there when a large herd of Western OG spiritual dinosaurs, said with the utmost respect, roamed the planet. Many were Chögyam Trungpa's companions, students, and friends: Alan Watts, Ram Dass, Jakusho Kwong Roshi, Jack Kornfield, Mirabai Bush, Sharon Salzberg, Allen Ginsberg, and many others as well. Some are still with us; many have departed this earth. I bow to all these great beings, named and unnamed here, known and unknown, offering deep thanks for their efforts to keep alive the genuine wisdom traditions of this world.

I have been fortunate, and I am honored, to have played even a small part in editing this book, helping to shepherd the sadhana and the commentary into this new and possibly final edition. Many of Chögyam Trungpa's students have played important roles in its presentation over the last half-century, and they have helped to create this book, gather together these teachings as a whole, and propagate these teachings.[9] I bow to all these servants of the dharma, who have helped to create a future for these precious teachings of the practice lineage.

Finally, let us bow with heartfelt thanks to Chögyam Trungpa, spiritual prophet of this age, who embedded so many tools of sanity and wakefulness in our world. Let us raise a HUM HUM HUM! May it help to liberate us all who dwell in the slime and muck of the dark ages.

Carolyn Rose Gimian

May 9, 2024

THE SADHANA OF MAHAMUDRA

*Which Quells the Mighty Warring of the Three Lords of Materialism
and Brings Realization of the Ocean of Siddhas
of the Practice Lineage*ⸯ

VIDYADHARA THE VENERABLE
CHÖGYAM TRUNGPA RINPOCHE

*This is the darkest hour of the dark ages.*ⸯ *Disease, famine and warfare are raging like the fierce north wind.*ⸯ *The Buddha's teaching has waned in strength.*ⸯ *The various schools of the sangha are fighting amongst themselves with sectarian bitterness; and although the Buddha's teaching was perfectly expounded and there have been many reliable teachings since then from other great gurus, yet they pursue intellectual speculations.*ⸯ *The sacred mantra has strayed into Bön, and the yogis of tantra are losing the insight of meditation.*ⸯ *They spend their whole time going through villages and performing little ceremonies for material gain.*ⸯ

*On the whole, no one acts according to the highest code of discipline, meditation and wisdom.*ⸯ *The jewellike teaching of insight is fading day by day.*ⸯ *The Buddha's teaching is used merely for political purposes and to draw people together socially.*ⸯ *As a result, the blessings of spiritual energy are being lost.*ⸯ *Even those with great devotion are beginning to lose heart.*ⸯ *If the buddhas of the three times and the great teachers were to comment, they would surely express their disappointment.*ⸯ *So to enable individuals to ask for their help and to renew spiritual strength, I have written this sadhana of the embodiment of all the siddhas.*ⸯ

*The sadhana is in three parts.*ⸯ

First, let the mind remain uncontaminated by the eight worldly concerns.༔ You must relax and stay in a quiet place with a good atmosphere to rest the mind on the great self-existing mandala of apparent phenomena and to take the refuge.༔

NAMO༔
Earth, water, fire and all the elements,༔
The animate and the inanimate, the trees and the greenery and so on,༔
All partake of the nature of self-existing equanimity,༔
Which is quite simply what the Great Wrathful One is.༔
In the spontaneous wisdom of the trikaya༔
I take refuge with body, speech and mind.༔
In order to free those who suffer at the hands of the three lords of materialism༔
And are afraid of external phenomena, which are their own projections,༔
I take this vow in meditation.༔

Meditate in that great simplicity which is beyond conceptions and see through the complexities of duality, in which apparent phenomena and the self are imagined to be separate.༔ The undercurrent of thoughts with all their pettiness and doubt and fear—all these must be overcome with that great assurance and fearless certainty which is the transcendental element of the voice of Manjushri, Mikyö Dorje.༔ So rouse that insight.༔ Be decisive, know what is, see clearly—these are the three kinds of confidence.༔

The spontaneous mahamudra mandala is now created from the wisdom of the fourth abhisheka.༔ This will be clarified by the following words:༔

HUM HUM HUM༔
In the boundless space of suchness,༔
In the play of the great light,༔
All the miracles of sight, sound and mind༔
Are the five wisdoms and the five buddhas.༔
This is the mandala which is never arranged but is always complete.༔
It is the great bliss, primeval and all-pervading. HUM༔

It is boundless equanimity, which has never changed.
It is unified into a single circle beyond confusion.
In its basic character there is no longer any trace
Of ignorance nor of understanding.
Nothing whatever, but everything arises from it,
Yet it reveals the spontaneous play of the mandala.

HUM HUM HUM
My whole being is Dorje Trolö
And my form is Karma Pakshi;
My speech is Mikyö Dorje
And my mind is Rangjung Dorje.
With that unwavering conviction
Fearlessly enjoy the mahamudra
And attain the experience of maha ati.
HUM HUM HUM

In the state of nonmeditation all phenomena subside in that great graveyard in which lie buried the complexities of samsara and nirvana. This is the universal ground of everything; it is the basis of freedom and also the basis of confusion. Within it, the vajra anger, the flame of death, burns fiercely and consumes the fabric of dualistic thoughts. The black river of death, the vajra passion, turbulent with massive waves, destroys the raft of conceptualization to the roaring sound of the immeasurable void. The great poisonous wind of the vajra ignorance blows with all-pervading energy like an autumn storm and sweeps away all thoughts of possessiveness and self like a pile of dust.

Whatever you see partakes of the nature of that wisdom which transcends past, present and future. From here came the buddhas of the past; here live the buddhas of the present; this is the primeval ground from which the buddhas of the future will come. This is the heavenly realm of the dakinis, the secret charnel ground of the blazing mountain. But you won't find ordinary earth and rocks here, even if you look for them. All the mountains are Buddha Lochana, who is the all-pervading wisdom of equanimity and unchanging stillness. This is the realm in which the distinctions between meditation and the postmeditation experience no longer occur. In this fearless state, even if the buddhas of the three times rise against you, you will remain in the indestructible vajra nature.§ The water which flows here is the Buddha Mamaki, who is the lake of the mirrorlike wisdom, clear and pure, as though the sky had melted.§ Here is the joyous river, which is the transcendent form of the eight kinds of consciousness.§ It flows into the great purity, which goes beyond clean and unclean.§

In the various parts of the charnel ground can be seen the terrifying trees, which are the protecting mahakalis: Rangjung Gyalmo, Dorje Sogdrubma, Tüsölma, and Ekajati.§ In these trees vultures, ravens, hawks and eagles perch, hungry for meat and thirsting for blood.§ They represent the concept of good and evil.§ Until you stop clinging to this concept the mahakalis will continue to manifest as friendly goddesses and harmful demons.§

Various animals roam about: tigers, leopards, bears, jackals and dogs, all howling and jumping up and down excitedly.§ These represent the different kinds of perception.§ Here too are the chötens of the awakened state of mind, where the great yogis live.§ They represent the supernormal powers which need not be sought.§

In the middle of this heavenly realm is a huge rock mountain, which arose from the corpse of the rudra of ego.§ It is triangular in shape and it pierces the skies.§ It is dignified and awe-inspiring and radiates the blue light of Vajrasattva.§ On top of this mountain is the red triangle which can accommodate all apparent phenomena and the whole of existence.§ This is the primeval ground where the question of samsara and nirvana does not arise.§ It is the beginning and the end of everything.§ The triangle radiates the blazing red light of inner warmth and compassion.§ Above the triangle is a beautiful flower, a hundred-petaled lotus in full bloom, exuding a delicate scent.§ It is the lotus of discriminating wisdom.§ Here is the moon of great bliss and skillful means.§ And here is the sun of wisdom and shunyata.§

HUM: The sonorous voice of silence is heard.§ From it appears the rainbow body of wisdom.§ This is the personification of the body, speech and mind of all the buddhas.§ He is the self-born teacher, the lord of the herukas, Padma Thötreng, the lama whose power extends over all apparent phenomena and the whole of existence.§ He is Karma Pakshi, in whom are unified the unchanging mind of the guru, the wisdom of the yidam, beyond waxing and waning, and the protectors—the confused thoughts which have returned to nakedness.§ He is dark red in color, symbolizing the oneness of everything within compassion.§ He is inseparable from peacefulness and yet he acts whenever action is required.§ He subdues what needs to be subdued, he destroys what needs to be destroyed and he cares for whatever needs his care.§ His anger, devoid of hatred, is as fierce and terrible as if the three worlds were on fire.§ His presence is overwhelming.§ His three eyes of wisdom are bloodshot and stare in all directions.§ They radiate light, outshining the sun and the moon.§ His expression is wrathful and he bites the lower lip.§ He has a black triangular beard, shiny and twisted into a point, emitting sparks of fire.§ In his right hand, raised to the heavens, he holds a nine-pointed dorje of meteoric iron, emitting a storm of red sparks, each in the form of the letter HUM.§ Thus he subdues spiritual pride.§ In his left hand he holds a phurba, also of meteoric iron, emitting a shower of sparks in the form of thousands of mahakalas.§ The phurba pierces through the heart of seductive passion.§ He wears the three robes of a bhikshu, signifying the accomplishment of discipline, meditation and wisdom.§ He is the originator and master of all buddha activity.§ Hence he wears the black crown, bright with gold and blazing with unceasing light, emitting a steady stream of discs of light in five different colors, which are the five buddhas.§ He stands on a dakini, in the form of a pregnant tigress, with his right leg bent and left leg extended in the heruka posture.§

Even the thought of him will destroy the mountain of conceptualizations.§ The sight of him dries up the ocean of dualistic clingings.§ He is immersed in flames which radiate the intense heat of compassion.§

In his forehead center is the unchanging form of Vairochana, who is Tüsum Khyenpa, the dharmaraja of the three worlds, clad in bhikshu robes, with his hands in the meditation posture, holding a dorje.§ He has white hair and a thin, dark face.§ His expression is wise and peaceful.§ He wears the black crown ornamented with a gold dharmachakra, which sends out rays of light.§ He is seated cross-legged on the back of an elephant.§

In the throat center of Karma Pakshi is Mikyö Dorje, the lord of speech, the unceasing voice of Amitabha.§ He is of orange color.§ He wears a tiger skin around his waist and a shawl of human skin around his shoulders.⸝ He wears ornaments of bone and jewels.⸝ In his raised right hand he holds the sword of wisdom, which cuts off the root of the universal unconscious.⸝ In his left hand, level with his heart, he holds the vessel which contains the treasure of the dharma.⸝ His face radiates friendliness.⸝ One glimpse of it suffices to open the door of confidence.⸝ The thought of him awakens memory.⸝ As the lord of the padma family he wears the black crown, ornamented with a golden lotus, radiating the red light of Amitabha.⸝ He is seated on a white lion.⸝

In the heart center of the Great Wrathful One is the king of the tathagatas, Rangjung Dorje, the Vajrasattva nature of never-ending awareness.⸝ He is blue in color with serene and friendly face expressing the state which transcends the boundary between meditation and nonmeditation.⸝ By a glimpse of his face the wisdom of the mind transmission is established in one's heart.⸝ His three eyes gaze into fathomless space.⸝ He has achieved the highest state of simplicity and is therefore seen naked, seated cross-legged, with hands in the meditation posture holding a skull cup filled with amrita.⸝ He is the king of kings and possessor of the indestructible vajra abhisheka, and therefore wears the black crown, bright with gold and ornamented with the vajra.⸝ The blue light of Samantabhadra, the All-Good, shines from the crown in the primordial state in which neither liberation nor confusion has ever arisen.⸝

Around Karma Pakshi a great host of the buddhas and the sangha, together with the utterance of the dharma, fills the sky.⸝ They are surrounded by the dharmapalas and dakinis.⸝ The sound of HUM and AH and PHAT shakes the sky.⸝ It is as though all the musical instruments of the universe were being played simultaneously.⸝ Whatever you see is the form of Karma Pakshi run wild; whatever you hear is the voice of Karma Pakshi let loose; whatever you think is the thought of Karma Pakshi unleashed.⸝ In the spontaneously existing state where meditation is effortless, all movements are the vajra dance and all sound is the vajra music.⸝ It is the great guru mandala.⸝

In this way rest the mind in the mahamudra of devotion with great trust and single-mindedness.⸝ One's mind should be free from pettiness and doubt.⸝

Here follows the supplication:

O Karmapa, lord and knower of the three times,
O Padmakara, father and protector of all beings,
You transcend all coming and going.
Understanding this, I call upon you—
Give thought to your only child.
I am a credulous and helpless animal
Who has been fooled by the mirage of duality.
I have been fool enough to think that I possess my own
projections,
So now you, my father, are my only refuge;
You alone can grasp the buddha state.
The glorious copper-colored mountain is within my heart.
Is not this pure and all-pervading naked mind your dwelling
place?
Although I live in the slime and muck of the dark age,
I still aspire to see it.
Although I stumble in the thick, black fog of materialism,
I still aspire to see it.

The joy of spontaneous awareness, which is with me all the time,
Is not this your smiling face, O Karma Padmakara?
Although I live in the slime and muck of the dark age,
I still aspire to see it.
Although I stumble in the thick, black fog of materialism,
I still aspire to see it.

At glorious Taktsang, in the cave
Which can accommodate everything,
Samsara and nirvana both,
The heretics and bandits of hope and fear
Are subdued and all experiences
Are transformed into crazy wisdom.
Is not this your doing, O Dorje Trolö?
Although I live in the slime and muck of the dark age,
I still aspire to see your face.

Although I stumble in the thick, black fog of materialism,⁞
I still aspire to see your face.⁞

The corpse, bloated with the eight worldly concerns,⁞
Is cut into pieces by the knife of detachment⁞
And served up as the feast of the great bliss.⁞
Is not this your doing, O Karma Pakshi?⁞
Although I live in the slime and muck of the dark age,⁞
I still aspire to see your face.⁞
Although I stumble in the thick, black fog of materialism,⁞
I still aspire to see your face.⁞

In the boundless space of nonmeditation⁞
He who performs the great dance of mahamudra⁞
Puts a stop to thoughts⁞
So that all acts become the acts of the guru.⁞
Is not this your doing, O Tüsum Khyenpa?⁞
Although I live in the slime and muck of the dark age,⁞
I still aspire to see your face.⁞
Although I stumble in the thick, black fog of materialism,⁞
I still aspire to see your face.⁞

When the current of thoughts is self-liberated⁞
And the essence of dharma is known,⁞
Everything is understood⁞
And apparent phenomena⁞
Are all the books one needs.⁞
Is not this your doing, omniscient Mikyö Dorje?⁞
Although I live in the slime and muck of the dark age,⁞
I still aspire to see your face.⁞
Although I stumble in the thick, black fog of materialism,⁞
I still aspire to see your face.⁞

The kingdom of no-dharma, free from concepts,⁞
Is discovered within the heart.⁞
Here there is no hierarchy of different stages⁞
And the mind returns to its naked state.⁞
Is not this your doing, O Rangjung Dorje?⁞

Although I live in the slime and muck of the dark age,⁞
I still aspire to see your face.⁞
Although I stumble in the thick, black fog of materialism,⁞
I still aspire to see your face.⁞

The father guru, the embodiment of all the siddhas,⁞
Is all-seeing and all-pervading.⁞
Wherever you look, his transparent body is there,⁞
And the power of his blessing can never be diminished.⁞
Although I live in the slime and muck of the dark age,⁞
I still aspire to see his face.⁞
Although I stumble in the thick, black fog of materialism,⁞
I still aspire to see his face.⁞

Living, as I do, in the dark age,⁞
I am calling upon you, because I am trapped⁞
In this prison, without refuge or protector.⁞
The age of the three poisons has dawned⁞
And the three lords of materialism have seized power.⁞
This is the time of hell on earth;⁞
Sadness is always with us⁞
And unceasing depression fills our minds.⁞

The search for an external protector⁞
Has met with no success.⁞
The idea of a deity as an external being⁞
Has deceived us, led us astray.⁞
Counting on friends has brought nothing⁞
But sorrow and insecurity.⁞
So now I have no other refuge⁞
But you, Karma Pakshi, the lotus-born.⁞

Think of us poor, miserable wretches.⁞
With deep devotion and intense longing⁞
I supplicate you.⁞
The time has come for you to arouse yourself and do something.⁞
The tradition of meditation is waning⁞
And intellectual arguments predominate.⁞

We are drunk with spiritual pride⁞
And seduced by passion.⁞
The dharma is used for personal gain⁞
And the river of materialism has burst its banks.⁞
The materialistic outlook dominates everywhere⁞
And the mind is intoxicated with worldly concerns.⁞
Under such circumstances, how can you abandon us?⁞
The time has come when your child needs you.⁞
No material offering will please you⁞
So the only offering I can make⁞
Is to follow your example.⁞

Chant the following as a celebration of identification with the guru:⁞

When the wild and wrathful father approaches⁞
The external world is seen to be transparent and unreal.⁞
The reasoning mind no longer clings and grasps.⁞
It is wonderful to arrive in your domain⁞
In the pure land of the blazing mountain⁞
Where every experience is full of joy.⁞
Hey-ho, the happy yogi!⁞

Every movement of the mind⁞
Becomes bliss and emptiness;⁞
All polarity disappears⁞
When the mind emerges into nakedness.⁞
This is the mandala in which⁞
The six senses are self-liberated.⁞
On seeing your face I am overjoyed.⁞
Now pain and pleasure alike have become⁞
Ornaments which it is pleasant to wear.⁞

The experience of joy becomes devotion⁞
And I am drunk with all-pervading blessings.⁞
This is a sign of the merging of mind and guru.⁞
The whole of existence is freed and becomes the guru.⁞
When such blessings descend, your child's depression⁞

Is entirely liberated into blissfulness.⁞
Thank you, great Karmapa! Thank you, father Padmakara!⁞
There is no separation between teacher and disciple;⁞
Father and child are one in the realm of thought.⁞

Grant your blessings so that my mind may be one with the
    dharma.⁞
Grant your blessings so that dharma may progress along the path.⁞
Grant your blessings so that the path may clarify confusion.⁞
Grant your blessings so that confusion may dawn as wisdom.⁞

*Repeat these "Four Dharmas of Gampopa" again and again.⁞ One should try to
give birth to the devotion of mahamudra by having complete trust in the guru.⁞
When the sense of devotion becomes very strong, then especially one should
realize that the guru is not external.⁞ That is to say, when a flash memory of
the guru arises, the mind becomes relaxed and opened out; or, when you relax
in meditation inseparable from the memory of the guru, the right atmosphere
is created and the mind becomes clear and naked.⁞*

*Sometimes, in order to make desires and attachments part of the path, you may
perform the following offering:⁞*

To the crazy-wisdom form of the buddhas of the three times,⁞
The unified mandala of all the siddhas, Dorje Trolö Karma Pakshi,
    I make this supplication.⁞
Desire, hatred and other hindrances are self-liberated.⁞
To the boundless rainbow body of wisdom, Padmakara Karma
    Pakshi,⁞
The heruka who, untouched by concepts, pervades all existence, I
    make this supplication.⁞
Whatever is seen with the eyes is vividly unreal in emptiness, yet
    there is still form:⁞
This is the true image of Tüsum Khyenpa, whom now I
    supplicate.⁞
Whatever is heard with the ears is the echo of emptiness, yet real:⁞
It is the clear and distinct utterance of Mikyö Dorje, whom now I
    supplicate.⁞

Good and bad, happy and sad, all thoughts vanish into emptiness
like the imprint of a bird in the sky:⁏
This is the vivid mind of Rangjung Dorje, whom now I
supplicate.⁏
The animate and the inanimate are the mandala of the glorious
mahasiddha, which no one can change;⁏
It always remains impressive and colorful. This mandala now I
supplicate.⁏
The hope of attaining buddhahood and the fear of continuing to
wander in samsara,⁏
Doubt that wisdom exists within one and other dualistic
thoughts—all these are my feast offering.⁏
Food, wealth, companionship, fame and sensual attachments—⁏
All these I offer for the elaborate arrangement of the mandala.⁏
Wantingness, desire, and passion I offer as the great ocean of
blood which comes from the killing of samsara.⁏
Thoughts of anger and hatred I offer as the amrita which
intoxicates extreme beliefs and renders them inoperative.⁏
All that arises within—wandering thoughts, carelessness and all
that is subject to ignorance—⁏
I offer as the great mountain of torma ornamented with the eight
kinds of consciousness.⁏
Whatever arises is merely the play of the mind.⁏
All this I offer, filling the whole universe.⁏
I offer knowing that giver and receiver are one;⁏
I offer without expecting anything in return and without hope of
gaining merit;⁏
I make these offerings with transcendental generosity in the
mahamudra.⁏

Now that I have made these offerings, please grant your blessings
so that my mind may be one with the dharma.⁏
Grant your blessings so that dharma may progress along the path.⁏
Grant your blessings so that the path may clarify confusion.⁏
Grant your blessings so that confusion may dawn as wisdom.⁏

Next comes the special supplication and taking of abhisheka.⁏

(This is composed by Guru Rinpoche himself:)

HUM HUM HUM⸘
In the cave of Taktsang Sengge Samdrup⸘
He who has subdued the evil forces⸘
And buried treasure in rocks and snow mountains in holy places of
    Tibet⸘
Shows kindness to the people of the future dark age.⸘
I supplicate you, Dorje Trolö;⸘
I supplicate you, Ugyen Padmakara.⸘

(The following four lines were composed by Karma Pakshi:)

HUM HUM HUM⸘
You are the lord of yidams and conqueror of the whole of existence
    and all apparent phenomena;⸘
You have subdued the viciousness of the Mongol emperor⸘
And overcome the energy of fire, water, poison, weapons and evil forces:⸘
I supplicate you, O Karma Pakshi.⸘

(The next four lines were written by Shamarpa:)

HUM HUM HUM⸘
You who fulfill all wishes⸘
And are lord of centerless space,⸘
You who shine with kind and luminous light,⸘
I supplicate you, Tsurphupa.⸘

(The next four lines were written by Mikyö Dorje himself:)

HUM HUM HUM⸘
AH! Mikyö Dorje fills the whole of space.⸘
HOH! He is the vajra joy which sends out luminous light.⸘
HUM! He is the energy of music and lord of messengers.⸘
OM! He is the wrathful action which cleanses all impurities.⸘

(The next five lines were written by an unknown author:)

HUM HUM HUM⁏
Seeing the bodhisattva Rangjung Dorje⁏
Is like discovering the wish-fulfilling gem.⁏
He removes the poverty of oneself and others;⁏
He is the source of all that is needed.⁏
I supplicate his wisdom body.⁏

(The next six lines were composed by Guru Rinpoche:)

HUM HUM HUM⁏
Whatever occurs in the realm of the mind—⁏
Such as thoughts of the five poisons—⁏
One should neither lead nor follow.⁏
Just let it remain in its true state⁏
And reach the liberation of dharmakaya:⁏
I supplicate the guru of self-liberated, perfect insight.⁏

Chant the triple HUM *as mantra over and over again.⁏ Then, by uniting your mind with the thoughts of the ocean of siddhas, their overwhelming presence and blessings are felt in great joy and emptiness.⁏ The visualization becomes just a mixture of colors.⁏ The dazzling rays of the five wisdoms are bright red, deep green, clear blue, pure yellow and bright white.⁏ They are not static but oscillating all the time, and they fill the whole of heaven and earth.⁏ They are so bright that they are hard to look at.⁏ At the same time, you can see a rain of amrita and many-colored flowers and you lose the clear-cut concept of "here" and "there" and become dizzy.⁏ Now you become the lord of the trikaya realm and receive the simple and ultimate abhisheka.⁏ You become one with the body, speech and mind of the siddhas.⁏*

Next recite the following verse (composed by Mikyö Dorje):⁏

HUM HUM HUM⁏
When the precious guru approaches⁏
The whole of space is filled with rainbow light.⁏
He sends out his emanations as messengers⁏
And a roaring flame of blessings shoots into the sky.⁏
Various meditation experiences and flashes of insight occur.⁏
Oh, the great guru!⁏

I follow your example;⁑
Please approach and grant your blessings.⁑
Bless this place!⁑
Give us the four abhishekas⁑
And clear all obstacles.⁑
Grant us the ultimate and relative siddhis.⁑
HUM HUM HUM⁑

Next follow the verses of the great leap into the void of panoramic awareness.⁑

HUM HUM HUM⁑
In the mandala of mahamudra⁑
Shines moonlight, pure and all-pervading.⁑
All apparent phenomena are the play of the mind.⁑
All qualities are complete within the mind.⁑
I, the yogi, am fearless and free from occupations;⁑
Hopes and fears of achieving and abstaining are all used up.⁑
I awaken into the wisdom with which I was born⁑
And compassionate energy arises, without pretense.⁑
Hey-ho, the self-existing rishi!⁑
I, the siddha, enjoy myself with great simplicity.⁑
A A A⁑

To end with, here are the auspicious final verses; so finish off by joyfully chant-ing these verses:⁑

The wisdom flame sends out a brilliant light—⁑
May the goodness of Dorje Trolö be present!⁑
Karma Pakshi, lord of mantra, king of insight—⁑
May his goodness, too, be present!⁑
Tüsum Khyenpa, the primeval buddha—⁑
Beyond all partiality—may his goodness be present!⁑
Mikyö Dorje, lord of boundless speech—⁑
May his goodness be present here!⁑
Rangjung Dorje, faultless single eye of wisdom—⁑
May his goodness be present!⁑
The Kagyü gurus, the light of whose wisdom is a torch⁑
For all beings—may their goodness be present!⁑

The ocean of wish-fulfilling yidams who accomplish all actions—ੰ
May their goodness be present!ੰ
The protectors who plant firm the victorious bannerੰ
Of dharma—may their goodness be present!ੰ
May the goodness of the great mind mandala of mahamudra be
    present!ੰ

*After practicing this sadhana, enjoy the presence of the guru and the energy of
compassion and devotion.*ੰ

*It is hoped that this sadhana will be practiced by those who are prepared to see
the living dharma within. The sadhana will help to purify the present degen-
erate state of philosophy and meditation practice. It will help to bring peace in
the warfare waged by materialism.*

> *In the copper-mountain cave of Taktsang,*
> *The mandala created by the guru,*
> *Padma's blessing entered in my heart.*
> *I am the happy young man from Tibet!*
> *I see the dawn of mahamudra*
> *And awaken into true devotion:*
> *The guru's smiling face is ever-present.*
> *On the pregnant dakini-tigress*
> *Takes place the crazy-wisdom dance*
> *Of Karma Pakshi Padmakara,*
> *Uttering the sacred sound of* HUM.
> *His flow of thunder-energy is impressive.*
> *The dorje and phurba are the weapons of self-liberation:*
> *With penetrating accuracy they pierce*
> *Through the heart of spiritual pride.*
> *One's faults are so skillfully exposed*
> *That no mask can hide the ego*
> *And one can no longer conceal*
> *The antidharma which pretends to be dharma.*
> *Through all my lives may I continue*
> *To be the messenger of dharma*
> *And listen to the song of the king of yanas.*
> *May I lead the life of a bodhisattva.*

The sadhana was written in 1968 by Chögyam Trungpa Rinpoche at Taktsang in Bhutan, where, about eleven hundred years ago, Guru Rinpoche meditated and manifested the wrathful form known as Dorje Trolö.

This sadhana was completed on the auspicious full-moon day of September 6, 1968. It was translated into English at Thimphu by Chögyam Trungpa Rinpoche and Künga Dawa.

PART ONE

The Embodiment of All the Siddhas

Karmê Chöling, Vermont, September 1975

The lineage of the sadhana is the lineage of the two schools put together: the two traditions of immense crazy wisdom and immense dedication and devotion. It puts the student's role and the teacher's role together into one powerful style. The Kagyü, or mahamudra, tradition, the tradition of Karma Pakshi, specialized in immense dedication and devotion. The Nyingma, or ati, tradition, the tradition of Padmasambhava, is the lineage of crazy wisdom. It is possible to put these two traditions together and work with both of them. The sadhana is a prototype of how emotion and wisdom can work together.
It's possible; it has been done.

—Chögyam Trungpa Rinpoche

1. Historical Commentary: Part One

It was most interesting in that my stay at Taktsang reflected that my being there had something to do with the Western world, since I had come there from England. I remembered England and thought about my work there and what I would have to do when I went back, so Taktsang was just a resting place for me. I knew I would have to go back to the West and present the vajrayana teachings to the rest of the world, so to speak. That concern was always intensely in my mind.

I would like to discuss the background to "The Sadhana of Mahamudra," in terms of the inspiration that developed in me from being exposed to both Western spiritual materialism and to the wisdom of the traditional Buddhist approach to reality.

The Vision of the Sadhana: Overcoming Spiritual Materialism

"The Sadhana of Mahamudra" was composed in Tibetan by myself, personally, and has been translated into the English language. The basic vision of the sadhana is based on two main principles: the principle of space and the principle of energy. Space here is related to the teachings of *dzogchen*, or ati, the ninth and highest yana of Buddhist tantra. The energy principle is related to mahamudra, from the *anuttarayoga* tantra; it is also a high level of experience. In the practice of "The Sadhana of Mahamudra" we are trying to bring space and energy together; we are trying to bring about some understanding and realization in the world.

This is a very confused world, a very corrupted world at all levels. I'm not particularly talking about the Orient or Occident; I'm talking about the world in general. Materialism and the technological outlook no longer come from the West alone. They seem to be universal. The Japanese make the best cameras. Indians make atomic bombs. So we are talking in terms of materialism and spirituality in the world at large. It's a universal situation. Therefore, as well, we can work together, East and West, in a very resourceful way.

The question that we need to look into is how we can overcome spiritual materialism fully and properly, without simply brushing it off as an undesirable consequence. The question is how we can actually work with the tendencies toward spiritual and psychological materialism that exist in the world today. How can we work with those things properly? How can we transmute them into livable, workable, enlightened basic sanity?

THE HISTORY OF COMPOSING THE SADHANA

I wrote this sadhana during a retreat in Bhutan in 1968.[1] My situation at that time was very unusual; you could almost say unique.

It was unique because I was in a position to see both cultures together. I had been in the United Kingdom for a long time, since 1963. I had seen that particular world and been in that particular atmosphere. When I returned to Asia and went to Bhutan, I also rediscovered its characteristics, which were extraordinarily familiar to me; but at the same time, the reference point, or contrast to Western culture, was very powerful and important.

I asked the queen of Bhutan, who was my hostess, whether I could do a short retreat at the Taktsang Retreat Center, at the site of the cave where Padmasambhava meditated. He actually became or manifested here as Dorje Trolö, his crazy-wisdom form. Taktsang is close to the second-largest town of Bhutan, which is called Paro. The queen was delighted by and appreciative of my request. She was hoping that I could encourage the temple keepers and bless the people, as well as the place itself. My student, Künga Dawa, and I went up there part of the way in a Land Rover, which had on it the flag of Bhutan and a license plate that said, "Bhutan One." Then, we traveled the rest of the way on horses and pack mules. When we got close to the cave, we had to dismount and climb down a very scary hill, which was a sheer drop of about eleven hundred feet if you went straight down. There were niches carved in the rock for our hands and feet. At the bottom, there was a little patch of grass that we walked across. We crossed a stream and came to the retreat center.

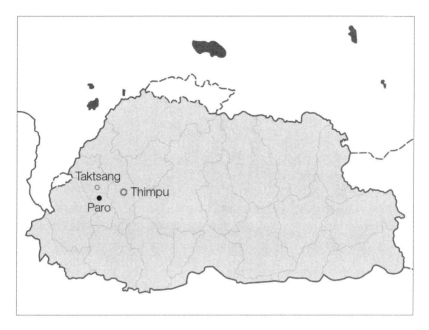

Map of Bhutan showing location of Taktsang. *Drawing by Chris Gibson.*

We were warmly received by the *kunyer*, or temple keeper. Several royal Bhutanese guards were also there, as well as various officials who had been sent to take care of us. In fact, there were quite a number of them—more than we needed. There were something like fifteen officials, and the place is very small. The site of the cave had been built up more than was necessary. The cave was below, and the temple where we stayed was built on top of it, on the rock. Something like nine temples and all kinds of shrines had been built around the cave. My bedroom was part of the ninth shrine of Amitabha, I believe. My friend Künga had a little cottage close to my room, which happened to be the hall of Karma Pakshi.

We settled in. We talked about the place and the air and the environment around there. At that point, I began my retreat. My experience there was extraordinarily casual. There was nothing at all extraordinary about it. Nothing really happened. There I was in a very special place that in my childhood I used to read about and talk about. Finally, I was in the very place where Padmasambhava actually became Dorje Trolö, where he manifested as a crazy-wisdom person. When I was a child of nine, I used to learn prayers to Padmasambhava by heart. I used to study many scriptures related to Padmasambhava; I used to read the story of Padmasambhava's life and study his teachings. But this place seemed to be an anticlimax. Nothing was happening. It was a nice hermitage, the service was excellent, and the landscape was beautiful. It was a nice temple and a nice view.

We couldn't walk around much because everything was built on a cliff. We could only sit and admire the view from the windows. We could walk up and down the staircase and through the various temples, and we could talk to the kunyer, the temple keeper, who we discovered was interested in collecting books of pornography. He also seemed to be interested in little business deals, but he didn't have much to sell. He was always trying to talk to Künga and trying to sell us this and that little thing, little trinkets, little goodies of all kinds.

Occasionally, we had visits from members of the royal family or from various dignitaries and visitors, ranging from Swedish doctors to German archaeologists to English historians. They used to come up there touring and exploring the place, which takes a few hours. Then they would have their picnic lunch and go away.

To our surprise, we learned that the reason we were so well fed was because the local people would bring us their firewood, eggs, meat, and their milk as part of their tax payment. By feeding the royal guest, they would get a reduction of their tax payments. It was very easy for them, because they wanted to relate with the holy man, the Tibetan *tülku*, the rinpoche. They felt good, and they also felt businesslike at the same time, that it was a very good deal for them. We had lots of eggs and lots of meat and lots of firewood and lots of milk—and nothing else. It was an interesting time, being there.

My so-called attendant, who had been appointed by the government, lived next door to me. Beyond that were the cook's quarters. My attendant and the cook used to sit around and throw dice and laugh and drink a liquor called *chang*, the local drink. Chang is similar to beer, somewhat. It's made from barley and yeast. But it's actually referred to as wine, barley wine. The word for wine made from grapes is *gunchang*; wine made from barley is called *nechang*. The cook and the attendant had a good time, because for a while they didn't have to serve as palace guards or be hassled by their palace duties. They were having their break, their chance to be away from the palace and to serve me for three weeks. So they had an extremely good time.

As far as I was concerned, there was no great revelation that I attained from that place apart from what was there, whatever it may be. It was most

LEFT: Chögyam Trungpa on a mule, on the way to Taktsang, 1968. *Photograph by Dan Russell and Künga Dawa; used by permission.* RIGHT: Photograph of Taktsang Cave, 1968. *Photograph by Dan Russell and Künga Dawa; used by permission.*

interesting in that my stay reflected that my being there had something to do with the Western world, since I had come there from England. I remembered England and thought about my work there and what I would have to do when I went back, so Taktsang was just a resting place for me. I knew I would have to go back to the West and present the vajrayana teachings to the rest of the world, so to speak. That concern was always intensely in my mind.

I conducted regular sadhana practices close to the big cave where Padmasambhava meditated.[2] Every day I practiced my sadhana with a few students of Dilgo Khyentse Rinpoche, who would prepare the shrine. We practiced together. It was a very pleasant living situation, but at the same time I had a sense of hauntedness: how to actually share this with others. I kept thinking about how I could actually communicate what I knew to others. That was a big stumbling block for me. I had a good time eating and drinking and everything, but at the same time, my mind was completely occupied. All the time, there was a concern about how this could be transmitted to others. I felt slightly depressed that I didn't have any bright ideas. No big gadgets popped up in my head. I racked my brains, and even though I was having a good time, I knew I was wasting my time.

"You're only here for three weeks," I kept telling myself. "What are you going to do after this, if you don't get something out of this fantastic, historic, blessed, highly sacred, powerful place? What if you don't get anything out of this?" That questioning took place continuously, each time I conducted the sadhana of Padmasambhava or visited the cave itself, which is a dark little dungeon. It smells of moss and rotten wood and decaying offerings; there is only a faint burning light. There is nothing particularly fantastic about it. It's just like getting inside a garbage pail—something like that. In spite of my respect for the place, it was still just going down to a dingy hole. I would just go back and forth between my room and that cave. Nothing was happening! I would try to think holy thoughts, but so what? It was very simple and very ordinary.

At that time, I started drinking more and more because I felt depressed. Bhutanese gin was being sent to us by the queen. She also sent us what is called Bhutanese golden drink, a liquor they produce in Bhutan. The queen was also constantly sending us all kinds of little chocolates and goodies and biscuits. Every day we got little goodies. I think she even sent me some Johnnie Walker Red, all of which was an interesting reference point for me.

One night—this is not a particularly extraordinary story—I got extremely drunk and frustrated. I looked out the window, and there was nothing but fireflies flying around. My cooks were snoring very loudly, and the statues in their little niches in my room were staring in their own way. The little butter lamps were burning; my bed was there, and my books were there. I felt such immense frustration that I actually yelled. I was extraordinarily drunk; it was a very intense, very personal experience. I was not yelling for help or for mommy or daddy; it was an internal yell, or shout. It created some kind of breakthrough, and also some understanding of alcohol at the same time. There is some kind of little click, a step that you can take between alcohol being possessed in your body or alcohol possessing your mind. Once your mind is clear, your body becomes uncomplicated. That was a particular point of realization, very quick, although I had no visions of any kind. Nothing extraordinary happened to me at all; the headlines of this sadhana just came up in my head, flashed in my mind. The whole headline flashed in my mind.

What was happening interested me a great deal. I felt that the experience might be some kind of leverage, some kind of handle or staircase through which I might be able to relate or communicate, by means of that particular discipline and message, which is said by nobody, but which was in my head. That message was very powerful and very important for me.

An understanding of alcohol took place at the same time. I was drinking Bhutanese gin, I think, as well as Bhutanese beer, which is atrocious. It usually makes you sick. It's a dishwater kind of substance; it doesn't taste so good. I was drunk on the combination of the two, or maybe it was three—whatever the third one was. Some understanding took place, and I wrote down the title of the sadhana that night. The next day I woke up quite clear, without any hangover. I was very happy and rejoiced; my whole mood had completely changed. My preoccupation with Taktsang, the feeling that I should make a big deal of the place, that I had to get something out of it, was completely gone.

We had lots of chilies in Bhutan, and Künga was feeling extremely painful. On that very day, he complained that he didn't want to eat this kind of food anymore. He just wanted some plain biscuits or meat. He asked me to translate his request to the cook. The cook said he had a problem with the pots: he couldn't cook two meals at once. He said he was cooking specially for me. He shouldn't have to cook especially for Künga; Künga was supposed to be my disciple, so he should eat what I ate. He shouldn't be treated as a VIP. I translated all that back to poor Künga, who was very depressed. So he had to stick with *ema*, which is the Bhutanese word for chili. Bhutanese cooking uses a lot of hot green chilies—it's like Szechuan food. Hot chilies were cooked with the meat. There was no curry powder or any other spice. It's very painful to eat, and it's good, too. The worst pain is when you go to the bathroom.

Getting back to the subject, I began to write the sadhana on that day, and I completed almost the whole thing. I wrote just a few words the following day. So altogether it took me about six hours to write the whole thing. I didn't have to think about what I was doing; the whole thing came out very fresh. After a while, the words began to churn in my mind and my hands began to ache. I tried to relax a little bit and rest my fingers. After that, I picked up my pen and just wrote spontaneously. That is how the sadhana was written.

THE PURPOSE OF THE SADHANA: JOINING ATI AND MAHAMUDRA

In writing the sadhana, I tried to bring together the devotion from the Nyingma tradition and the Kagyü tradition. That is the basic idea of the sadhana: to bring together the ati and mahamudra traditions. There's no conflict at all between the two. The contemplative approach of the Kagyüs is somewhat dramatic and perhaps too power oriented. In order to tone it down, I added something from the Nyingma tradition, in order to create a better soup stock, by adding another flavoring. Bringing those two traditions together actually makes a lot of sense. Karma Pakshi, who is the main figure in the sadhana, is regarded in the sadhana as the same as Padmasambhava, who is the founder of the Nyingma lineage. It was Padmasambhava who introduced the Buddhist teachings to Tibet. He was also a tantric master. Karma Pakshi was a less powerful or famous person historically. He was just a crazy-wisdom person in the Kagyü tradition.

My purpose in writing the sadhana was to build a bridge between the two contemplative traditions. Even the wording of this sadhana, how each sentence and the whole thing is structured, is based on that idea of trying to bring together in a harmonious way the mahamudra language of the newer school of tantra and the ati language of the older school of tantra.

Underlying both mahamudra and maha ati is a basic foundation: the practice of surrendering, renunciation, and devotion. That brings the whole thing together, very much in a nutshell. You have to surrender, and you actually have to develop devotion. Without that, you can't see or hear or experience the real teachings properly and fully. We could go into the details of that later on.

DISCUSSION

The reference to "warring sects" in the sadhana.

Question: At the beginning of the sadhana, in the introductory remarks before we begin chanting, the sadhana speaks of warring sects, schools of the sangha fighting among themselves. Were you referring to the conflict between the Nyingmas and the Kagyüs?

Chögyam Trungpa Rinpoche: Not necessarily. Warring or fighting refers to all the schools—to everything, to everybody. The Theravadins were at odds with the Sarvastivadins; the Burmese were quarreling with the Sinhalese.

Relationship of mahamudra and ati.

Q: Are mahamudra and ati two different sects, related to the Kagyü and Nyingma lineages?

CTR: They are not regarded as being different in terms of being in conflict, but the mahamudra tradition of the Kagyüs was often regarded as less advanced than the highest level of the Nyingma tradition, which is ati. The Kagyü tradition actually does accept the ati teachings.

Reconciling the Kagyü and the Nyingma lineages in the sadhana.

Q: I was deeply impressed by the process, more than I was by the climax or the content of what we're striving to understand. As you told the story, with my Western ears, I heard you saying that you went in and out of the garbage pail, and you came to this place and made a primal scream, and out came the thing that you were looking for. So I'm curious as to what motivation you felt, as sort of the filter or the transmitter of Buddhism, to create this reconciliation of two schools.

CTR: Well, that reconciliation evolved on its own. For example, the third Karmapa, Rangjung Dorje, was the embodiment of both traditions. At the same time, the Kagyü and the Nyingma lineages both continued separately. So I don't particularly have to invent a new lineage. Jamgön Kongtrül the Great also realized that the two traditions are very close, that they work hand in hand. The Kagyü tradition is more energetic and the Nyingma tradition is more spacious; nevertheless, they work together.

Carrying the profundity of the sadhana into everyday life.

Q: The sadhana is a highly inspiring piece of literature. It speaks of how the phenomenal world in all its simplicity and mundane quality represents the very highest, the most profound, truths. There's an exciting quality to performing the sadhana; at the same time we could have some intuitive sense that our mind in its naked state could actually be Dorje Trolö—that it could be of the nature of self-existing equanimity. That simplicity is very exciting, but at the same time, that exciting simplicity is over when the gong rings three times and we go back to our simple, mundane world. We don't think anymore in terms of Dorje Trolö or self-existing equanimity. Yet that is what the sadhana is about: seeing the profundity in everyday experience.

CTR: We have an artificial problem there. I don't see any real problem. It's a question of what we're going to do afterward. We just do what we do, and when the security of our inspiration gets exposed to city life or just ordinary life, it is very painful for us. But we have to submit to that situation; otherwise we would have no way to understand ourselves. I don't see any big problems, particularly. We just have to do it, just do it very simply. And when we do it, we are able to feel it properly. If we have any complaints, that is a sign that we didn't do it properly. So it's very simple to deal with our artificial problem. We have to do it. We have to do it.

Reference in the sadhana to the waning of the Buddha's teaching.

Q: You wrote at the beginning of the sadhana that the teachings of Buddha were waning, and that spiritual materialism was getting stronger. Was that in reference to your experience at the temple at Taktsang?

CTR: It was in reference to many things. We definitely had a lot of spiritual problems in my country. People just conducted their little spiritual business affairs: they conducted marriage ceremonies; they conducted funeral ceremonies; they conducted ceremonies for the sick; they conducted ceremonies for the unfortunate. However, there was no real practice going on; it was a big racket. It was no wonder the communists decided to take over; they were right from that point of view. They had a perfect right to destroy that superficial and highly theocratized society, which had no real theocracy, no real religion, no real insight. All those things were true. In fact, I think the dissolution of the Tibetan kingdom was very fortunate for Buddhism. We are finally here; we are face-to-face with somebody else, with another real world. I'm beginning to feel that Tibetan teachers who escaped from communist oppression could hopefully conduct their business very honestly. They don't have to continue the old ways—over and over, again and again.

So as far as I'm concerned, I have pulled my own trip together from that point of view. I just tell people the truth: that to begin with, life is painful— that it's not blissful to begin with. I tell people they have to do things properly, that they have to sit a lot. That's the basic point. If people want to get into tantra, I tell them that it's a very long way for them, that they're not ready for it, and so forth. What we have been discussing under the heading of the sadhana is that people corrupt the teachings in the name of holiness. It has happened in the past, in the Catholic tradition as well as in other high church traditions. It seems to be always the same problem. What we are getting into here is hopefully reformed Buddhism. What happened in Tibet did not happen in the name of deception; there were very honest and fantastic teachers, great teachers like Jamgön Kongtrül. But there were a lot of other people who were trying to make fifty cents into a dollar. It was a complex situation.

Q: I'm very glad you're here.

CTR: Thank you. You got your money's worth.

2. Devotion and Crazy Wisdom

The crazy-wisdom tradition puts a lot of emphasis on the sense of sudden intoxication, that ordinary mind can be suddenly transformed into no-mind. The mahamudra devotional school puts its emphasis on gradual intoxication, telling students that they have to take their time, take it sip by sip, so to speak, and find their own level. Both approaches have truth in them... There is a need for both approaches together. That makes the whole thing completely workable for students.

Next we could discuss the relationship between crazy wisdom and devotion. That relationship underlies "The Sadhana of Mahamudra."

Devotion

Hero Worship versus Genuine Devotion

The ordinary notion of devotion is based on some kind of parental relationship, a relationship between a father or mother and a child. On the part of the child, it involves security, admiration, and hero worship. That is why a lot of people think that devotion means putting a picture of their own favorite football player or rock star on their wall, along with photos of their favorite admired gurus. Jumbling them together that way seems to be their idea of hero worship, the worship of the ultimate achievement of a spiritual and physical superman. That kind of devotion is very questionable. There is no real substance or intelligence there, in terms of relating with the reality of personal growth; it's purely hero worship, a dream world. That kind of adoration actually weakens the notion of heroism.

In the Kagyü tradition, the notion of devotion is an absolutely fundamental and, at the same time, full commitment. Devotees do not regard
the object of their devotion as purely an object of admiration. They don't
simply admire somebody because that person has great talent, and therefore
should be a good person to be put on their list of heroes. There is enormous
simple-mindedness in that approach, which is why we are not really able to
appreciate art or fine craftsmanship or true sanity with that approach. We
usually put everything together in one big garbage pail; we feel that anybody
who is not quite in keeping with our own clumsiness has got to be good. So
let us worship all these great football players or great presidents along with
our great spiritual teachers. That approach seems to be starting out on the
wrong footing; we could quite safely say that we are beginning at the wrong
end of the stick.

Any real sense of devotion or dedication comes not from comparing, but
from personal experience. We have actually committed ourselves. Maybe
the closest example of devotion that we could come up with would be the
way we feel about our lover, who may not be a great musician or a great
football player or a great singer. That person may not even be all that great
at keeping their domestic life together. There is just something about that
particular person, who doesn't fit any of the usual categories of heroes. He
or she is just a good person, a lovable person who has some very powerful qualities in themselves. That seems to be the closest analogy that we
could come up with. But at the same time, devotion in the spiritual context
involves something more than that. Our lover may have some kind of physical beauty or may be able to offer us some sort of security. He or she may
be able to create an accommodating nest for us personally, which would be
a fantastic idea. But somehow, in real devotion, we are even transcending
that situation.

Real devotion is connected with some sense of ground, in which we relate
with our own mind. Often you may not be able to do so with your lover,
since your lover is the object of too much admiration. The object of devotion, the guru, is not so much an object of admiration, not a superman. We
are not expecting everything to be absolutely right. At that point, we take
another step in our relationship with our guru, our teacher, who is not a
football player, not a great musician, a great singer, or even a great lover.
We have gone to another level. We simply begin to realize that some kind
of love affair is taking place between us and the teacher, not at the football
player level or even at the wife or husband level; something else is taking

place. That something else is difficult to explain and very hard to describe; that something else has immense clarity and power. We don't usually like our lovers to have too much power over us; we don't usually like our heroes to have too much power over us. We would simply like to idolize them. That way it's our choice rather than something coming from that angle. The complete devotion of the relationship between teacher and student is a unique situation.

The Two Aspects of Devotion

Longing. There are two aspects to devotion: longing and humbleness. The first one is longing, in the sense that you would actually like to get into the mind of your teacher. You would like to experience your teacher's mind fully and completely; you wish you could get inside the teacher's brain and look out. Then you could say, "Wow! This is how the teacher sees it. It's fantastic!" You would like to get inside his or her brain first and then look at yourself. You're a little disciple sitting there in your teacher's mind and looking at the world from his point of view. You climb over his brain and you poke a little hole in his skull so that you can look outside. But although you are unable to do that, you still feel a kind of fascination and a fantastic longing: you would like to mix your mind with his or her mind. That longing is the first kind of devotion.

Humbleness. The second aspect of devotion is humbleness. Humbleness in this case means absence of ego, absence of arrogance. When you worship a football player or your great daddy or your great mother, that worship is somewhat arrogant: you think that you will inherit their great genius. You would like to associate with great poets, great artists, great geniuses. But when you relate with your teacher spiritually in terms of devotion, there is very little room for arrogance. You have a sense of humbleness and an absence of uptightness.

Uptightness is also arrogance. Arrogance is thinking that you know what you are going to do; you are completely involved in your male chauvinistic trip or your female chauvinistic trip. You think that as females or as males, you have the right to a complete description of what spiritual disciplines you might be receiving. That kind of chauvinism is what's known as arrogance. People who might mock other people's chauvinistic trips would never criticize themselves. They would say about others, "*You* are a bitch; you are a pig." The others are in the wrong, obviously. That is always the problem. When there is arrogance, there is no communication. So the obstacle to humbleness is too much chauvinism, and not paying enough attention to who you are and what you are. The only way to overcome that obstacle is to develop a sense of humbleness. Genuine humility doesn't mean that you have to faithfully follow an Oriental trip of bowing every other minute or every other second. You don't have to kneel down and lick your teacher's feet as an expression of devotion. Sometimes when people can't experience devotion properly, they just try to act it out physically. They are always trying to please, trying to maintain some kind of format or protocol, which is highly questionable. Often such people are extraordinarily arrogant.

Real humbleness is not allowing any kind of backbone in oneself. You are completely flexible from head to toe. You are without a backbone, without any bones at all in your body. You would just like to kneel down. You are flexible like a good fish that has been cooked; you are completely flexible, like a worm. You don't have the arrogance of sticking your little corners out and saying, "No, no! You can't touch my ribs. No, no! You can't touch my neck. You can't touch my back, my shoulders, my leg. It hurts! Don't touch me." You are totally reduced to a piece of raw meat, a completely flexible piece of raw meat. You are willing to do anything. You are willing to get into anything; you are willing to actually open yourself up and be at the mercy of your teacher.

So those two aspects of devotion—longing and humbleness, the absence of pride or arrogance—are the basis or foundation of the sadhana. They are also a description of how you could actually follow your path.

CRAZY WISDOM

Going further, another aspect of the tradition of the sadhana is crazy wisdom, which is a very unusual topic. How can we say that craziness and wisdom would exist together? We could say quite safely that the expression *crazy wisdom* is not structured correctly; it is purely a linguistic convenience. We could say instead that wisdom comes first and craziness comes afterward, so "wisdom crazy" is more accurate. In relation to the idea of journey, wisdom is an all-pervasive, all-encompassing vision or perspective. It is highly powerful, clear, and precise. You are able to see things as they are, in their own right; you have no biases at all; you see things as they are, without any question. Out of that, you begin to develop craziness, which is not paying attention to all the little wars, the little resistances that might be put up by the world of reference points, the world of duality. That is craziness.

So "wisdom crazy" is the better term. It involves a sense of immense control, immense vision, and immense relaxation occurring simultaneously in your mind, all the time. You might ask how that is possible. Ordinarily, if you exercise too much control, you can't relax. You think that in order to be in control, you have to be tight. So how can you have immense control and immense relaxation at the same time? How can you see clearly at the same time? But that dichotomy is too conceptual; you can achieve immense control and immense relaxation and immense clarity all at the same time.

JOINING CRAZY WISDOM AND DEVOTION

The lineage of the sadhana is the lineage of the two schools put together: the two traditions of immense crazy wisdom and immense dedication and devotion. It puts the student's role and the teacher's role together into one powerful style. The Kagyü, or mahamudra, tradition, the tradition of Karma Pakshi, specialized in immense dedication and devotion. The Nyingma, or ati, tradition, the tradition of Padmasambhava, is the lineage of crazy wisdom. It is possible to put these two traditions together and work with both of them. The sadhana is a prototype of how emotion and wisdom can work together. It's possible; it has been done.

This particular tradition or lineage has developed quite recently, starting about 160 years ago. It was founded particularly by the Tibetan master Jamgön Kongtrül the Great. He had developed a deep understanding of the ati and mahamudra principles, and he had become the lineage holder in the contemplative traditions of Tibetan Buddhism. His tradition or system is called the Rimé school, which literally means "unbiased." There is no favoritism toward a particular school of thought, but it combines the contemplative traditions. The meditative traditions were brought together at that point. The initial inspiration for the Rimé school came from Karma Pakshi, the second Karmapa, who lived in the thirteenth century. Karma Pakshi was a teacher of the Kagyü lineage. He received teachings from the Nyingma tradition as well as from his own tradition.

Rangjung Dorje, the third Karmapa, the reincarnation of Karma Pakshi, brought the two traditions together still more. He had the very clear and precise understanding that the mahamudra teaching of devotion and the maha ati teaching of crazy wisdom could be brought together. The tradition became very eminent. It was a very important revelation for the two contemplative traditions of Tibetan Buddhism.

Openness and craziness became one approach at that point. In the Kagyü tradition, there were people like Milarepa, who was a very hard worker. He was extraordinarily diligent and devoted to his own particular discipline. On the other hand, the holders of the Nyingma lineage, like Padmasambhava, were wild and crazy and fantastically expansive. They were visionary on a larger scale; they had their own particular style of relating with the world. Bringing those two styles together is like making a good cup of tea. You boil some water and you put a pinch of tea in it, which makes a good cup of tea. You put a dash of milk in it and you drink it up.

So what we are talking about is a very beautiful blend of the two situations put together. It's an ideal situation. Quite possibly, I could say that it's the best thing that has happened to Tibetan Buddhism. It's a fantastic, magnificent display of total sanity, of basic enlightenment. Both traditions also have developed a sense of ruggedness and openness, expansiveness, and craziness put together. My personal teacher, Jamgön Kongtrül of Sechen, who was the embodiment of both traditions, handed down the teachings to me, so I feel extremely worthy and very personal about discussing this subject.

I feel that being able to discuss these things is a rare opportunity for us. The crazy-wisdom tradition puts a lot of emphasis on the sense of sudden intoxication, that ordinary mind can be suddenly transformed into nomind. The mahamudra devotional school puts its emphasis on gradual intoxication, telling students that they have to take their time, take it sip by sip, so to speak, and find their own level. Both approaches have truth in them.

However, it is best to start with the gradual process; otherwise you get an upset stomach—or even sudden death. In any case, you would experience sudden chaos. So whichever of these two traditions a person is involved with does not really make any difference at this point. Younger students are not able to handle the abruptness or suddenness. Therefore, they should be trained in hinayana first, then in mahayana, and only later in vajrayana. They should be prepared slowly and gently, and when they are ready to actually take the leap, then you push them off the cliff and make them fly. That is precisely how the mother eagle trains her young. The first few weeks she feeds them with all kinds of meat and worms and what have you. And only later, when they are still playing games with their mother, when they still want food and are getting fat without any exercise, when they are ready to use their wings, the mother pushes them out of the nest. In that way the young eagles begin to fly. They begin to take pride in their abilities. That approach to training actually makes sense.

Our lineage is quite fittingly referred to as the "children of the garuda," which is a mythical bird in Indian mythology. When the garuda egg hatches, the young garuda is all ready to fly. In the Rimé tradition, the ideas of sudden birth and gradual birth work together.

That question of gradual or sudden enlightenment exists in the Zen tradition as well. In Zen, people talk about experiencing satori and suddenly being able to do anything you want. But at the same time, you are expected to do a lot of sitting practice; a lot of training is needed. So that seems to be the general pattern of spiritual development: that there is a need for both approaches together. That makes the whole thing completely workable for students. If it were not for the mahamudra, or devotional, tradition, the maha ati, or crazy-wisdom, tradition might produce a lot of fanatics, a lot of neurotics, quite possibly even a lot of suicides. It is common knowledge that there is a high suicide rate among Zen practitioners. It is also quite possible that the gradual school would end up just running on its own regular nonsense if there were no crazy-wisdom school to save people from their wormlike trip, chewing their way through their own little tree, going round and round and round and finally dropping dead, completely dried up.

So bringing the two traditions together saves both, and their combination seems to be one of the most workable situations that has ever developed. It's no wonder the great teachers of the past came to that conclusion; I would say that they were very smart, as they deserve to be. They were, and they still are. That approach is still working in our own time.

DISCUSSION

Gelukpa tradition and the use of old tantras.

Question: Do they use the old tantras in the Gelukpa tradition?
Chögyam Trungpa Rinpoche: They miss a lot of big chunks, so they have no crazy wisdom; they're afraid of it. That's why in Western literature they are called the reformed tradition. Charles Bell and other scholars all call them "reformed."

Q: Last night you used the word "reformed" when you were speaking about the Kagyü tradition coming to America.

CTR: Well, this is real reform. We're not threatened by anybody, so we are doing it properly.

Devotion to discipline versus devotion to the teacher.

Q: You mentioned devotion—devotion to the teacher and devotion to discipline. I wonder if the teacher is the embodiment of discipline.

CTR: The teacher is the embodiment of discipline.

Q: Can one be devoted to discipline?

CTR: Sure, to a discipline that is given by a teacher. You can't get away with that!

Heroism of crazy wisdom.

Q: It seems to me that the concept of crazy wisdom has something very heroic about it. The crazy-wisdom person can do anything he wants; he's very powerful. He's a hero just like a football player is.

CTR: Well, I think that he *is* a hero rather than someone who is hero-worshipped. That's the difference. Obviously, he is powerful. When you possess power, you don't have to say, "I am powerful," because you are powerful already. So the difference between being hero-worshipped and being a hero on the spot is that you don't have to be qualified as a fantastic and powerful person. You are already.

Q: I have to think about that.

CTR: You'd better think about that before you get out of here.

Mahamudra and ati in the nine yanas.

Q: Why is maha ati the ninth yana and mahamudra the sixth yana?

CTR: Let's make it very simple. There are six tantric yanas that come after the first three yanas: *shravakayana, pratyekabuddhayana,* and *bodhi-sattvayana.* Those first three yanas make up the hinayana and the mahayana together. Then, there are six further yanas, or stages, of the vajrayana. Mahamudra includes the next three yanas,[1] which are the first three tantric yanas. Anuttarayoga tantra, which is basically the fruition of the sixth yana, is particularly predominant. Beyond that, you are approaching the area of ati, or crazy wisdom, the three higher tantric yanas: *mahayoga, anuyoga,* and *atiyoga.* The ninth yana is maha ati, or ati mentality.[2]

Advisability of starting the path with ati.

Q: I would like to ask your opinion of following a path that starts with ati. Or do you see the merging of the two traditions as being the best way for us?

CTR: It's very difficult to attain ati experience immediately; it takes a long time. So you find yourself following mahamudra, basically. That's what Rangjung Dorje, the third Karmapa, discovered himself. Many of the great teachers of the ati tradition, Jigme Lingpa and Longchen Rabjampa for example, constantly refer back to the nine-yana structure. You might think that you are doing ati-type discipline, that you belong to that particular style. Nevertheless, you always find that you have to start from scratch, which is unavoidably the mahamudra principle. So we don't have to give them labels, particularly, but what the whole thing amounts to is that you're starting from mahamudra experience in any case.

Seeing every experience as a manifestation of the guru principle.

Q: Rinpoche, could you talk about mahamudra and its connection with devotion and humbleness, and mahamudra and its connection with the visual aspect of the world, as a way of seeing reality as something vivid and colorful?

CTR: That's a very good question. Thank you. I wondered if somebody would catch on to that. You did. Devotion is not only devotion to your guru alone; it is also devotion to the manifestations of the guru that exist throughout your life, all the time. If you are drinking your tea, if you slipped a disc in your back, if you're crossing the river in a ferry, if you're flying in an airplane, if you step in dog shit—whatever you might do in your life—everything is a manifestation of the guru principle. Because there is such a powerful love affair between you and your vajra master, everything becomes extraordinarily vivid and extraordinarily personal.

You might sometimes feel like complaining about the whole thing; you might try to avoid the whole situation altogether. But somehow that doesn't work. There is a constant haunting quality to your experience, and when you try to forget your guru, he only becomes more prominent. When you try to pursue your guru, he only fades away into the background. That kind of process continually happens, and that actually creates the colorful perceptions of mahamudra experience. So the whole thing begins with devotion. That seems to be the basic point.

There is need for the vajra master in any case, whether you are part of the ati tradition or the mahamudra tradition. Particularly in the ati tradition, you need to have a lot of guidance and a sense of commitment to the vajra master. So the more commitment you have to the vajra master in the mahamudra tradition, the more ati-type experience will begin to take place. So it's saying the same thing in some sense.

Mahamudra automatically carrying over into action.

Q: That was the next thing I wanted to ask. It would seem that if you lived according to a mahamudra style, it would automatically carry over into action, without the normal reference points. So the traditions are very close together.

CTR: Well said, son of noble family.

Difference between the two schools in terms of luminosity and emptiness.

Q: Is the difference between the two schools a statement—not so much that "form is emptiness" and "emptiness is form," but that "form is luminous" and "luminosity is empty"?

CTR: How do you know about that?

Q: Does that make any sense, or is—

CTR: It does make sense, it does make sense. But did you read about that, or did you think about it?

Q: I thought about it.

CTR: Oh, that's great! That's been done already. That seems to be the tantric notion of the whole thing. Instead of saying "empty," you say "luminous."

Q: Well, I read that part in *Cutting Through Spiritual Materialism*.

CTR: You did? That's too bad.

Personalities in relation to mahamudra and ati.

Q: Why did the two schools arise? It wasn't just the personalities, was it?

CTR: It was the personalities, sure. People have different ideas: some people would like to be pilots and fly airplanes. Some people would like to be playboys. The playboy people are mahamudra people; the pilots are ati people. But maybe the playboys would like to fly airplanes, and the pilots might like to be playboys. Those are the two basic kinds of vision: one is so expansive, and the other is so intense and colorful—a love affair.

Spaciousness and demand in mahamudra practice.

Q: But in order to experience mahamudra, wouldn't your practice have to be very spacious as well?

CTR: In some sense. But if you find yourself in the middle of anuttarayoga disciplines, they are very demanding. They reduce you to nuts and bolts; with your mudras, your mantras, and your visualizations, you don't know where you are. It's a very demanding practice. You can't eat this; you can't eat that. You must eat this; you must drink that. You are constantly bounded within a very small area. But that is necessary because each time you practice, it is a process of shedding something.

Getting into the tantric world is a very full experience—overwhelmingly demanding. Some people's idea of tantra is just drinking ordinary liquor and having a good time, having a freestyle love affair. But that's not quite so. Demands are made on you in a particular way; the whole process is extraordinarily demanding. The whole point is to scrape away your basis, so that you don't have any ground to walk on. It is like scraping meat off bones: your emotions begin to float to the surface like fat boiled in water.

Q: But as you practice and the demands become greater and greater, shouldn't some kind of spaciousness always be required?

CTR: Not necessarily. As you become greater and greater, you could discover more and more possibilities of things that you could put into that greatness. If you become a millionaire, you buy lots of property and lots of furniture. You buy a big house and you fill it with pictures and photographs and furniture. That's how the whole thing goes. When you have a bigger style of thinking, you would like to decorate your world that way, because you feel that passion is your style. Maybe you should visit the homes of rich people and see how they handle themselves, particularly in America, which is a notoriously crude country. All kinds of things are going on in rich people's homes. Spaciousness doesn't mean that when you clear a space, when you open up a space, that nothing will occupy it. It usually happens that when you have more space, you put more stuff in it.

Q: So the big danger is of this intoxication becoming intoxicated.

CTR: Yes, that's right. You got it.

In order to connect with this material, it would be good if you can put more emphasis on disciplining yourself and on the sitting practice of meditation. That will make what we are discussing much more workable and immediate and realistic for you.

3. The Mandala of the Siddhas

That whole process of visualization is based on the unique world which is created by bringing together the contemplative traditions of the two schools. There is no need to borrow from any other tradition; we have a self-existing world that is created from the unique bringing together of the Kagyü and Nyingma traditions, very closely and properly.... One school has the brains and one school has the heart, so to speak. The brain represents the ati tradition; the heart is the mahamudra tradition. Joining the two together makes a perfect human being—something even more than that, a higher human being, a fantastic superman, a vajra superman of our age.

What we discussed in the last chapter covered the background of the two disciplines of the practice lineage. The language used in the sadhana is based on those two experiences: the highest level of devotion and the highest level of wisdom combined. Today, we could go beyond that to a more detailed understanding the sadhana itself.

The Opening of the Sadhana

The sadhana is composed of various sections, according to a traditional pattern. At the beginning is taking refuge and the bodhisattva vow. The first section also creates an atmosphere of self-realization or basic potentiality, which is an ongoing theme in the sadhana. In tantric language, that is called vajra pride. Your basic existence, your basic makeup, is part of enlightened being, a part of the enlightened principle. You are already basically enlightened, so you need only recognize or realize and understand that. That is done in the first lines of the sadhana.

CREATING THE MANDALA OF THE SIDDHAS

The Charnel Ground

The next part of the sadhana is the creation of the mandala of the siddhas, Karma Pakshi and Padmasambhava, who are embodied together. Beneath Karma Pakshi Padmasambhava is a triangle, which rests on a rock, which is built on the property of the charnel ground, which is a symbol of no-man's-land. It is the ground where birth and death take place; it is prelife and postlife experience. The idea of the charnel ground is that all kinds of experiences coexist simultaneously; you are working with that kind of no-man's-land. You no longer belong to any particular situation; you no longer belong to any particular lifestyle. You are completely open and basic. That fundamental principle is the nature of buddha mind, in fact. Buddha mind, or buddha nature, is like the space where birth and death take place. Discontinuity, or dissolving, and continuity take place constantly in that space. From that basic mandala of the charnel ground, the siddhas arise.

The Inner Mandala

There are two types of mandala: there is the elaborate setup of the geographical mandala of the charnel ground, and there is the mandala that is created out of one's own body. The various parts of the body mandala are the forehead center, the throat center, and the heart center. The body mandala is connected with what is known as inner yoga: you don't actually have to arrange anything; the mandala is already developed in your own existence. Your body could be regarded as sacred ground or property already. At that point the figure of Karma Pakshi and Padmasambhava arises as one person, the great wrathful one, the embodiment of crazy wisdom.

That basic principle is not particularly visualized in the way that orthodox sadhanas prescribe. In this case, the qualities and the visualization are taking place simultaneously. The qualities, or symbolism, and attributes of all kinds are described one by one.

Traditionally, in tantric visualization practice, the visualization is created, and after that the higher principles descend to bless the visualization. The jnanasattvas bless the existing visualization, called the samayasattva, and merge with it. But in this sadhana, samayasattva and jnanasattva are embodied together. The symbolism is described first, and then the attributes of

Dorje Trolö Karma Pakshi thangka. *Painted by Sherab Palden Beru; used by permission.*

the symbolism are described, throughout the whole visualization. The basic point is that Karma Pakshi and Padmasambhava are one, and their attributes are continuous. In addition, there are various centers in the body: the forehead center, the throat center, and the heart center, which are important places.

The head center represents the physical plane, the world of form, the tangible, solid world—as opposed to the confused world. The confused world, to use an ordinary metaphor, is like a chicken without a head. That chicken is very freaked out and runs all over the place. But a chicken with a head might be a better chicken. So the head chakra—or actually, somebody with a whole body including the head—is the idea of solidity, definiteness. The throat center is connected with the idea of speech, communication, reference point. You have to speak in order to connect the body and the mind. The heart center is related with the mind.

In the forehead center we have Tüsum Khyenpa, who represents the vajra principle. He was the first of the Karmapa line. He was a great ascetic, a great meditator, and a great penetrator, which is the vajra principle. In the throat center we have Mikyö Dorje, the eighth Karmapa. He was a great scholar, a great theologian (so to speak), and a great grammarian. He represents speech, the voice or the proclamation of the teachings. In the heart center we have Rangjung Dorje, who was the third Karmapa. He was the one who actually brought the ati tradition and the mahamudra tradition together. He was a lineage holder in both the Nyingma tradition of Longchen Rabjampa and others, and in the Kagyü tradition, obviously, since he was a Karmapa himself.

Bringing Together the Contemplative Traditions of Mahamudra and Ati

That whole process of visualization is based on the unique world that is created by bringing together the contemplative traditions of the two schools. There is no need to borrow from any other tradition; we have a self-existing world that is created from the unique bringing together of the Kagyü and Nyingma traditions, very closely and properly. We could call the central figure of Karma Pakshi Padmasambhava "Karma Padmasambhava." He is the same person, one person. The first name is Karma and the surname is Padmasambhava, which is saying that it is the same person, with the same basic character. He represents the fact that the two traditions are extremely

Tüsum Khyenpa, Mikyö Dorje, and Rangjung Dorje. *Detail from the thangka on p. 47; used by permission.*

close. There is no sectarianism or bitterness at all between them. There is a saying in Tibet that the separation between the Kagyü and Nyingma traditions doesn't exist in the same way that your left eyeball and your right eyeball do not compete with each other. You see with both eyes. The two traditions are always together and always synchronized in their disciplines.

Getting back to the sadhana, around Karma Pakshi are a great host of buddhas and the sangha, the utterance of the dharma, the protectors, and so on. They legitimize the visualization as being the embodiment of the three jewels: Buddha, dharma, and sangha. The dakinis, the *dharmapalas*, and the protectors are all included. That's the important point.

The text continues:

> Whatever you see is the form of Karma Pakshi run wild; whatever you hear is the voice of Karma Pakshi let loose; whatever you think is the thought of Karma Pakshi unleashed.

That is a very important point here. The whole approach is that there is a sense of not holding back. Not holding back doesn't mean vomiting out sickness or churning out buckets of diarrhea. This is a very sane approach: we are talking about how to let go within the whole thing, how to open. You suddenly discover a sense of immense freedom when you connect with the wisdom of those two beautiful schools put together.

One school has the brains and one school has the heart, so to speak. The brain represents the ati tradition; the heart is the mahamudra tradition. Joining the two together makes a perfect human being—something even more than that, a higher human being, a fantastic superman, a vajra superman of our age.

The best of the two worlds had been put together in combining the two great contemplative traditions: that was the message that came to me from my teacher, Jamgön Kongtrül. He transmitted a lot of information and teachings to me. I also received teachings from many other teachers; I probably had something like fifteen gurus altogether. And all of the teachings agreed. I understood that there was no problem, no chaos, no confusion in putting those two schools and their wisdom together. They don't even have to be put together, actually; they simply dissolve into each other—simultaneously. That dissolving is a product of "let loose," "let go," and "unleashed." There is a sense of immense power and immense discipline at the same time.

SUPPLICATION: LINKING WRETCHEDNESS AND GLORY

The next section is the supplication. In the supplication, we are basically trying to relate with each of the basic centers, or focal energies—body, speech, and mind—as well as with the sadhana as a whole, or with Karma Pakshi Padmasambhava. In these verses we are asking to be admitted or accepted into that condition of gloriousness. Our own condition is highly wretched. So we are trying to link together wretchedness and gloriousness.

It is usually very difficult for us to do that. If we don't have a greater vision, we can't bring those two worlds together at all. The world seems very divided to us; we are so depressed and so wretched that when we even think about that gloriousness, we feel more depressed. Oy vey! And when we are into the gloriousness, we don't want to have anything to do with the wretchedness. It seems to us that wretchedness has not yet come, or else that we have already gone through it; we have already abandoned it behind our back.

Making a separation between gloriousness and wretchedness is our biggest problem. The purpose of this sadhana is to bring those two poles together, which is not particularly impossible. Wretchedness brings us down to earth, and gloriousness brings us up, makes us expansive, gives us more vision. So the idea of the supplication is to bring about a combination of those two situations.

Supplication in the Nontheistic Tradition

Supplication is not asking something of some divine principle that exists somewhere else—upstairs in the loft. It doesn't mean trying to get that person to descend on us. Here, supplication is the fundamental principle of the simultaneous existence of depression and excitement; we try to relate to both of them. Whenever there is too much excitement, depression may become very useful. Whenever there is too much depression, some excitement may be workable and uplifting. One of the problems with the theistic tradition is a constant attempt to cheer up, to try to compete with heaven or with granddad. We try to become completely like him; we try to forget how wretched we really are. Then, when we finally realize how wretched we are, we punish ourselves or we are afraid of being punished, flagellated. The theistic tradition seems to be very schizophrenic; it is unable to accept that the human condition and the divine condition are really one.

In the Buddhist nontheistic tradition, we don't have that problem. The divine principle, however glorious it may be, is still very depressing. And depression, however depressing it may be, is still glorious. We don't actually have to jump back and forth like a flea. We could stay on our own meditation cushion; we could simply sit and be. We could wash our dishes in the kitchen sink; we could drive our car; we could go to nine-to-five jobs—we could do all the things that we are supposed to be doing. We could earn our bread that way. But at the same time, we don't have to jump back and forth anymore. We can simply stay where we are.

Where we are is what we have and what we might be, what we will be and what we have done. Everything is included. This very moment is everything. We don't have to jump back and forth comparing our own little wretchedness—how tiny we are, how little we are, how dirty we are—with how great *they* are, how fantastic they are, how expansive they are, how overwhelming they are, how glorious and mighty they are. If that is what we are thinking, then we are having a problem with our thinking system. If we try to put those two poles together, we get spiritual indigestion forever.

Very few theologians have actually come to that point of joining the two, with the exception of Martin Buber, who actually has something to say about this. He says that the two poles of the conflict exist because human beings are no longer able to accept simplicity. That seems to be the basic point, which comes through quite truly, quite rightly in Mr. Buber's writings.

The Thick Black Fog of Materialism and the Slime and Muck of the Dark Age

The supplication section of the sadhana describes our own condition, which is "wretched" and "miserable." We are surrounded by a "thick black fog of materialism"; we are bogged down in the "slime and muck of the dark age." It's like a description of an urban ghetto. There is so much pollution, so much dirtiness, and so much greasiness in this existence, not only in cities, but also in the country—maybe much more so. We experience the whole world that way.

There is a somewhat metaphysical meaning behind the two descriptions: "slime and muck of the dark age" and "thick black fog of materialism." "The slime and muck of the dark age" has the connotation of an overwhelming environment, one that we often feel we are unable to relate with. We have a sense of the world's hostility and aggression, as well as passion; everything is beginning to eat us up. And "the thick black fog of materialism" refers to the basic wrongness or problems of the environment. So a general sense of the environment and the reference point of our relationship to it are put together.

These two types of corruption correspond to the description of two types of experience in the Buddhist tradition. The first type is called "neurotic crimes." We are constantly trying to patch things up. We don't want to see the embarrassing holes in our existence, we would like to cover them with patchwork. We are constantly rushing and running so fast that we begin to stumble over our own feet.

The second type of experience is called "blockages" or "obscurations." We have a sense of uncertainty that results from our own speed. There is a fundamental kind of wrongness in our actions because we are so involved in running, speeding. Those two principles are what is referred to as the slime and muck of the dark age and the thick black fog of materialism in this section of the sadhana.

Disillusionment with Spiritual Materialism

The next passage in the supplication is about our disillusionment with the world of spiritual materialism. It reads:

> The search for an external protector
> Has met with no success.
> The idea of a deity as an external being
> Has deceived us, led us astray.

The verse goes on from there.

There are all kinds of spiritual materialism, but theism seems to be the heart of spiritual materialism. The problems created by theism have been somewhat solved by the humanists, by the development of the Darwinian theory of evolution, the basic scientific discovery that the creation of the world was independent of God. Charles Darwin quite suspiciously presented his case, which has somehow served the purpose of human individuality. So the humanistic psychology approach makes the basic nontheistic or humanistic point. But having understood that, it gives us no guidelines for conducting our lives. That seems to be the problem.

People feel a lot of disappointment in their own culture. They are constantly rejecting their own culture—needlessly. But in some sense they do it from a sense of genuine need. The traditional culture and the traditional hierarchy that they inherit come from their parents. Their parents believe in a hierarchical setup of authority, which comes from their priests, their religious background. It comes from the first and foremost great-great-great-granddad, who said that law and order was God, who handed down traditions: how you should eat, what your table manners should be, how you should sit on your toilet seat. You are supposed to behave well; you are supposed to be good boys and girls. All that comes from great-great-granddad. People resent that, obviously. If you can't even relate with your own parents, and then you find that there are even greater parents—100 percent more so, 200 percent more so, 500 percent more so, 1,000 percent more so—if your parents have been magnified to such a gigantic scale, that obviously becomes a source of pain; it becomes a problem. That kind of heavy-handed authority is what has led American psychology, or Western psychology in general, to a journey toward nontheism. That is the newest spiritual development, as far as the Western world is concerned.

The various things discussed here, the institutional corruptions and the traditional idea of trust, are based on nothing but confusion. All these things are related with the theistic problems that exist in our world. But we can't be too fatalistic about this situation: it also has a lot of potential, immense potential. The complaints and the reaction against our parents and our granddad and our great-great-granddad are well founded. That new kind of wisdom of asserting our own intelligence is quite right; it seems to be the vanguard of the nontheistic tradition, which is just about to give birth. One of the most important and interesting points that we have discussed here is that everything which seems to go wrong with our life, the mismanagement of the dharma and all the other things—the list goes on and on—all seem to be related with that problem of theism.

Theism and Buddhism

That theistic problem is not a problem for theists in the literal sense alone; it is a problem for many Buddhists as well. When Buddhists begin to deify their beliefs, when they start to believe in divine providence, when they revert to a primitive level of belief, they are corrupting Buddhism immensely; they are simply worshipping an external deity.

Very conveniently we have lots of *yidams*, lots of dakinis, dharmapalas, buddhas, and bodhisattvas. In fact, the Buddhists of this age think that if they don't like one deity, they can choose another one. They have an immense feast of choices. In the Judeo-Christian tradition, there's only one divine person, which makes it very difficult. But Buddhists, or Hindus for that matter, find it delightful to jump back and forth. If they don't like one deity, they can associate with somebody else. In that way, Buddhism has become a theistic religion, which is a sign of corruption, a sign of the dark age.

Part of our work here is to try to solve that problem. We are trying to reform that primitive and corrupted way of looking at things. We are trying to reintroduce the style of the early Buddhists, the purity of the Buddhism that first came to Tibet and that was first introduced in India at the time of Tilopa, Naropa, Marpa, and Milarepa. We are trying to turn back history, to purify ourselves, to reform Buddhism. That is our basic approach. It's a question of dealing with the spiritual materialism that exists both within Buddhism and outside of it.

Theistic beliefs have been seeping into the Buddhist mentality, which should be nontheistic; that has brought with it a lot of corruption and problems. There has been too much worship and too much admiration of deities, so much so that people can't experience the awakened state of mind properly; they can't experience their own sanity properly. In fact, one reason I wrote the sadhana at all is because such problems exist both within and outside of the Buddhist tradition, and because the spiritual scene all over the world is going through that kind of corruption. The whole world is into fabricating its spiritual mommies and daddies.

If you don't like father figures, you decide to have a female yidam like Tara. "I like her because I'm a woman," you say. "I'm a mother, and maybe I should relate with her. She seems to be kind and motherly, and I don't like these wrathful people." Or if you feel that Tara is somewhat too corny and you would like to have someone juicy and gutsy, then you relate with those wrathful people. There are so many trips about the whole thing. It's like a society woman telling her neighbor about her new hat. "What kind of yidam do you have?" "Who gave you that yidam? Oh, that's nice. I was just about to have so-and-so yidam, but my teacher said, 'You should have this one. It's good for you!'" The marketing of yidams, the auctioning of yidams, is mind-boggling. So the purpose of the supplication is to reawaken people from their trips. At that point, inner experience can begin to come up.

IDENTIFICATION WITH THE GURU

The next section, which is connected with that awakening, begins:

> When the wild and wrathful father approaches⁞
> The external world is seen to be transparent and unreal.⁞
> The reasoning mind no longer clings and grasps.⁞

You are arriving in new territory. In spite of the depressions of theistic overhang, or hangover, in spite of the theistic diseases that even Buddhists or other traditions can catch, you finally begin to realize that you don't have to dwell constantly on your pain. You begin to realize that you can go beyond that level. Finally you can celebrate that you are an individual human being. You have your own intelligence, and you can pull the rug from under your own feet. You don't need to ask somebody else to do that. You don't need to ask someone to pull up your socks—or your pants, for that matter.

The next theme in this section is the idea of the merging of one's mind with the guru's mind. It says in the sadhana at this point:

The experience of joy becomes devotion‡
And I am drunk with all-pervading blessings.‡
This is a sign of the merging of mind and guru.‡
The whole of existence is freed and becomes the guru.‡

It's not that the guru is a deity that you bring into your heart, whom you become one with. It's not like artificial insemination, particularly. It is very personal and spontaneous; you are what you are, and you realize that your own inspiration exists in that particular intelligence and immense clarity. With that encouragement, you begin to wake up. You begin to associate yourself completely with the dharma; you identify completely with the dharma; you become one with the dharma. You no longer depend on any external agents to save you from your misery; you can do it yourself. That is just basic Buddhism. It could be called the tantric approach, but it's just basic Buddhism, which starts from the hinayana level of the first noble truth, and so forth—especially the third noble truth, I suppose.

The Four Dharmas of Gampopa

The next section is the "Four Dharmas of Gampopa." You could study the teachings that I've given on those, in connection with this. The first dharma is "Grant your blessings so that my mind may be one with the dharma."[1] You become completely one with the dharma. It's not so much that you follow the dharma, but that your mind *is* dharma. The second dharma is "Grant your blessings so dharma may progress along the path." When your mind has become one with the dharma, then practice becomes the natural behavior pattern that exists in you. The third one is "Grant your blessings so that the path may clarify confusion." The confusion that you brought to the dharma, to the path, and to your life does not exist anymore. That confusion has been clarified. The last dharma of Gampopa is "Grant your blessings so that confusion may dawn as wisdom." You are beginning to have a very clear perception that the world is created out of no-mind—properly and fully. The world does not have to be based on strategy anymore; the world can be based on your own experience and on clear vision, clear insight.

Offering

Then we have the offering section. It is quite simple. You have tried to make connections; you have tried so hard; you have tried to open up immensely. At that point, you no longer have to try so hard to be ingratiating. You finally realize that you have something to give, something to offer, rather than offering nothing and asking for nothing. What you have to give is your own ego—ignorance, aggression, passion. We have all that juicy stuff, very rich, very fertile, very potent, and very smelly. The idea is to give these things, to offer them and not to be embarrassed. You can actually appreciate your own particular experience.

It is like entertaining a guest with your ethnic cooking. You don't have to feel bad about being Italian or Jewish or Chinese or Tibetan or Japanese or whatever. You just cook your meal for your guests. You do it in your own 100 percent ethnic style, and your guests might like it fantastically. Those ethnic qualities in you, those provincial or local qualities in you, are the ground for fantastic color and fantastically good ideas. They could be offered as a great feast, a fantastic feast. That is what the idea of offering boils down to.

Padmasambhava/Guru Rinpoche

The next section is the *abhisheka*.[2] It begins:

> HUM HUM HUM:
> In the cave of Taktsang Sengge Samdrup:
> He who has subdued the evil forces:
> And buried treasure in rocks and snow mountains in holy places
> of Tibet:
> Shows kindness to the people of the future dark age.:
> I supplicate you, Dorje Trolö;:
> I supplicate you, Ugyen Padmakara.:

That verse was composed by Guru Rinpoche, Padmasambhava himself. Dorje Trolö was the eighth aspect of Padmasambhava.[3] We have no idea of the real meaning of the word *Trolö*. It is a very enigmatic word. Some scholars say that it is the Tibetanized version of Krodhaloka, the wrathful lord of the world. *Trolö* doesn't have any particular meaning in Tibetan.

Tro sometimes means "wheat" and sometimes means "beige"; *lö* sometimes means "loose." Basically, Dorje Trolö is the embodiment of a real, true crazy-wisdom person.

Padmasambhava manifested as Dorje Trolö near the end of his life at Taktsang in Bhutan, which at that time was in Tibet. Sengge Samdrup is the name of the guardian deity there, so the cave was called Taktsang Samdrup, meaning the cave of Sengge Samdrup. *Sengge* means "lion," and *samdrup* means "wish-fulfilling." We might wonder how he did the whole thing, how he actually became a crazy-wisdom person. Nobody knows, since there is nobody here to tell us the firsthand account. As far as we know from history and from lineage gossip that has been handed down from generation to generation, he actually changed his outlook and his behavior pattern at that point.

He became very wild and crazy, seemingly. He was able to manifest himself in that way in order to override the immense speed that exists in neurosis. He was much faster than our ordinary neurosis; therefore he could bypass our ordinary speed. However fast our speed might be, whether it be as fast as a rocket or as fast as a jet plane, he would go much faster—quite possibly a hundred times the speed of sound. In that way he was able to communicate with people and catch them, catch their neurosis. That is the idea of crazy-wisdom manifestation here, of wisdom so powerfully up-to-date that even the newest inventions of our own conceptual mind and speed can't match that. The crazy-wisdom person is super-superhuman.

The idea of Padmasambhava cutting through craziness and manifesting crazy wisdom here is partially that he had conquered the Tibetan national craziness or nationalism of the Tibetan people. At the time, Tibet was completely dominated by theism; people worshipped various local deities. There was a lot of arrogance in spite of the inadequacy in the country. Padmasambhava was able to overcome those problems.

Burying scriptures as a time capsule.[4]

Padmasambhava was a very visionary person; when he came to Tibet, he buried scriptures. Those buried scriptures were the ancient equivalent of the time capsule. He constructed containers in which sacred scriptures and various ritual objects and household articles could be stored, and he buried them in certain places, so that future generations could appreciate and emulate those things, so that people of the culture of the golden age could

Dorje Trolö. *Line drawing by Glen Eddy; used by permission.*

appreciate those examples of quality and wisdom. That was one of the most important and powerful things that Padmasambhava did. He had so much concern for people who would be born several centuries after him; therefore he buried a lot of scriptures and texts, like *The Tibetan Book of the Dead*, which many of you have. Having that now is a product of Padmasambhava's work of burying manuscripts.

The people who discovered such texts later on are actually connected with a spiritual discipline of the Nyingma tradition. They would have a vision and some sense of feeling, and so they would begin to excavate in certain areas and dig up these treasures.

We were thinking of doing a similar thing to what Padmasambhava did. I asked one of my students, Steve Roth, to look into buying a time capsule; that would be the modern style of burying scriptures, or terma. We could collect instructions on how to meditate; we could write them quite simply. Maybe we could include a *zafu* and *zabuton*, and we could bury them somewhere. As we go further, as students go through further development, we could do similar things at a more advanced level. Further instructions could be buried that actually might be helpful to somebody in the future. That's a possibility.

It turns out that the company that builds time capsules went bankrupt, so we have to find another company. We have that project lined up to do at some point. If you have any suggestions as to how we can do that, if you have any suggestions as to what we could put in the capsule apart from a zafu and zabuton, your ideas are very welcome. In that way, we could take part in making history—in the future.[5]

The next stanza is

> HUM HUM HUM:
> You are the lord of yidams and conqueror of the whole of
>   existence and all apparent phenomena;:
> You have subdued the viciousness of the Mongol emperor:
> And overcome the energy of fire, water, poison, weapons and evil
>   forces::
> I supplicate you, O Karma Pakshi.:

Karma Pakshi was a very strange person. He was very sturdy and sometimes fierce, but he was also humorous. He went to China to visit the emperor, accompanying a Sakya lama who was at the time the ruler of Tibet, the equivalent of the Dalai Lama. They went to China together. Apparently, Karma Pakshi had a goatee; he was quite mysterious. The Chinese emperor is supposed to have remarked, "The Sakya guru is quite good, but how about the other one, the one with the goatee?" Karma Pakshi was supposed to have been an extraordinarily powerful person, and the emperor was very impressed by him.

Karma Pakshi. *Line drawing by Glen Eddy; used by permission.*

Subjugating the Mongol emperor is an important point about Karma Pakshi. Later on, he became the emperor's guru. The Mongolian emperor was supposed to have put him through all kinds of trials: he was thrown into a pitch pit teeming with fleas or mosquitoes or some other insect; he was abandoned in a cold cellar, one of those little cellars or holes where they used to throw prisoners. At one point, Karma Pakshi was hung up from the ceiling by his goatee. But he survived all those trials and tribulations. Each time, he became more and more powerful, more and more impressive and dignified. Finally the emperor gave up. He surrendered to Karma Pakshi, and he became a great emperor. He actually became Karma Pakshi's student. He even became a lineage holder in one tradition of the Kagyü tradition. He became a great practitioner of the six yogas of Naropa. It's quite amazing that such a softened emperor could be made into such a hardened practitioner.

There are a lot of stories about how Karma Pakshi overcame the energy of fire, water, poison, weapons, and evil forces. The main idea is that Karma Pakshi possessed power over phenomena. His basic qualities were fearlessness and abruptness; his actions were unpredictable. But his approach was very direct and precise.

Tüsum Khyenpa

Next the text reads:

> HUM HUM HUM⋮
> You who fulfill all wishes⋮
> And are lord of centerless space,⋮
> You who shine with kind and luminous light,⋮
> I supplicate you, Tsurphupa.⋮

This stanza supplicating Tüsum Khyenpa was written by Shamarpa, a disciple of Tüsum Khyenpa. *Shamarpa* means "red hat person." *Tsurphupa* means the "person from Tsurphu," referring to the Karmapa's seat in Tibet. Tüsum Khyenpa was a very interesting person: he was supposed to look like a monkey. His jaws protruded; his whole face jutted forward like a monkey, an ape or gorilla. He was quite old at this time. In fact, other sects made fun of both Gampopa and Tüsum Khyenpa. They said that Gampopa looked like a goat and Tüsum Khyenpa looked like a monkey. He was a very earnest student of the practice. He came from East Tibet, where there were many traders; it was a very rich province. He went all the way from there to Central Tibet in order to study with Gampopa.

He built his square hut the length of his own body, five feet in all its dimensions, and he spent something like six years meditating there. That hut was on the ground of Tsurphu, Karmapa's monastery. Tüsum Khyenpa was known as "the good sitter," and quite rightly so. He was a very good sitter, a great practitioner of meditation.

He had a lot of influence on the various political problems of his time. He was able to arrange a number of peaceful settlements between local warlords. At that time, Tibet was a divided country; there was no one king. Everything was in the control of the warlords. So Tüsum Khyenpa was a great meditator and, I would say, a great statesman. He actually reshaped the history of Tibet; he was able to make peace between warring factions. At the same time, he was very much into practice.

Toward the end of Tüsum Khyenpa's life, he and two other disciples of Gampopa got drunk and danced outside the cave of the Gampo hills. They were singing a song of mahamudra, and the *gekö* of the monastery decided to kick them out, because nobody was allowed to drink liquor inside the monastery compound. Gampopa was very upset about that. He said, "If you kick my main students out of the monastery, I'm going with them." One of Gampopa's songs says, roughly, "Come back. Come back. We're going to create a vajra establishment in this place; you should not leave. Come back. We should not trust in these organizations; we have our own kingdom of mahamudra." It's a very moving song, which is part of the *Kagyü Gurtso*; it has been translated as one of the songs in *The Rain of Wisdom*.[6]

Mikyö Dorje

Next the sadhana reads:

> HUM HUM HUM:
> AH! Mikyö Dorje fills the whole of space.:
> HOH! He is the vajra joy which sends out luminous light.:
> HUM! He is the energy of music and lord of messengers.:
> OM! He is the wrathful action which cleanses all impurities.:

Mikyö Dorje, who is being supplicated here, was an interesting person. He was a great scholar, a great grammarian, as I mentioned before, and a great practitioner. He worked a great deal to bring together the mahayana and the vajrayana philosophies of the Buddhist tradition. That was one of the landmarks of his achievement. The understanding of shunyata and many other mahayana traditions were brought together by him in a vajrayana-like tradition. He was a great figure in the *svatantrika* tradition. He introduced the idea that emptiness is the same as luminosity. For a long time that concept had been lost in Buddhist philosophy. People had forgotten about the idea of luminosity; they just talked about emptiness, and emptiness being the same as form. Mikyö Dorje played an important role in reintroducing the awareness of luminosity.

Mikyö Dorje also visited China, where he became the imperial teacher. He was also a great artist and craftsman. At one temple in Tibet, he carved a seventy-five-foot Buddha and the Buddha's throne, as well as a bas-relief of the life of the Buddha. The whole thing was made of sandalwood. He was also a great caster. Many statues were cast under his direction. There is a tradition of fine craftsmanship among the Karmapas, to which the Sixteenth Karmapa is an exception.[7]

Rangjung Dorje

The next stanza of the abhisheka portion of the sadhana is

HUM HUM HUM
Seeing the bodhisattva Rangjung Dorje:
Is like discovering the wish-fulfilling gem.:
He removes the poverty of oneself and others;:
He is the source of all that is needed.:
I supplicate his wisdom body.:

We have no idea who wrote this verse supplicating Rangjung Dorje. Rangjung Dorje was the third Karmapa. It was he who brought together the ati and mahamudra traditions; we owe him a great debt. In fact, the whole inspiration for the Rimé tradition of joining together the Nyingma and Kagyü traditions is due to Rangjung Dorje. His idea was to expand from the mahamudra experience of the Kagyü tradition, the orthodox mahamudra experience of purely dwelling on deities and working with conceptual ideas, into the ati experience of the next further level, the complete spaciousness of discipline. Rangjung Dorje was a truly fantastic person. He was also a great craftsman: he was a great painter, woodcarver, and embroiderer. A lot of tapestries were produced under his direction. We used to be able to see his tapestries in Tibet, but I suppose those things are gone now.[8]

We'll conclude our discussion of the abhisheka section of the sadhana in the next chapter.

DISCUSSION

Colorfulness of the sadhana and the phenomenal world; its relationship to luminosity and ati.

Question: Rinpoche, last night you said that the vivid and colorful qualities of the sadhana were a result of taking what was happening with your guru very personally. In that way, the whole phenomenal world becomes very vivid and colorful. When you say that form is luminosity, does that sense of luminosity come from the ati tradition of expanded vision?

Chögyam Trungpa Rinpoche: I think it basically comes from the ati tradition, but it also comes from the mahamudra tradition. There's some sense of brilliance and of precision. That sense of luminosity certainly doesn't come from the pure mahayana tradition, which is somewhat nihilistic.

According to the mahayana tradition, everything is empty. It's like the black zafus and black robes of the Zen tradition, which is pure mahayana: there is no room for white. The idea of luminosity is that there is room for white, some kind of white. The brightest color that the Zen people can come up with for their *roshi's* zafu is brown—dark brown. That is as far as their tradition is willing to go toward light, so to speak. I think that the idea of luminosity is highly influenced by some kind of faint understanding of the ati tradition.

Q: Perceiving vividness and colorfulness sounds like a very personal experience, and the experience of luminosity sounds more like the kind of perception that comes from awareness practice.

CTR: That experience of luminosity is also supposed to be an ati expression at some point. It may be underdeveloped in individual experience, but it's still the same thing. It could be crude, just the flicker of one's own neurosis, but that neurosis has some root of sanity behind it.

Humanistic psychology and the nontheistic approach.

Q: Rinpoche, you mentioned humanistic psychology. If I understood you correctly, you were saying that it was clearing the ground for the nontheistic approach—that it was an expression of revolt against the dominant culture, and in that sense it was a healthy revolt. Or were you being critical?

CTR: It is healthy in the sense that it is nontheistic, which means Buddhistic. But the problem with humanistic psychology is that it doesn't have any direction. It's like women's liberation or men's liberation, without anything else going on around it. You have to have a tradition, a discipline to follow up the basic insight. But I don't think we can blame the humanistic people; I think they are very brave and very good. They have at least provided a foundation for nontheistic spirituality—and that's fantastic!

The relationship of equanimity and wrath.

Q: I would like to ask you about the opening lines of the sadhana:

> Earth, water, fire and all the elements,
> The animate and the inanimate, the trees and the greenery and so on,
> All partake of the nature of self-existing equanimity,
> Which is quite simply what the Great Wrathful One is.

What is the relation between equanimity and wrath, or this Great Wrathful One?

CTR: What's the problem?

Q: Well, I get the feeling that all through the sadhana great wrath is important. But I can't connect it with equanimity and self-existing suchness. I just can't make the connection.

CTR: I think you have a preconceived idea of wrath. Wrath doesn't mean anger; it's just wrath. Can you imagine being angry without aggression? It's just a sense of power. You can't say that fire is angry, but it still burns you.

Q: Are all the elements like that?

CTR: No. The idea is that each of the elements has its own quality. Water is unyielding; if you drown, you can't say that the water was too aggressive. You can't blame the water; you can't sue the water, the river, or the lake. It is the same with earth and earthquakes. If you fall down the mountain, you can't say it was the earth's fault. Each of the elements has its own self-existing quality. They can't be blamed as being like somebody's deliberate aggression or neurosis. It is the same with the basic wrath of the wrathful one. The brilliance and powerful vibrating quality that exist in that energy are not directed toward any particular aim or object. It simply exists.

Lofty concepts, like mahamudra and ati, in contrast to one's limited personal experience.

Q: Rinpoche, in my own experience, space or luminosity, mahamudra or maha ati, seem very far away, very foreign. I don't think I've ever experienced those things, and I feel that I'm not good enough to know what they are. It seems like wishful thinking and that it might be better just to sit and not have such a glorious idea of what's out there.

CTR: Well said, sir. You should sit, and those things might come sometime. They might never come. Take that attitude. The more you give up the possibility of fruition, that much closer it will be. It's quite naughty of me to say that. But it's far away and it's very close. Because it's far away, it's very close.

Practicing the sadhana in connection with phases of the moon.

Q: Rinpoche, why is the sadhana always read in connection with the phases of the moon?

CTR: Well, you might go crazy on that day. That's true, actually. When the moon changes phase, when it begins to wax and wane, certain psychological shifts take place. That is traditional.

Choice in Chögyam Trungpa Rinpoche's own path.

Q: What element of choice did you have in your path? We are here because we choose to be here. We are here through some karmic coincidence or because of some mistake—who knows why? But your path was already chosen for you soon after you were born. Did you at any point have any choice to get out or take another direction?

CTR: I could always have escaped, sneaked out. Apart from that, there wasn't much choice. I thought of escaping occasionally; I even planned it, but somehow it didn't work. I was always thrown back to the same thing. I had a tutor, who was constantly pressuring me to learn more and study more. I finally asked him to resign, which was quite a brave step to take. And when he wasn't there to put pressure on me, I came back by myself. I didn't want to leave the monastery anymore. I realized that the only thing I wanted to get rid of was my tutor. I was quite happy with what I was doing, and I could say the same thing now. I am quite happy with what I am doing.

4. Joining Insight and Devotion in the Rimé Tradition

Once you begin to realize the essence of the lineage, the backbone of the lineage, you will find that the greatest accomplishment of the Rimé tradition has been to bring together emotion and insight. Insight becomes more emotional, and emotion becomes more insightful. I would say that that is the best possible contribution to our world.

I would like to complete the description of the sections of the sadhana, which began in the last chapter. The sadhana involves the creation of a mandala, with deities and offerings. In traditional sadhanas, the practitioner, the deities visualized, and the principle of energy that descends upon the visualization, called jnanasattva, are usually separate realities. But this sadhana takes a somewhat ati approach, which is what is known as the umbrella approach. Instead of the practitioner yearning upward, energy comes down as the understanding of the self-existence of wisdom, which never needs to be sought. The sadhana ends that way as well.

There is also an element of mahamudra in the sadhana, of further intense admiration of the guru and the gloriousness of it. That admiration reflects the mahamudra approach; it is based on *intense* devotion, rather than on purely traditional devotion.

Conclusion of the Abhisheka

Chanting the Triple HUM

At a particular point in the abhisheka, the chanting of the triple HUM, that intense devotion becomes fuzzy and vague. The boundary between you and your guru becomes vague, and you are uncertain whether or not a boundary exists at all. At that point, there is the possibility of being one with your guru. And that possibility increases as you get closer to the end of the sadhana.

Concluding Abhisheka Verse

The next verse begins:

> HUM HUM HUM༔
> When the precious guru approaches༔
> The whole of space is filled with rainbow light.༔

It continues from there. This verse is a direct quotation from the sadhana of Mikyö Dorje, written by himself. It is as if there is an immense traffic jam: the practitioner begins to experience all kinds of energies. You feel intense devotion, intense longing, which tends to make sense of all the thought patterns that go through the mind. You experience all your mental activities as sacred, blessed by the guru. You experience great openness. You also realize that the worshipper and those being worshipped are one, which is ati. It's a question of totality.

This last part of the sadhana is part of what is known as receiving abhisheka. In traditional sadhanas, the visualization is dissolved at this point; it enters into the practitioner's body. But in this sadhana, the visualization remains; there is no dissolving. This last section is the final crescendo of the whole sadhana, the final feast.

Verse of Confirmation

Next comes a short verse that is a commentary on what has been happening throughout the sadhana:

> HUM HUM HUMꞋ
> In the mandala of mahamudraꞋ
> Shines moonlight, pure and all-pervading.Ꞌ
> All apparent phenomena are the play of the mind.Ꞌ
> All qualities are complete within the mind.Ꞌ
> I, the yogi, am fearless and free from occupations;Ꞌ
> Hopes and fears of achieving and abstaining are all used up.Ꞌ
> I awaken into the wisdom with which I was bornꞋ
> And compassionate energy arises, without pretense.Ꞌ
> Hey-ho, the self-existing rishi!¹Ꞌ
> I, the siddha, enjoy myself with great simplicity.Ꞌ
> A A AꞋ

This verse is a confirmation of the whole thing, the final ati stamp of approval, that real things have taken place in the proper way. The point is that the chanting and meditation that we have done in the sadhana are unnecessary—in essence, everything's done already. These verses cut through any possibility of potential spiritual materialism. Beyond that, they are meant to inspire further appreciation of the lineage and the wisdom of the lineage.

Verse of Auspiciousness

Then we have the last verse, which is a traditional ending:

> The wisdom flame sends out a brilliant light—Ꞌ
> May the goodness of Dorje Trolö be present!Ꞌ
> Karma Pakshi, lord of mantra, king of insight—Ꞌ
> May his goodness, too, be present!Ꞌ
> Tüsum Khyenpa, the primeval buddha—Ꞌ
> Beyond all partiality—may his goodness be present!Ꞌ
> Mikyö Dorje, lord of boundless speech—Ꞌ
> May his goodness be present here!Ꞌ

Rangjung Dorje, faultless single eye of wisdom—⁈
May his goodness be present!⁈
The Kagyü gurus, the light of whose wisdom is a torch⁈
For all beings—may their goodness be present!⁈
The ocean of wish-fulfilling yidams who accomplish all actions—⁈
May their goodness be present!⁈
The protectors who plant firm the victorious banner⁈
Of dharma—may their goodness be present!⁈
May the goodness of the great mind mandala of mahamudra be
    present!⁈

This ending is an acknowledgment of the process that you have gone through in reading the sadhana. It is also preparation for the postsadhana level of practice, for beginning to relate again to your daily life situation. The experience of Dorje Trolö, Karma Pakshi, Mikyö Dorje, and all the others are part of the great feast, part of the great insight. So at last we have gone through the whole sadhana.

JOINING MAHAMUDRA AND ATI: DEVOTION AND CRAZY WISDOM

I would like to remind you again and again of the necessity of understanding and bringing together the highest aspects of devotion and crazy wisdom. You might find that devotion and crazy wisdom were somewhat arbitrary concepts if you didn't have any experience of the practices of our lineage.

Joining Emotion and Insight

But once you begin to realize the essence of the lineage, the backbone of the lineage, you will find that the greatest accomplishment of the Rimé tradition has been to bring together emotion and insight. Insight becomes more emotional, and emotion becomes more insightful. I would say that that is the best possible contribution to our world. When we have insight alone, it tends to become dry and high-floating[2] and full of the sophistries of conceptual mind. And when we become purely emotional, we have no way of relating properly with our world, in terms of the visionary aspect of the world. We care only about ourselves and those who are very close to us.

We want somebody in particular to be with us rather than the whole world to be with us. That problem of possessiveness is always prominent.

Bringing insight and devotion together at the tantric level has been a very powerful contribution to buddhadharma. The Rimé tradition has succeeded in bringing together the illusory world of mahamudra—with its understanding of the color and emotional implications and vividness of experience—with the all-pervasiveness, spaciousness, and larger-scale thinking of the ati tradition. There is an almost patronizing quality to the ati tradition, which is valuable, too. At the ati level, the journey and the maker of the journey are not even important, because the journey itself is not important; it has already been made. Therefore, the only journey we could make would be to acknowledge that we have already made our journey, that we have already arrived at whatever place we wish. At the same time, we have no reference point as to how we have made our journey; we are caught in a very powerful and interesting dichotomy.

Chögyam Trungpa's Unique Joining of Mahamudra and Ati

My presentation of Buddhism in America particularly has been an expression of bringing together mahamudra and maha ati indivisibly. There is the general perspective of ati, the flavor of ati, even starting from the hinayana practices of shamatha and vipashyana. Those basic practices have an ati flavor of spaciousness, which seems to be their saving grace, in some sense. Then we have the mahamudra experience of paying attention to details and to our lifestyle and personal situation. We learn to appreciate those things. We develop a sense of humor and begin to relate with the world—not just as something to get rid of, but as something to appreciate. From there we develop a sense of dedication and devotion to the lineage and a feeling of pride: we belong to this particular lineage and we are following its traditions wholeheartedly. So in that way, everything is brought together.

The teachings are capable of reaching people's minds properly, without any cultural sophistries and problems of that nature, because of the saving grace of both of those wisdoms. Those teachings transcend the conceptual level: they are able to communicate with us as human beings. The teachings are a direct link from one human being to another; they are not borrowed culture. That cultureless quality is very much connected with an aspect of both schools.

DISCUSSION

Understanding how Buddhism is a "spiritual" path.

Question: I used to think that spirituality was something beyond mind, that it was metamind. I thought it was the reception and transmission of some kind of invisible energy. However, my understanding of the teachings, as you have presented them, is of a quest or training for a more profound perceptual process, for a perceptual change in the way we govern ourselves. Why then is it called a spiritual path? What is "spiritual" about our training and about our endeavor?

Chögyam Trungpa Rinpoche: That's a good question, actually. We are not talking about "spirituality" in the name of "spirit," which has a theistic origin. We are talking about spirituality in terms of picking up some kind of vibe or energy of spirit—high spirit—rather than spirit as a ghostly being. That seems to be the difference. We are speaking of "spirit" not "spirits." We are talking about heroism and self-respect and a high sense of understanding. Spiritual discipline, from that point of view, is not dependent on anybody's feedback; you depend on yourself. You have to develop yourself in any case. That's the idea of heroism and trust in your own resources.

Q: So it's heightened path?

CTR: Yes, something like that. High strung.

Karma Pakshi as the heruka who exists independent of people's belief.

Q: There is something in the sadhana about Karma Pakshi being the heruka who exists independent of people's belief.[3]

CTR: That's a nontheistic remark. People's beliefs are usually somewhat theistic. They think that Jehovah exists because somebody once saw him and brought all kinds of messages down from heaven. The more people acknowledge his existence, the more they worship him, the more powerful he becomes. That is the theistic concept. But in the case of nontheism, something can exist independent of belief; it is self-existing. That doesn't mean to say that Karma Pakshi is an external deity, as such, but he exists free from conceptual mind. And being free from conceptual mind is in itself experience.

Q: So it is connected with the vajrayana tradition of visualizing aspects of awakened mind?

CTR: Yes, definitely.

Nyingma-Kagyü lineage holders of Rimé; Nyingma attitude toward Kagyü and Mahamudra.

Q: Rinpoche, the Trungpa lineage seems to be primarily Kagyü. And the Kagyüs integrated Nyingma teachings. But have there been any Nyingma lamas who have integrated mahamudra with ati? Are there any Nyingma-Kagyü holders of the Rimé lineage?

CTR: There is a Nyingma master, Yungtön Dorje Pel, who was of both the Kagyü and the Nyingma lineages. He actually brought the two traditions together. Also, the first Trungpa, Künga Gyaltsen, was a disciple of Trungmasé, who was originally trained in the Nyingthik tradition of the Nyingma lineage. Trungmasé went to visit the fifth Karmapa, Teshin Shekpa, and became his disciple. So his monastery was formally established as within the Kagyü tradition. Nevertheless, that Nyingma background is part of the history of the Surmang tradition. So there were many teachers in the Nyingma tradition who were open to the possibilities of working with the mahamudra tradition. But on the whole, the Nyingma tradition or the teachers took a somewhat patronizing attitude toward the lower tantras.

That superior attitude used to come up quite frequently. In fact, when I studied with Jamgön Kongtrül, many of his Nyingma students would say, "You mahamudra people"—as if we were some little ethnic group. They had a definite tendency toward snobbishness. That's a fact. But the interesting thing is that the Kagyü people, the mahamudra people, never showed any resentment of that.

They took it for granted that, if you have a primitive understanding of the mahamudra tradition, that it was not as great as the ati tradition. This was completely understood.

Q: Similarly, it seems that sometimes there is an indirect kind of chauvinism among vipashyana students in their attitude toward shamatha. It's a kind of elitism.

CTR: If you like, sure. It's harmless. Why not? Why not have chauvinism? It doesn't hurt a flea.

Groundlessness and skillful means in the sadhana.

Q: When I hear the sadhana, I have a feeling of groundlessness.

CTR: Obviously, you feel groundless because the sadhana doesn't offer you any possibilities of entertainment or any security. It is itself groundless. At the same time, it is very practical and pragmatic. It's not wishy-washy, particularly. It deals very directly with situations; it embodies skillful means. If you have truly perceived things as they are, then you automatically develop skillful means. So skillful means is a byproduct, rather than something you aim for. That is one of the differences between the sutra or mahayana teachings and the tantric teachings. In the tantric teachings, the virtues that are described in the sutra teachings are seen as by-products rather than as the direct result of practice. So the sadhana is groundless, but at the same time it's pragmatic.

Verses of the sadhana written by other teachers.

Q: When you were writing the sadhana, did you spontaneously remember the verses that were written by Mikyö Dorje and Guru Rinpoche and so on?

CTR: Well, they came up at appropriate times. I also thought that I should include some of the verses composed by great teachers, so that the whole thing wouldn't become my own production. What I was doing was honoring their existence, not only at the conceptual level, but at the historical level as well.

It is my wish that what you have learned here—if anything—does not become purely conceptual. Hopefully, you will be able to translate it into practice, especially the sitting practice of meditation. Thank you, everybody.

PART TWO

"The Sadhana of Mahamudra"

Karma Dzong, Boulder, Colorado, December 1975

There is basic ground that we all believe in and live on, and out of that, we create an extraordinary landscape. Out of that comes further extraordinary imagery, which is not just basic sanity alone, but basic wakefulness within sanity. Sanity can be reasonable, but there has to be something very wakeful about the whole thing. That wakefulness is embodied in the crazy-wisdom principle, embodied in the yidam, which is not necessarily a native of that particular landscape or, for that matter, he is not a nonnative, either. He is just there. You might feel threatened because the environment is very spooky. You have to give up your arrogance, which we talked about already in connection with devotion. Giving arrogance up is connected with devotion. Having related with longing and with the absence of arrogance, you have to surrender completely. In other words, everything takes place in the charnel ground. It is a place of birth and a place of death.

—Chögyam Trungpa Rinpoche

5. The Guru Principle

On the Buddhist path, the development of the teacher-student relationship is analogous to bringing up infants, relating with teenagers, and finally relating with grown-ups. Those are the three examples. . . . I would like to present the notion of devotion, or faith, properly. Faith here is not worship; the guru is not particularly regarded as Christ on earth, our only link to God. The guru is regarded as a spiritual elder, spiritual friend, and vajra master. He has ways and means to create situations in accordance with our own receptivity, our own particular style.

The discussion of "The Sadhana of Mahamudra" is basically a vajrayana-oriented topic. At the same time, it has a lot of implications for, and connections with, the basic practice and understanding of hinayana and mahayana Buddhism. In this discussion, I would like to explain the basic nature of the Buddhist journey that we're taking, as it relates to the Buddhist style of meditation practice and spiritual discipline as a whole.

The first topic is devotion, which is the basis of the sadhana. Any practice of this nature cannot be properly understood without appreciating the sense of hierarchy, if you like, in the relationship of the teacher and the student, or the guru and the *chela*, or disciple. Devotion is the basis of that relationship; it is its most important aspect. But you can't have a proper relationship to devotion unless you have some understanding of the guru principle altogether.

Parent-Child Relationship as a Model

To begin with, as human beings, we believe it is necessary to have some kind of babysitter, or to have our parents acting as our babysitter. We need someone to change our diapers, give us a bath or a shower, change our clothes, put us in pajamas. We need to have someone who can tell us how to eat—whether to use a spoon or a fork and how to relate with cups and plates—and how to sit up, and who will provide us with some kind of seat, called a baby seat. That's the beginning point, the first reference point in our lives for a hierarchical relationship with another human being. I'm not particularly coming at this topic from a higher level, an arrogant level. But if we want to function properly in our life, we have to have such a starting point as we begin to grow up. As children, we must have experienced that ourselves. It has happened to us already. That basic human experience is an analogy for the teacher-student principle as it develops through the three yanas. On the Buddhist path, the development of the teacher-student relationship is analogous to bringing up infants, relating with teenagers, and finally relating with grown-ups. Those are the three examples that we could use as reference points for our discussion, quite simply, without further complicating the issue.

THE HINAYANA TEACHER AS ELDER

In discussing the student-teacher relationship, the first point is the hinayana relationship to hierarchy or to a parental figure. On a very elementary level, that is the beginning point of the journey that this sadhana is presenting.

Our ordinary sense of the growing-up process, whatever we think it entails, is based purely on our dreams. We have to face that fact. We have to acknowledge that we think we're going to become PhD candidates without even knowing how to speak or write or read, without even being toilet trained. That's the kind of ambition we usually have: we don't want to be hassled by little embarrassments here and there. We say to ourselves, "Of course I can push them aside; I can just grow up, and soon I will be accepted in the mainstream of the respectable, high-powered world. I'll just do my best. I'm sure I can do it." That's our usual approach. Many people believe that professionalism means having a self-confident but amateurish approach to reality, which is not quite true. We're not talking about being "professional" Buddhists in this sense. We're talking about how to actually become adults in the Buddhist world. We have to grow up as adults rather than being kids who appear to be grown-up. We actually have to grow up, and we have to face the problems that exist in our lives. We have to learn to grow up—we have to learn to develop a sense of the subtleties, a sense of understanding our reactions to the phenomenal world, which are our reactions to ourselves at the same time.

In order to do those things, we need some kind of parental figure to begin with. In the hinayana tradition, that parental figure is called a *sthavira* in Sanskrit, or *thera* in Pali, which means "elder." The elder is somebody who has already gone through being babysat and has graduated from that level of experience to become a babysitter. In ordinary life, that person is very important for our development, because we have to be told what will happen if we put our fingers on the hot burner. We have to be warned. Or if we decide to step on a pile of shit or if we decide to eat it up, we need to know the consequences, what's going to happen to us.

All those seemingly unimportant little details are quite trivial, but they provide a very important background for us. We have to learn the facts and figures and the little details that exist in our lives: what is good, what is bad, what should be done, what shouldn't be done. Some kind of discrimination is important, but not in order to bring everything down to promises and punishment as such. We are not talking about the Christian concept of original sin. But we do need to have a basic understanding of how things are done in connection with natural forces. If you walk out into the snow without any clothes, you will catch cold—obviously. That's a natural fact. If you eat poison, you will die. Those simple little facts and figures are important.

There are spiritual facts and figures as well. As a practitioner, you might regard yourself as grown-up. You might say, "Well, *I* don't need a babysitter. I can take care of my business. I'm fine—no thanks." But in terms of spiritual discipline, even that reaction is very infantile. You are completely closing off large avenues of learning possibilities. If you reject those possibilities, then you have nothing to work with. You have no idea even how to begin with the ABC level of basic spirituality.

So in the hinayana tradition, the notion of *acharya*—meaning "master," "teacher," "elder," parent figure, and occasionally babysitter—is always necessary. That person's purpose is not to teach us what's good and what's bad— how to hate the bad and how to work toward the good—but the point is how to develop a general sense of composure. That is very important as a first step; it is the beginning of devotion, in some sense. At that point, at the hinayana level, devotion is not necessarily faith at an ethereal or a visionary level, particularly. Devotion and vision come purely from a sense of practicality: what it is necessary to do and what it is necessary to avoid. It's just a simple, basic thing.

The First Noble Truth

So at the hinayana level, to begin with, the teachings tell you that your view of the world is an infantile view. You think you're going to get ice cream every day, every minute. As a baby and a young child, you are always crying and throwing temper tantrums, so that your daddy or your mommy or your babysitter will come along with a colorful ice-cream cone and begin to feed you. But things can't be that way forever. What we are saying here is that life is based on pain, suffering, misery. A more accurate word for that experience of *duhkha*—usually translated as "suffering"—is *anxiety*. There's always a kind of anxiousness in life, but you have to be told by somebody that life is full of anxiety, to begin with. The elder helps us to relate with that first thing, which is actually called a truth. It is truth because it points out that your belief that you can actually win the war against pain, that you might be able to get so-called happiness, is not possible at all. It just doesn't happen. So the elder, parent, thera, or sthavira tells us these facts and figures. He or she tells us that the world is not made out of honeycombs and big oceans of maple syrup. That person tells us that the world has its own unpleasant and touchy points. And when you have been told that truth, you begin to appreciate it more. You begin to respect that truth, which actually goes a very long way—all the rest of your life. And you begin to have some feeling for your teacher as a parental figure.

For the elder, such truth is just old hat: he or she knows it already, having gone through it. Nevertheless, the elder doesn't give out righteous messages about those things. She or he simply says, "Look, it's not as good as you think, and it is going to be somewhat painful for you—getting into this world. You can't help it; you're already in it, so you'd better work with it and accept the truth." That is precisely how Lord Buddha first proclaimed the dharma. His first teaching was the truth of suffering. So when you are at the level of being babysat, having the teacher as a parental figure, you are simply told how things are. Being told about the truth of suffering is like having your diapers changed—your nappies. This is an example of the trust and faith in the teacher that develop in the early stage of the teacher-student relationship, when the teacher acts as a babysitter.

THE MAHAYANA TEACHER AS SPIRITUAL FRIEND

At the second level of your relationship with your teacher, having already understood the first noble truth, you no longer see the teacher as a hassle or as overwhelming, unpleasant, or claustrophobic. At that point, your relationship with your teacher begins to evolve into a different level.

He or she becomes the *kalyanamitra*, a Sanskrit word meaning "spiritual friend" or "friend in virtue." The kalyanamitra is less heavy-handed than the elder or parent, but on the other hand, he is much more heavy-handed. He is like a rich uncle who provides money for the rest of his family, including his parents. He becomes a big deal to his relatives because he doesn't want them to just lounge around and live off his money. The rich uncle would like to be more constructive than that; he would like to have very industrious relatives, so that he can promote his capital.

Unlike a rich uncle in ordinary life, the bodhisattva's approach, the mahayana approach, is not based on self-aggrandizement. It isn't self-centered. It is a much closer relationship. The teacher has become a friend, a spiritual friend. When relatives give us advice, we have a certain attitude toward their advice: we know that we are just being told the *relative* truth. That truth has some value, it has some application, but it is still relative truth. But when friends give us advice, it is much more immediate and personal than relative-like truth. If we are criticized by our parents, we think that it's their trip, or we think something is wrong with their approach, so we take it very lightly. Sometimes we are very resentful, which helps us to push those criticisms aside. But if we are criticized by our friends, we feel startled. We begin to think that maybe there's some element of truth in what they are saying.

Working with Others: The Six Paramitas

So in the mahayana, the approach to the student-teacher relationship is that the teacher is a spiritual friend. He or she is much more demanding than the purely relative level. The spiritual friend makes us much more watchful and conscientious. At that point, relative truth has already become somewhat old hat. We already know about the four noble truths: pain, the origin of pain, cessation, and path. So what's next? At this point, the spiritual friend tells us, "Don't just work on yourself. Do something about others. Relate with your projections rather than with the projector alone. Do something about the world outside and try to develop some sense of sympathy and warmth in yourself."

That is usually very hard for us to do. We are already pissed off that life is painful; we're resentful about our world. We are a bundle of tight muscles; we're very uptight. It's very hard to relax, to let go of that. But it can be done; it's being done in the present, and it will be done in the future. So how about giving an inch? Just letting go a little bit? Opening a little bit? We could be generous and disciplined at the same time. Therefore we should be patient and exert ourselves, be aware of everything that is happening, and be clear, all at the same time.

That is what is called the six paramitas, the six transcendent actions practiced by the mahayana practitioner, or bodhisattva. Practicing the paramitas is a tall order in some sense. How can we practice all six of them simultaneously? It seems like you have to be a fantastic actor who doesn't believe what he is doing, or else you have to become an idiot who purely follows the rules, someone who gives things away, who is disciplined and patient and hardworking. But there are other more genuine ways of practicing the paramitas. That practice puts us in the spotlight, so to speak. We have a general sense of wanting to open for the very reason that we have nothing to lose. Our life is already a bundle of misery and chaos. And since we already have nothing to lose, we might in fact gain something by just giving, opening. That seems to be the trick, the point at which the transition between elder and spiritual friend takes place.

The spiritual friend acts like a rich uncle who throws us into the street, not giving us any pocket money. He might give us a few pencils and tell us to go out and sell them. We might say, "I'm sorry, I need a warm coat. I can't go out like this." And he will say, "First you have to sell your pencils. Then you get a coat. You have to buy a coat for yourself; I'm not going to provide you with one. You have to earn the money yourself." That's a very rough example; please don't misunderstand me. But that seems to be the general pattern of the relationship.

The Vajrayana Teacher as Vajra Master

At the next level, the vajrayana level, your relationship with the teacher becomes very complicated, very tricky. Your teacher becomes what is known as the vajra master, and your relationship with him or her has a different slant entirely. In some sense, he becomes a combination of the elder and the spiritual friend. The process is the same; the line of thinking is the same, but it has its own particular twist. The vajra master is not an elder, a parental figure, a spiritual friend, or a rich uncle. He is a born warrior who accepts only a few students. He will not accept students who are sloppy and unreceptive.

The Meaning of Vajra

Vajra is a Sanskrit word meaning "indestructible," adamantine, or diamond-like. According to Indian mythology the vajra was the scepter of Indra, the king of the gods. It was such a powerful weapon that it could destroy anything. Having once destroyed, it would return to his hand. It had the power to destroy not only once, but in many situations. This weapon was indestructible because it could not in any way be cracked, bent, or destroyed. So the idea of vajra mind is that it is completely well put together. It does not have any cracks anywhere; it cannot be criticized. You cannot bring any confusion into it because it is so well guarded—not out of paranoia, but out of its own existence. It is self-guarded, so to speak.

The Vajra Master as Samurai

The closest analogy for the vajra master is the samurai. Such a teacher is ferocious, but at the same time he or she has the qualities of a parent, an elder, and a friend. He could be very passionate, very warm and sympathetic, but he doesn't buy any bullshit, if we could speak American at this point. Studying with such a person is very dangerous, and it is a very advanced thing to do. You might actually progress much faster on the path. But if you start with the expectation of going faster, then you might actually go slower. The vajra master's approach to teaching is to create successive teaching situations in your life. Having already gone through the hinayana and mahayana, you are well trained and disciplined.

At this point, the vajra master demands complete, unconditional trust and openness from you, without any logic behind it. Maybe some kind of little logic applies, but the rest of it is simple and straightforward: "Would you like to come along with me and take part in this historic battle? Come along, here's your sword." Of course, you have room to chicken out. But once you have chickened out you could go through a lot of problems, unspeakable problems. The more you are a coward, that much more the vajra master will try to terrify you. I don't want to paint a black picture of the vajra master, but that is the simple truth. The more you try to escape, the more you will be chased, cornered.

However, the more you work with the vajra master, the more you will be invited to join that fantastic feast and celebration and mutual dance. The notion of celebration here is that of feast. It is not the idea of indulging, having parties and eating a lot. Feasting means sharing together rich experiences of all kinds. Sharing together in that way is the only way that the vajrayana teachings come alive and become very appropriate. But if you were not ready for that, then the vajra master might send you back to your spiritual friend or, if necessary, to your elder, your rabbi.

The Vajra Master as Inner Guru

The level of your commitment to the vajra master, the samurai, is not purely to the external person alone; it has possibilities of commitment to the internal guru as well. I heard that Dr. Herbert Guenther said that toward the end of your relationship with the kalyanamitra, the spiritual friend, you discover your inner guru. I must contradict that statement. That is not the case, even though Dr. Guenther is a great professor. At that level, you have not yet discovered the inner guru.

Something beyond that outer level takes place only when you meet the vajra master. At that point, you begin to experience a greater level of heroism, fearlessness, and power. You begin to develop a sense of your own resources. But that journey takes much, much longer than you would expect. The vajra master doesn't want to give you any chance to play out your trip. Otherwise, you might decide to reject your irritating and overwhelming vajra master. You could purely internalize by saying, "I don't have to deal with that person anymore. I can just do it on my own."

Nontheistic Devotion

The point here is that, at this level, there is a sense of magic, power, and immense devotion. That devotion is quite different from devotion in the theistic tradition, devotion to Christ or Krishna or whoever you might have. In this case, faith and devotion are very much based on the sense of not giving up completely, but taking on more things, taking all sorts of examples and insight and power into yourself. At this point, you can actually be

The *vajra*, or scepter. This vajra belonged to Chögyam Trungpa. *From the collection of the Shambhala Archives. Photograph by Marvin Moore; used by permission.*

initiated—that is precisely the word—you can receive abhisheka. You can be abhisheka-ed, to coin a verb.

Faith and devotion in the theistic tradition have a very remote quality. Somebody is out there all the time—not a person, not a teacher, not an elder, not a parent, but something greater, someone who will feed you, who will make you feel secure. Everything is somewhat on an ethereal level, as they quite precisely call it, on the level of otherness. That particular thing is going to save you. You might not necessarily believe in an old man with a beard, but you still believe in something out there somewhere, playing tricks on you. The reason why lizards exist, the reason why snakes coil themselves, why rivers run to the ocean, and why trees grow tall—the reason for all this mysteriousness must be because of "him" or "it."

That theistic belief actually keeps you from understanding real magic. It keeps you from trying to understand how things come about or from finding out how you can do something in your own way. When you think that the world must be someone else's work, or creation, you begin to feel as though the whole world is run by a gigantic corporation, including the weather. But we run our own corporation, according to the nontheistic tradition of Buddhism. In order to have access to our world, so that we can run our own corporation, we need to have the vajra master give us manuals, systems, techniques, and instructions. And if we are dumb, if we are not exuberant, he might actually put us into a very difficult situation.[1]

So that is the general preparation of the ground for our discussion of the sadhana. I don't want to give you too much material at this point. I would like to present the notion of devotion, or faith, properly. Faith here is not worship; the guru is not particularly regarded as Christ on earth, our only link to God. The guru is regarded as a spiritual elder, spiritual friend, and vajra master. He has ways and means to create situations in accordance with our own receptivity, our own particular style. And you could create a whole situation and relate with that.

DISCUSSION

Working with disillusionment toward the teacher.

Question: Rinpoche, what does the student do when heavy disillusionment with the kalyanamitra or the acharya or the vajra master sets in? How does he relate to that?

Chögyam Trungpa Rinpoche: I suppose it's up to you.

Q: Is there any sense of direction?

CTR: Well, maybe the whole relationship was conducted wrongly at an early stage. There is some need for undoing and going back. You should go back to the elder.

Q: How do you find the elder again?

CTR: Sit a lot. Practice diligently, without visualizing anything.

When to trust completely in the guru.

Q: How would a person know when it's appropriate to assume that complete trust without logic? How would a person know when it's time to start relating to a guru in that way?

CTR: I think at that point, your teacher might begin to direct you. He might begin to throw you into a different phase.

Q: But isn't it possible that you might feel appropriately that you weren't really ready for that?

CTR: Well, I think there has to be some kind of faith and trust in the physician.

Q: Isn't it dangerous to jump into that kind of faith and obedience too soon?

CTR: It depends on you, too. In the early stages, you look for an appropriate parent. If you make a mistake at that level, then you keep on making mistakes all down the line. You have big disasters and you end up in a loony bin, or something like that.

The interplay between critical intelligence and faith.

Q: At other times you have stressed being very critical, keeping one's critical intelligence at all times. Is there a point along the path where you give up that critical quality toward the teacher or the teachings? Is there a point where this faith is different from that critical quality, or do you keep that critical quality? Do they go together?

CTR: Well, I think that critical quality still goes along with your faith, but your criticism becomes more of an introverted than extroverted critical attitude. It begins to turn inward and it begins to dissolve.

The role of opening up in practicing the paramitas.

Q: I have a question about the paramitas. When you open up, you just step into open space. Does that create the space for the paramitas to sort of go through you, to happen, or is there some element of endeavor in doing them?

CTR: I think that it comes naturally, but at the same time there is obviously a need for some kind of push. You can work with yourself as well as with your spiritual friend. The two go together.

How cynicism and trust work together in relating to the teacher.

Q: If you maintain this cynicism up to the last moment, it seems that you would realize that your trust in this person could actually be another self-deception. At that point, you might only surrender because you knew that even if it were self-deception, it wouldn't matter anyway.

CTR: I think it works both ways. Your critical input and your surrendering are working together at the same time. They're not working against each other. The more you get input and the more you develop, the more you question even those things. So there is some kind of dance taking place between the teacher and yourself. You are not particularly trying to switch off one area and switch on another area. The two are synchronized together. It shouldn't be purely a kill-or-cure situation. You think that you have to be very naive or terribly cynical to the point of being ready to drop the whole thing. But that somehow doesn't have any bearing. Those two attitudes have to work together.

Q: Do you sort of flicker from one state to the other?

CTR: You have a general sense of cynicism to begin with, and a general sense of openness at the same time. They work together, simultaneously. So at the same time that you appreciate what you have received as a great gift, you continue to question it.

Theistic and nontheistic approaches to the world as a giant corporation.

Q: You said that, according to the theistic view, the world is run by a gigantic corporation, but that we could run our own corporation if we had a manual from the guru. I'm confused about the laws of the corporation, and the taxes, and how everything works together.

CTR: I don't see any problems with that particular way of looking at things. We are already involved in some idea of totality. As Suzuki Roshi says, big mind is the biggest one of all. Small mind needs to be trained to become big mind. Jews and Christians would say that you have to submit, you have to surrender to this big creation. You are simply the creatures of it. The problem lies in distinguishing "big" versus "small" rather than in who runs the household. You use very subtle logic: if you are the mother superior of a particular nunnery, then you have your little kingdom. But then the people under you simply become reflections of yourself, your own extension of security rather than the cosmic level.

What we are discussing here is the difference between theistic and nontheistic attitudes at a cosmic level. The nontheistic approach would be, obviously, that somebody has to take control of the whole situation. It could be anybody: the head of a meditation center, the head of the whole organization, or somebody who runs the building. All those people are necessary, but they are not particularly regarded as gods. They are just ordinary people who are confused or on the way up or on the way down. They are just little beings working with their little brains. However, the theistic idea of the world as a huge scheme is very tricky. Once you click into that idea, you discover that it doesn't give you any room for anything at all. You are just part of that huge scheme, so you might decide to murder somebody, according to the will of the scheme. That is going a bit too far. This isn't just a farfetched example. That logic could go very far; it has been done in the past. Or you could just create little areas in the name of the huge scheme. That becomes problematic.

Importance of personal contact with the teacher; role of the sangha.

Q: In terms of relating to the guru as a parent, kalyanamitra, or vajra master, it seems that relationship implies a lot of personal contact. Sometimes I wonder whether you have to use your own fantasy about where you are in this relationship, when you don't have personal contact. Perhaps that's a silly question.

CTR: It's not that silly; it's very potent. It is in the air in many ways, which makes it a good question. I quite agree with you: personal contact is important. But what do we mean by personal contact? That's the question. You have some kind of understanding and experience of how far such an elder, kalyanamitra, or vajra master has the composure to communicate on a level that could be understood. The communication could be nationwide; it could even be at a cosmic level. The communication is not at the level of individual worship or experience alone, but many students are working on that particular level. They are beginning to pick up that particular type of sanity, that particular kind of openness. They are beginning to create an environment of sanity. So the concept of sangha is a very important part of that particular notion of communication between teacher and student. The sangha is a group of people who don't lean on each other; they stand on their own feet and they propagate the teachings. They are capable of expanding themselves.

So the message that individuals receive from the teachings can be expanded, and the whole thing can be done very honestly. If any problems come up, they can be handled by direct authorization, direct contact with your elder or your spiritual friend. Overall, creating an atmosphere of sanity is a very important part of that. Otherwise the teacher-student relationship becomes just like a buying and selling trip. Everybody comes to the cash register[2] and pays his money, and the cashier makes the change. The whole thing becomes very petty and it takes too much time and space and sanity.

Knowing which level of teacher-student relationship is appropriate.

Q: I got confused about the rich uncle and the father. How does one know what level you are on, when there's so much interpenetration of all the levels? We're told that there's not necessarily a definite distinction between hinayana, mahayana, and vajrayana. Or is that incorrect?

CTR: Those levels are largely a matter of a student's discipline, his or her sense of practice, which is largely based on the sitting practice of meditation to begin with. Beyond that, it's a matter of commitment to giving up individual freedom and dedicating oneself to a much wider level of practice. It's a matter of personal choice.

Q: I was wondering whether all three of those levels happen at once.

CTR: Not necessarily. The first two might happen at once, but the last one, the vajrayana, happens in a very single-handed way, which is the only way. It's a very special one.

6. Crazy Wisdom

The crazy-wisdom body, or form, is related with the basic notion of enlightenment. We say in the opening line of the offering in the sadhana: "To the crazy-wisdom form of the buddhas of the three times." So crazy wisdom is part of the general scheme of enlightenment. . . . But in this case we are talking about a larger form of crazy wisdom, which is cosmic crazy wisdom. It is part of the enlightened attitude of the whole situation, which is already crazy, continuously crazy—and wise at the same time. Primordial wisdom is continuously taking place. That is a very crazy thing, in some sense.

We have discussed the three levels of the teacher-student relationship in terms of the student's development. Now, I would like to discuss those to whom we're relating in the sadhana. We have a sense of relating with somewhat ideal, ethereal beings, who are known as Dorje Trolö or Karma Pakshi. These are people who have already existed, who have lived and died in the past. How can we relate those people to the present situation? And how is that different from worshipping Jesus Christ, for that matter?

That is an interesting question. Dorje Trolö and Karma Pakshi represent the notion of the embodiment of the siddhas. *Siddha* is a Sanskrit word that refers to those who are able to overpower the phenomenal world in their own enlightened way. A siddha is a crazy-wisdom person.

DEFINITION OF CRAZY WISDOM

Crazy wisdom in Tibetan is *yeshe chölwa*. *Yeshe* means "wisdom," and *chölwa* is literally "gone wild." The closest translation for *chölwa* that we could come up with is "crazy," which creates some further understanding. In this case "crazy" goes along with "wisdom"; the two words work together well. So it is craziness gone wise rather than wisdom gone crazy. So here, the craziness is related with wisdom.

Wisdom

The notion of wisdom here is very touchy, and we will have to get into the technical aspect of the whole thing. Wisdom is *jnana* in Sanskrit and *yeshe* in Tibetan. *Yeshe* refers to perception or to enlightenment, which exists eternally. *Ye* means "primordial," and *she* means "knowing," so *yeshe* means "knowing primordially," knowing already. The idea is that you haven't suddenly acquired knowledge. It isn't that somebody has just told you something. Knowledge already exists; it is already here, and we are beginning to tune in to that situation. Such a thing actually does exist already. Wisdom isn't purely manufactured by scholars and scientists and books.

So the notion of enlightenment is the same as that of wisdom. Being a buddha is not so much being a great scholar who knows all about everything and therefore is enlightened. Being a buddha, being enlightened, is actually being able to tune our mind in to that state of being which already exists, which is already liberated, a long time ago. Our only problem is that we have covered it over with all kinds of hiding places and shadows and venetian blinds—whatever we have covering us. We are always trying to cover it up. As a result, we are known as confused people, which is an insult.

We are not all that confused, stupid, and bewildered. We have possibilities—more than possibilities. We actually inherit fundamental wakefulness—all the time. So that is the notion of enlightenment, as well as the notion of yeshe. We are eternally awake, primordially awake, cognitively open and insightful. That is the notion of wisdom.

Crazy

The notion of "crazy" is connected with relating with and dealing with individual situations. When wisdom has been completely and thoroughly achieved at the fullest level, then it has to relate with something. It has to relate with its own radiation, its own light. Ordinarily, when light begins to shine, it reflects on things. That is how we can tell whether the light is bright or dim. The light is reflected in our eyes; we see it, and so we can tell there is light. Therefore, when light is very brilliant, it projects and reflects on things properly and fully. Then we know that there is some kind of communication taking place. In terms of the expression of wisdom, that communication is expressed by the intensity of the wisdom light shining through. That communication is traditionally known as buddha activity or compassion.

Compassion is not so much feeling sorry for somebody, feeling that you are in a better place and somebody else is in a worse place. Rather, compassion is not having any hesitation to reflect your light on things. That reflection is an automatic and natural process, an organic process. Since light has no hesitation, no inhibition about reflecting on things, it does not discriminate whether to reflect on a pile of shit or on a pile of rock or on a pile of diamonds. It reflects on everything it faces. That nondiscriminating reflection is precisely the nature of the relationship between student and teacher. When the student is facing in the right direction, then the guru's light is reflected on him. And when the student is unreceptive, when he is full of dark corners, the teacher's light is not fully reflected on him. That light does not particularly try to fight its way into dark corners.

So that nonhesitating light reflects choicelessly all the time; it shines brilliantly and constantly on things. Craziness means not discriminating and being without cowardice and paranoia. "Should I shine on this object, even though this other object is facing toward me?" Not at all. As it says in the sadhana:

> He is inseparable from peacefulness and yet he acts whenever action is required.§ He subdues what needs to be subdued, he destroys what needs to be destroyed and he cares for whatever needs his care.§

So the definition of crazy wisdom is that whatever is needed will be done and what is not needed is not done. That idea is quite different from the Christian notion that everybody should be converted to Christianity—even stones and grass and meat eaters. It isn't our duty to go around the corner and convert someone. This is a different approach. Whatever needs to be reflected on is reflected on, and whatever needs to be done is done—on the spot.

Maybe that idea doesn't seem to be particularly crazy from your point of view. You might think that if somebody is crazy, he won't leave you any space at all. He will just roll all over you, vomit all over you, and make diarrhea all over you. He will make you terribly crazy, too; he will extend his own craziness. But here this craziness is not so neurotic. It is basic craziness, which is fearlessness and not giving up on anything. Not giving up on anything is the basic point. At the same time, you are willing to work with what is there on the basis of its primordial wakeful quality. So that is the definition of crazy wisdom, which is sometimes known as "wisdom gone wild."

THE SPACE OF COMPLETE SANITY

Crazy wisdom is not only connected with reflecting on things, but it is also connected with the space around things. The crazy-wisdom person provides immense space or environment around things. That environment is completely thronged with the energy[1] of its own fearless wisdom. When a crazy-wisdom person decides to work with you, when he decides to liberate you, you become his victim, choicelessly. You have no way to run away from him. If you try to run backward, that space has been already covered. If you try to run forward, that space has also been covered. When you have a feeling of choicelessness in regard to the particular teacher that you relate with, if you give in to that, your relationship becomes very natural and open. So the crazy-wisdom teacher is somewhat dictatorial. The space he creates is thronged, filled with a strong charge of heavy enlightenment, heavy primordial sanity.

That is usually our problem: we can't handle too much sanity. We would like to have a little corner somewhere for neurosis, a little pocket, just a little puff here and there. If we run into too much sanity, we say, "Boy, it was heavy!"

That heavy sanity is basically what the sadhana is all about. Its purpose is to create just such an atmosphere of claustrophobic sanity, claustrophobic enlightenment in this world, particularly in North America. Western Europe, too, is somewhat hopeful. The idea is that the practitioner of this sadhana should have that kind of understanding or appreciation of sanity. He should be willing to commit himself to an intense experience, which is usually called "freaky."

Let's discuss and dissect the notion of freakiness. What do we mean by "freaky"? The word has two aspects. When sane people get into insane situations, they say that it is freaky. But when insane people get into sane situations, that is also known as freaky. It's just the other way around. So the word *freaky* by itself doesn't mean anything very much; it's just common jargon for when we don't like such situations. We find them threatening to us, whether they are right or wrong, sane or insane. We would like to actually demonstrate or indulge in our own thingy, which is not allowed in those situations. We could say that crazy wisdom actually charges toward us and develops its own direction. There is a sense of openness and a sense of confusion at the same time.

We have a great fear of complete sanity. Let's face it! We don't like being completely sane, completely awake. We really don't like it! We would like to have a little home touch at this level, at that level, at all kinds of levels. We would like to have a home touch so that we can indulge in ourselves, as well as inviting somebody else to indulge in us. We would like to take a break here and there. That is always the case: we don't want to be completely sane.

We have no idea how to be fully sane, fully balanced, fully awake. We have no idea at all. We have never done so. Occasionally, when we are feeling good and religious and prayerful, we would like to go up to our loft. But at the same time, the basement is more attractive. We actually feel as though we have a better reference point and learning situation if we are allowed some indulgence in our neurosis, as long as we're also doing a good job on the other side, on the level of wakefulness.

Sometimes, when we have been quite heroic, quite sane for a long time—if such a thing is possible at all—and then we return to our previous situation, it is more refreshing for us to see things at the so-called gut level, dirty-spoon level, greasy-spoon level. We have some kind of neurotic love for our ethnic claustrophobia. That ethnic claustrophobia applies not only to the Jews and the Chinese and Italians; it applies to everybody's little ethnic world—our grandmother's cookies and our mother's temper tantrums and our father's businesslike style. All those little things that make us glad to return home, to be comfortable at home, are very nostalgic. We would like to return home and feel those good old things. Maybe that's why antiques are very expensive in America.

The vajrayana approach to reality demands complete sanity. It demands not being afraid of sanity. It demands highways and highways and highways of sanity, skies and skies and skies of sanity, fold after fold of it. The vajrayana demands not being afraid of that.

At the first Naropa Institute course on tantra, in the final lecture, I talked about the blue pancake.[2] That is a similar approach. The idea is not so much a round pancake on your plate; rather the whole sky is a self-existing pancake, dough after dough, roll after roll of pancake. That is the space that is always there.

THE CRAZY-WISDOM BODY

The crazy-wisdom vision is very crazy, too. It gives us a sense of direction, a sense of heroism, a sense of reality, a sense of compassion, and so forth down the line. It also includes our doubts as part of that crescendo. So the crazy-wisdom body, or form, is related with the basic notion of enlightenment. We say in the opening line of the offering in the sadhana: "To the crazy-wisdom form of the buddhas of the three times." So crazy wisdom is part of the general scheme of enlightenment. The crazy-wisdom guru is not some Rasputin of Buddhism gone wild who does crazy things, who churns out a crazy-wisdom cult. You might think, "Padmasambhava went to Tibet and got drunk and went crazy. He hyperventilated in the mountain air after being in India." Or, "Karma Pakshi went to China and got turned on by being an imperial teacher. Because of that, he went crazy."

But in this case, we are talking about a larger form of crazy wisdom, which is cosmic crazy wisdom. It is part of the enlightened attitude of the whole situation, which is already crazy, continuously crazy—and wise at the same time. Primordial wisdom is continuously taking place. That is a very crazy thing, in some sense.

Dorje Trolö

We have two personality types in the sadhana: Dorje Trolö and Karma Pakshi. Dorje Trolö is Padmasambhava. Padmasambhava attained enlightenment at birth. He was an Indian Buddhist saint, a siddha, a *vidyadhara*, or "wisdom holder," and a great teacher who brought Buddhism to Tibet. There was already some element of Buddhism there, but Padmasambhava actually brought the full swing, the full force of Buddhism to Tibet.

He manifested as a crazy-wisdom person particularly when he was meditating in Tibet, in a cave called Taktsang Sengge Samdrup, which is now in Bhutan. (In those days, Bhutan was part of Tibet, in the province of Mön.) In order to relate with the savageness of the Tibetans and their own little ethnic samurai mentality, he had to appear in that manifestation. So he manifested himself as an enlightened samurai, a savage person, a crazy-wisdom person known as Dorje Trolö.

According to the iconography, Dorje Trolö rides on a pregnant tigress. He wears the robes of a bhikshu, or Buddhist monk, and he wears a kimono-like garment underneath. He holds a vajra in his right hand and a three-

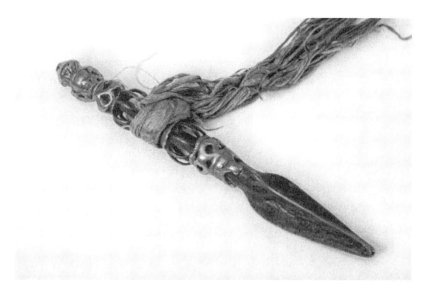

The *phurba*, or ritual dagger. This phurba, carried by hand out of Tibet by Chögyam Trungpa, is an important relic belonging to his lineage, thought to have belonged to Padmasambhava himself. *From the collection of the Shambhala Archives. Photograph by Marvin Moore; used by permission.*

bladed dagger in his left hand. He represents the aspect of crazy wisdom that doesn't relate with gentleness in order to tame somebody. In order to tame someone, you can approach the person abruptly and directly. You can connect with his or her neurosis, his or her insanity; you can project sanity on the spot. That's the notion of crazy wisdom.

Karma Pakshi

Karma Pakshi was the second Karmapa. The Karmapas are the heads of the Karma Kagyü lineage, the practice lineage, to which we belong. Since Karma Pakshi was recognized as a great master, he was invited to the Chinese court as part of the entourage of the Dalai Lama, who in those days was the head of the Sakya sect and was not known as the Dalai Lama. This abbot, the Sakya teacher, was going to become the imperial teacher to the Chinese emperor. Karma Pakshi was just going along as part of the group.

Karma Pakshi was always very strange; his style was not in keeping with the protocol expected of emissaries to the Chinese imperial court. During the journey to China, he played a lot of little tricks; everybody was concerned about his power and his naughtiness, so to speak. There was a lot of intrigue. The Sakya abbot who was supposed to become the Chinese imperial teacher didn't like Karma Pakshi's tricks, and so had him thrown in jail. By means of his miraculous powers, Karma Pakshi turned his prison into a palace. He was able to manifest himself as a real crazy-wisdom person. He proved that politeness and diplomacy were not necessary in order to convert the Chinese emperor, who was Mongolian in that era. He showed us that straight talk is more effective than gentle talk. He didn't say, "Buddhism would be good for your imperial health." He just wasn't into being diplomatic. The rest of the party got very upset; they were afraid that he might blow the whole trip, so to speak. And apparently he did!

Toward the end of his visit, he became the real imperial teacher. The Chinese emperor supposedly said, "The Sakya guru is fine, but how about the other one with the beard? How about him? He seems to be a very threatening person."

The energy of crazy wisdom is continuously ongoing. Karma Pakshi was always an unreasonable person—all the time. When he went back to Tibet, his monastery was still unfinished, so he ordered it to be built on an emergency basis. In that way Tsurphu monastery was founded. It was the seat of the Karmapas in Tibet. It is interesting that such energy goes on throughout the whole lineage.

If I may, I would like to inject a bit of our own vision, here and now, in connection with this aspect of crazy wisdom. For us, it is like wanting to buy a huge building, which may be out of the question, in some sense, but on the other hand, it is a possibility.[3] And we are going to do it! That seems to be Karma Pakshi's vision, actually. He would have done a similar thing.

Suppose a fantastically rich person came along. All of us might try to be nice to this particular guy or this particular lady—or we might blow his or her trip completely—to the extent that this person would be completely switched! Although the person's notion of sanity was at the wrong level, he or she might become a great student if we were willing to take such a chance. So far, we haven't found such a person, who would be rich enough and crazy enough and bold enough to do such a thing. But that was the kind of role Karma Pakshi played with the emperor of China. Karma Pakshi was known for his abruptness and his dedication. He possessed the intelligence of primordial wakefulness.

Tüsum Khyenpa

Then we have another interesting person in the sadhana: Tüsum Khyenpa, who was the first Karmapa, before Karma Pakshi. He was an extraordinarily solid person, extraordinarily solid, sane, and contemplative. He spent his whole life teaching and negotiating between various warring factions. There was a lot of chaos at that time; all kinds of squabbles erupted among the Tibetan principalities. By his efforts, their fighting was finally subdued. He was basically a peacemaker and a very powerfully contemplative person.

Mikyö Dorje

Then we have Mikyö Dorje, who was the eighth Karmapa. He was a great scholar and a great teacher, and he was very wild in his approach to reality. Once he said, "If I can light fire to the rest of the cosmos, I will do so." That kind of burning prajna was in him all the time.

Rangjung Dorje

Rangjung Dorje, the third Karmapa, was a key person: he brought together the higher and lower tantras. He was an extraordinarily spacious person, and one of the most powerful exponents of mahamudra, which is at a very high level of vajrayana enlightenment experience. He was a great exponent of the ati teachings as well.

Connecting with the Crazy-Wisdom Lineage through the Sadhana

I'm trying to introduce these people to you tonight. And I'm sure they're very pleased to meet you as well. They are such powerful people! It's such a powerful idea! And that powerful idea is not of the past or of the present or of the future; it is simply living experience at every level. All those ideas which presently exist have existed in the past—obviously. Otherwise, we wouldn't be able to discuss them. And since such experience did exist, does exist, we have some way of relating with that. We can capture the vision of those people and their fearlessness.

How are we going to do that? The only way to do so seems to be to have some kind of connection, a means, a way to link ourselves to that. That way is the sadhana itself. I'm not talking about tripping out, taking LSD and reading the sadhana in the afternoon, trying to visualize Dorje Trolö and Karma Pakshi, trying to bring them into your world. I'm not talking about getting them on your side when you are particularly depressed or in need of help. The approach in vajrayana is not the popular Christian principle of inviting God to be on your side because your side is right. That is precisely the kind of problem with the Arabs and the Israelis. We're not putting up a fight, so no one has to be on our side or on the other person's side. There is no other person to fight with. We're on our own side, and "they" are we.

So those people in the sadhana are not regarded as ghosts, as holy ghosts. And they are not particularly regarded as the Christ principle. They are not regarded as larger spirits that we have around us. They are simply regarded as states of being that express ourselves in our awakened state.

DISCUSSION

Fate of the Chinese emperor.

Question: Rinpoche, with all due respect to Karma Pakshi, can you tell me what happened to the Chinese emperor?[4]

Chögyam Trungpa Rinpoche: I think he was saved. There's a story that the Chinese emperor became one of the lineage holders himself. That's not bad for a Chinese, eh? [Laughter]

Relationship of figures in the sadhana to the vajra master.

Q: Are all these people the same as a vajra master? If you get into it with the vajra master, are you getting into it with them?

CTR: Yes, absolutely! It's like studying with somebody who is fully soaked in his or her own tradition, like a poet. It's as though you could meet a living poet who has all the feelings and inspiration of his tradition. It feels as if you could actually meet Shakespeare, as if you could meet Yeats or another great poet on the spot. Unfortunately, the world of poets is slightly different from the world of Buddhist practice, which is constantly being transmitted from generation to generation.

Rangjung Dorje's integration of ati and mahamudra.

Q: Rinpoche, you mentioned that Rangjung Dorje integrated the ati and the mahamudra traditions. Was he a holder of the ati lineage as well as the mahamudra? And along those lines, is the sadhana an integration of the Nyingma and the Kagyü traditions? And do the Nyingma lamas incorporate the practice of mahamudra?

CTR: Yes. He was in the ati lineage. The sadhana is supposedly in the Kagyü tradition, which has a lot of ideas borrowed from the Nyingma tradition. That's the case with almost any sadhana in the Kagyü tradition. The Nyingma tradition also incorporates the practice of mahamudra.

The difference between jnana and prajna.

Q: What is the difference between jnana and prajna?

CTR: Jnana is basic, primordial wakefulness. And prajna is a tool that you use throughout the whole journey, starting from the *pratyekabuddha* level of the hinayana up to the vajrayana level. It is a constant examination: you are constantly trying to find out the way things are. So prajna is more intellectual, and jnana is more experiential.

The word *intellectual* has a very limited meaning in the English language. I don't know about its meaning in the other European languages. In English it means just relating with books and facts and figures. But in this case, "intellectual" means seeing things very precisely, as much as you can. It means perceiving further and transcending your own perceptions at the same time. That is not quite a meditative state. It's not a state: it's working with your mind.

Q: Is jnana like something that has been given to you already, and prajna like something that you develop?

CTR: Jnana is your inheritance. Prajna is a sympathetic inheritance which you work toward.

Q: I don't quite understand what you mean by sympathetic.

CTR: It's something that you already have with you. You could say prajna began when you were born, when you learned how to suck your mother's nipple. It begins from that level, which is already an inheritance, in some sense.

Q: But it's also something you develop.

CTR: Yes.

Q: Do you develop more and more prajna?

CTR: You don't suck your mother's nipple forever; you just grow up.

How crazy wisdom relates to being human.

Q: Could you talk about how crazy wisdom relates to being a human being? Are we manifestations of crazy wisdom refusing to see itself, or something like that?

CTR: Yes.

Q: There must be more to it.

CTR: That's it!

Interrelationship of the incarnations of the Karmapas.

Q: Rinpoche, if Tüsum Khyenpa was the first Karmapa, Karma Pakshi was the second Karmapa, Mikyö Dorje was the eighth Karmapa, and the Sixteenth Karmapa is the one we know,⁵ are all these people the same person?

CTR: Well, it's like trying to say which sky is the real sky: the one above New York City or the one above Boston. It's difficult to say.

Difference between an ordinary crazy person and a crazy-wisdom person.

Q: I usually think of a crazy person as being kind of out of control and kind of dangerous because I can't reason with him, I can't control him. Is there that feeling about the crazy-wisdom person?

CTR: With the crazy-wisdom person, wisdom is already wise. In other words, if you become wise, you become a wisdom person. Trying to control someone who is crazy is obviously not wise. Such a person doesn't know anything about wisdom; he is just being crazy. That seems to be the problem. If you don't have a touch of wisdom, a dash of wisdom in your craziness, you are just flat crazy. It's very dangerous, sure.

But a crazy-wisdom person is not particularly dangerous. On the other hand, he could be dangerous. It depends on how crazy *you* are. If you are more crazy, then the crazy-wisdom person is more dangerous. It also works the other way around. When an ordinary person is crazy, if he is less crazy, he is safer. He is not as much of a threat, right? I hope so. Is that logical? But at the crazy-wisdom level, if you are more crazy, then the crazy-wisdom teacher is going to be more dangerous for you. He is going to try to cut through the aorta of your neurosis.

Q: Does that relate to what you were saying earlier in the talk about a feeling of freakiness? Kind of feeling half insane and half sane?

CTR: Yes, something like that.

Q: When you feel that freakiness, is that the time to let go more? Is that the time for a leap?

CTR: The letting go has to be based on some kind of wisdom. You see, the point is that first you get wisdom; then you get crazy. That's what the crazy-wisdom direction is all about. In ordinary cases, first you get crazy, and then you get wisdom. That is the mad philosopher style.

Integration of ati and mahamudra in the sadhana.

Q: Rinpoche, in the sadhana, is there some point where the ati and the mahamudra traditions are integrated, or is that happening all through the sadhana?

CTR: All through the whole thing.

What you are battling against in the vajrayana?

Q: I wonder if you could reconcile something from the last talk with something you said this time. Tonight you spoke about there being no sides. But last night, in describing the relationship with the vajra master, you said something about the vajra master inviting the student: "Here is your sword. Come join the battle." Who is the battle against?

CTR: The two things are saying the same thing. The battle is simply not being afraid to fight, to use your sword. Sometimes people become petrified when they are given a weapon. They are afraid they might cut themselves by tripping on it, if they're wearing a long coat or something. People are afraid of all kinds of things; they are so cowardly. If they have a sword, they are constantly in fear of having an accident. But if you are given a sword, you should be able to handle it. That is what we have been discussing tonight.

Q: I still don't understand. What are you going to do with the sword?

CTR: You fight with it.

Q: But what is it that you fight? Or is this the sword of Manjushri?

CTR: That is also a sword. You battle with your neurosis, which battles back. It's not just chopping down neurosis, which is quietly lying there. It's not all that simple, you know. This whole world is coming toward you.

Relationship of openness and not giving up.

Q: You talked about openness, and you talked about jnana as not giving up anything. I don't see how the two go together.

CTR: I don't see any problems with that. Openness is not giving up. When you're open, that means that you don't reject anything. It's not refusing to give up in the sense of working very hard to get something. We're not talking about laboring. Not giving up doesn't have to become a crusade.

Fear of sanity and how to overcome it.

Q: You said that we don't want to be completely sane. Is that because of our fear? And if so, why are we afraid, and what can we do about it—other than sitting?

CTR: You are afraid because you like the smell of your own armpit. You find it very attractive, very homey. Doing something about that would be taking a shower, trying out the perspective of freshness instead of your smelly armpit. That is opening up. That is not indulging your own little thingy. You just get out! That seems to be the point.

Q: That has to do with familiarity, which is a very safe feeling. But I don't understand how that relates to overcoming fear.

CTR: Well, nothing is going to be familiar in an area where we have never gone. Nothing is going to remain very familiar. But at this point, familiarity is not the criterion. The criterion is just general wakefulness. That is going to be very alien to a lot of us, but we've got to do it.

Q: So is that the leap?

CTR: Yes. You've got to do it.

7. The Charnel Ground

Having discovered that the charnel ground is not unworkable, it actually becomes our working basis. It is the expression of our neurosis, which we have to work with. We begin to find that there is enormous strength and power behind it. We are not trying to get away from the charnel ground. We also don't build a Hilton Hotel in the middle of it. We don't shut the doors in order to seal off completely the smell of rot and the chaos outside, so that we could enjoy ourselves on the wall-to-wall carpeting. Building the mandala is actually part of the charnel-ground principle.

We have discussed the principle of crazy wisdom, and hopefully we now have some understanding of what that is. I would like to go further in discussing what kind of world, what kind of universe, is connected with the crazy-wisdom mandala.

Mandala as the Expression of Our Basic Being

The interesting point is that such a mandala, or such a world, is not built on any form of uncertainty at all. It has very specific and definite patterns and directions. It is simply the expression of our own particular state of being, which constitutes the basic world of pain and pleasure, chaos and order, neurosis and sanity, and so forth. This kind of mandala setup is used in "The Sadhana of Mahamudra" as it is in many traditions of tantra, particularly the anuttarayoga and mahayoga levels of the tantric teachings.

We have a basic background, which is actually speakable, workable, and communicable. And on that basic ground, which we share with each other, the teachings can be founded. If the teachings were founded on virgin territory, there would be no communication whatsoever with our ordinary, everyday-life situation. In that case, teaching would be out of the question. Nobody would be able to understand properly; nobody would be able to practice properly. Because the practice of buddhadharma exists within our own state of being, our own world, it is very powerful. The teachings speak our own language, rather than some divine language, some language of transcendence.

People get excited when spiritual language is used as a foreign language that has nothing to do with them personally or with their everyday life. Everything is expressed in extraordinary language, and people try to relate to that as if they were eating a new dish or wearing a new costume. They think of it as something exotic or special, something they are not used to. Such indulgence is completely fake because it has nothing to do with their lifestyle or their state of mind. They simply would like to have something different for a change.

Some people find that ordinary life is too dull, that the environment is too predictable. They decide to go to India or Japan for a change. When they get to those countries and discover such familiar landmarks as Coca-Cola bottles or ice-cream cones, they feel completely insulted. They feel insulted, not because they're culturally impeccable, but because they were looking for something other than their own experience. They're shocked that their territory has been invaded, and they blame it on those countries. They didn't expect such places to be Americanized, Westernized. And when they begin to realize that the Japanese don't always sit on low cushions, that they use tables and chairs and eat with knives and forks, it's terrible. They are so insulted. When they begin to realize that Japanese wear suits and ties and ordinary clothes rather than kimonos, they are so insulted.

This is not so much a puritanical approach to the world or to culture, although you present it that way because that's the only way that you can present it. But it is a personal invasion. You are looking for an ideal new world, a brand-new world completely different from your world. But when you begin to relate with the larger world, the world on a global level, you discover that the technical or mechanized aspect of Westernization is always prominent. You begin to realize that your ideal world is not intact, which is very difficult for people to relate with. We hear all kinds of stories when people come back from other countries. Sometimes they're very disappointed. Sometimes they're not all that disappointed because they have gotten something out of it, but still they make jokes about Coca-Cola bottles with flowers in them sitting on the shrine. In 1974, hundreds of people in Boulder made fun of His Holiness the Sixteenth Karmapa drinking Sprite while he was giving blessings. They thought it was very cute, kind of a collage of artistic improvisation. Some people thought it was not so good; they thought that even the Karmapa was beginning to be corrupted by such things.

So we have that notion of wanting to change our world completely. When we get into a different tradition of spiritual discipline, we think we're getting into another cultural setup altogether. We would be highly confirmed in our expectations if the rest of the world, other than this world, walked on the ceiling instead of on the floor. That would be regarded as a fantastic thing to do. We would like to learn that particular martial art of sitting and walking, even sleeping, on the ceiling. Those things should be regarded as just dreams. There is a touch of cheap magic about them. Those expectations and attitudes are what is known as spiritual materialism. We think that somebody has a higher level of psychic ability and can tell us where our missing coin is. That approach is just a simple version of a comic book brought to life; nothing is happening there.

THE CHARNEL GROUND

I am discussing this particular point because in the sadhana we talk about the whole mandala being created on the charnel ground, where birth, life, and death take place. It is a place to die and a place to be born, equally, at the same time—a wasteland of some kind. The closest thing to a charnel ground in this country is a hospital, a place where you give birth and where death occurs. But the charnel ground is much more than a hospital situation. It is simply our basic raw and rugged nature, the ground where we constantly puke and fall down, constantly make a mess. We are constantly dying, we are constantly giving birth. We are eating on the charnel ground, sitting on it, sleeping on it, having nightmares on it. That basic ground which we use all the time is what is known as the charnel ground.

A traditional description for the charnel ground is an abandoned place where nobody would want to hang out. But it's so truthful. It does not try to hide its truth about reality. There are corpses lying all over the place: loose arms, loose hands, loose internal organs, and flowing hairs all over the place. Jackals and vultures are roaming around, each one devising its own scheme for getting the best pieces of the corpses, the next finger or toe. That is precisely what we are doing in this country and in this world.

When I say this country, I do not mean the USA alone, but the ordinary, usual world that we live in. Whether it is an Occidental or an Oriental situation, it's exactly the same thing. There is always a charnel ground of some kind where we try to catch each other's toes and bite each other's tails. This is called business mentality or competitiveness, friendship, or any of the many words that we use. This is the charnel ground, and that is why we don't like it. We want to get into a higher level of something or other, where we might be able to attach ourselves slightly differently. But unfortunately, according to the vajrayana teachings, we can't do that. According to basic Buddhism, in fact, we can't do it. Everything starts from the first level of the truth of suffering and the origin of suffering. And studying our particular state of mind—the five skandhas and the twelve nidanas and all the topics that we discuss as part of the basic teachings of hinayana and mahayana—is simply an attempt to understand the notion of charnel ground properly and fully.

Those who are known as bodhisattvas—the brave people who can actually tread on the path of enlightenment, who can dance with it—are also treading on the charnel ground. They realize that the world they are treading on and working in is filled with intense neurosis, intense chaos, intense ugliness and unpleasantness—all the time. Bodhisattvas are actually inspired to work with such chaos, to tidy up a little bit, without disrupting the generally inspiring qualities of those untidy areas. They just work with what is there.

This sadhana follows the traditional pattern of first laying the ground of the mandala. If you are going to build a castle or a house, you build it on a battlefield, which is a somewhat medieval concept. In some sense, you could say that people fight for their land, slaughter some of their enemies, and drive the rest away—which creates a charnel ground. Once you capture that particular land, you say, "This is my property. I'm going to build my castle on it, my house on it."

Creating the mandala of the sadhana is the same kind of experience. First there is need for a rugged, raw, and straightforward relationship with the world. You have to overcome a certain hesitation toward that particular relationship. The interesting point is that, having dealt with the rugged and raw situations, and having accepted them as part of your home ground to begin with, then some spark of sympathy or compassion could begin to take place. You are not in a hurry to leave such a place immediately. You would like to face the facts and realities of that particular world; you would like to go back and try to build on your home ground. So the chaos that takes place in our neurosis is the only home ground that we can build our mandala on.

If we are looking for something else, then we want to reject that ground and find a better, higher, more loving, less aggressive place. If we are looking for an ideal spot, we never find it. It is like shopping for an apartment; we never come up with an ideal place to live. We have to make modifications: sometimes we modify the situation, sometimes we begin to accept it. Our constant desire is to look for luxury, but such luxury doesn't happen without our dealing properly with the rugged aspects of our life.

That seems to be the first message, which may be very grim. But it is also very exciting. Large areas of our life have been devoted to trying to avoid discovering our own experience. Now we have a chance to explore that large area which exists in our being, which we have been trying to avoid. We have further possibilities of discovering a good site on which to build our castle of enlightenment. When people are unable to accept this message, some people go too far: they commit suicide. They say, "This particular life is too hopeless. There is too much charnel ground. Hopefully the next life will be better." But the same thing goes on in the next life, too, from that point of view. We inherit our previous charnel ground; it is doubled, tripled, a hundred times exaggerated.

Once I gave a talk at the Asia House in New York City, and the old ladies and old gentlemen there were very upset because I discussed the charnel ground. I also discussed the way people relate to art purely in terms of buying and selling it. I said that regarding Buddhist art purely from that point of view is nothing but spiritual materialism. They were very upset; they didn't like the subject at all. It hit them very deeply.

Having discovered that the charnel ground is not unworkable, it actually becomes our working basis. It is the expression of our neurosis, which we have to work with. We begin to find that there is enormous strength and power behind it. We are not trying to get away from the charnel ground. We also don't build a Hilton Hotel in the middle of it. We don't shut the doors in order to seal off completely the smell of rot and the chaos outside, so that we could enjoy ourselves on the wall-to-wall carpeting. Building the mandala is actually part of the charnel-ground principle.

THE ROCK OF SANITY AND FAITH

The notion of the immense sanity that exists within the charnel ground is symbolized in the sadhana by rock. That monumental rock is a symbol of solid and sane ground. It is obsidian or flint, very sharp and accurate. It is a monument that we can build within the charnel ground, as part of this particular environment of neurosis. So there could be a monumental rock in the middle of the charnel ground. Why not? In this case, it is not an ego-centered monument, but a powerfully personal and fully awake aspect of that ground. And that monument is called faith, devotion, trust. We decide to work with our charnel ground rather than running away from it, because there is so much devotion and faith and trust in our own sanity already. Our sanity automatically becomes a rock.

This is similar to the concept of Saint Peter's Basilica. The idea was that the foundation of the church should be built on some kind of solid foundation of real faith, unshakable faith.[1] Unfortunately, that only happened in Rome and doesn't exist anymore. However, in this case, this rock is not in Rome; it is everywhere, in every one of our hearts.

A mahayanist analogy for this rock of sanity is that everyone possesses Buddha in themselves. There is a perfect, beautiful, well-preserved Buddha image in everyone's heart. That doesn't necessarily mean that, if you dissect yourself, you will find a little statue inside. Buddha in your heart is a symbol of faith: you could be immaculate and perfect, as perfect as Shakyamuni Buddha himself. That possibility already exists in you.

What is faith? Is it blind or real? In ordinary terms, the concept of prayer in the Christian tradition is an expression of faith. Once you have said a prayer, you have faith that something will happen to you or that something will actually be transmitted to somebody else, one way or another. It makes sense to you that what you want to happen will happen. And if you are in the wrong, you will be punished. You should take that also as a message. But in this case, faith has nothing to do with praying to somebody. Faith is a sense of dignity. Meister Eckhart talks about faith and prayer in the sense of awake—being present and mindful and aware of the situation. Faith is seeing things as they are—whatever they might be—precisely, directly, and without any hesitation. We have already experienced our neurosis faithfully and properly. We have no way of avoiding our neurosis. Acknowledging that is one step toward faith. We know how much pain is involved, how many problems there are already.

We are already well versed in our own problem of reality, the facts and figures and the truth of reality. That is a step toward faith.

Working with our own reality brings us the realization that it is workable: it is not as bad as we thought. In fact, it is highly possible to work with our reality, our neurosis. That brings a further level of faith, that we can actually be with ourselves and our neurosis, and we can experience openness. Faith is not so much connected with promises: "Everything's going to be okay. Just have faith. You're going to get a million dollars tomorrow. There's nothing to worry about. Just have faith."

You might be disappointed when you go to your mailbox tomorrow. That kind of faith is future oriented. It is not that you should have faith and therefore you'll be given your reward. But faith is the conviction that something is actually happening this very moment, that something is taking place right now, therefore it is so. It is tonight, it is nighttime, the sun isn't shining. It is winter; there is snow on the ground. We are indoors, we have electricity, and we have lights shining on us—very simple. That's the kind of faith we're talking about. It's actual faith as opposed to promised faith, which is a different approach. Nothing is related with any reward.

That notion of reward reminds me of one of those scientific experiments that trains rats to eat at a certain time. If you program them in a certain way, they do what you want. The same thing is being done with monkeys and dolphins. But spiritual discipline is not particularly a zoological practice. Buddha or God doesn't regard human beings as zoological specimens or as an interesting study program. People are real. We'll have to ask Jehovah about that, whether or not he agrees with us.

THE TRIANGLE OF COMPASSION

Faith is very solid when it is based on the experience of now rather than on future proof. So the rock we are talking about is very solid and very basic—absolutely basic. On top of that rock sits a red triangle, which is a symbol of the feminine principle. The triangle represents the cervix, the gate of birth. It is a very popular tantric image. Once you have faith, then you can give birth—properly, freely, fantastically. You can actually give birth to everything. But if you were in the charnel ground without faith, you would be constantly confused; you would be completely sterile. You couldn't be a proper mother or father; you would be completely castrated. You would be just a freaky wind, blown by the incense of rotting bodies and the stench of jackals. You would be completely confused by the whole thing.

This triangle is just a triangle, a red triangle. It could be made of plastic or ruby. Compassion radiates constantly from this triangle, which is the notion of relaxation or openness. When you're willing to give birth to reality, you can't begin by fighting for your territory. You can't say, "This is my baby; that is your baby," and put stamps on their foreheads. You can't categorize which babies belong to whom. That doesn't necessarily mean that you have to abandon your baby at the hospital and take someone else's baby. That would be too literal. I am mentioning this just in case. I respect your sanity; nevertheless, there could be occasional people who are too literal.

In this case, the triangle represents a much more general and basic approach—a more sane approach. Such compassion is giving, opening. What has been happening so far in the charnel ground is a self-exploratory process, constant personal exploration. But beyond that, there is just giving, opening, extending yourself completely to the situation, to what is available around you, being fantastically exposed. That sense of openness can take place when you have faith and when you have developed dignity and a sense that you can give birth to another world. Then you are ready to open up and perform your duty.

To end, I'd like to share the passage from the sadhana that we've been discussing this evening:

> In the state of nonmeditation all phenomena subside in that great graveyard in which lie buried the complexities of samsara and nirvana.⁑ This is the universal ground of everything; it is the basis of freedom and also the basis of confusion.⁑ Within it, the vajra anger, the flame of death, burns fiercely and consumes the fabric of dualistic thoughts.⁑ The black river of death, the vajra passion, turbulent with massive waves, destroys the raft of conceptualization to the roaring sound of the immeasurable void.⁑ The great poisonous wind of the vajra ignorance blows with all-pervading energy like an autumn storm and sweeps away all thoughts of possessiveness and self like a pile of dust.⁑
>
> Whatever you see partakes of the nature of that wisdom which transcends past, present and future.⁑ From here came the buddhas of the past; here live the buddhas of the present; this is the primeval ground from which the buddhas of the future will come.⁑ This is the heavenly realm of the dakinis, the secret charnel ground of the blazing mountain.⁑ But you won't find ordinary earth and rocks here, even if you look for them. All the mountains are Buddha Lochana, who is the all-pervading wisdom of equanimity and unchanging stillness.⁑ This is the realm in which the distinctions between meditation and the postmeditation experience no longer occur.⁑ In this fearless state, even if

the buddhas of the three times rise against you, you will remain in the indestructible vajra nature.᾿ The water which flows here is the Buddha Mamaki, who is the lake of the mirrorlike wisdom, clear and pure, as though the sky had melted.᾿ Here is the joyous river, which is the transcendent form of the eight kinds of consciousness.᾿ It flows into the great purity which goes beyond clean and unclean.᾿

In the various parts of the charnel ground can be seen the terrifying trees, which are the protecting mahakalis: Rangjung Gyalmo, Dorje Sogdrubma, Tüsölma and Ekajati.᾿ In these trees vultures, ravens, hawks and eagles perch, hungry for meat and thirsting for blood.᾿ They represent the concept of good and evil.᾿ Until you stop clinging to this concept the mahakalis will continue to manifest as friendly goddesses and harmful demons.᾿

Various animals roam about: tigers, leopards, bears, jackals and dogs, all howling and jumping up and down excitedly.᾿ These represent the different kinds of perception.᾿ Here too are the chötens of the awakened state of mind, where the great yogis live.᾿ They represent the supernormal powers which need not be sought.᾿

In the middle of this heavenly realm is a huge rock mountain, which arose from the corpse of the rudra of ego.᾿ It is triangular in shape and it pierces the skies.᾿ It is dignified and awe-inspiring and radiates the blue light of Vajrasattva.᾿ On top of this mountain is the red triangle which can accommodate all apparent phenomena and the whole of existence.᾿ This is the primeval ground where the question of samsara and nirvana does not arise.᾿ It is the beginning and the end of everything.᾿ The triangle radiates the blazing red light of inner warmth and compassion.᾿ Above the triangle is a beautiful flower, a hundred-petaled lotus in full bloom, exuding a delicate scent.᾿ It is the lotus of discriminating wisdom.᾿

Discussion

Allowing the energy of crazy wisdom to enter you.

Question: In terms of opening up to perform our duty, as you said, did you mean to open and allow the enlightened energy to come through us as the action of a bodhisattva?

Chögyam Trungpa Rinpoche: I'm talking about something more than purely being a bodhisattva. You allow the energy of crazy wisdom to come inside you.

Q: So it's not obligatory as much as it is a natural sort of evolutionary—

CTR: Well, it is obligatory, in some sense, because you have to push yourself. You might have some hesitations about it. Nothing will arise easily; there has to be some kind of effort. That's where faith comes in: your faith has to be a rock. It couldn't just be cotton wool or papier-mâché in the shape of a rock. It has to be a real rock, and some real effort has to be put in. Good luck.

Hesitation and faith.

Q: In terms of faith and hesitation, do you have to be able to get past hesitation before faith happens? I sort of got that impression.

CTR: Well, that would be very difficult to do.

Q: So there's some sense of working with the hesitation as part of the faith, or something?

CTR: Yes. Otherwise, you'll never get anywhere. Hesitation *is* faith. You have faith in hesitation. If you have faith in something, you can work with it. You could even have faith in drinking a cup of tea, or you could drink vodka in the same way.

Relationship of faith and discipline.

Q: Rinpoche, what about the question of discipline and faith? How are they integrated?

CTR: Faith is discipline. You can't have faith if you don't have discipline. Discipline is trying to work with the situation that you have faithfully worked out. Then you have faith. They go hand in hand, needless to say.

Q: Does that give birth to anything? In that process of discipline, is there any sense of the birth of the situation taking place as a result of those two things coming together?

CTR: I hope so, sir. You'd better—we'd better—do it, whatever the case.

Relationship of the charnel ground to crazy wisdom.

Q: Is the charnel ground crazy wisdom?

CTR: It's just charnel ground. We can't dress up our charnel ground; it's simply charnel ground. The charnel ground has wisdom and craziness at the same time, but I wouldn't say that the charnel ground *is* crazy wisdom, particularly. There's a lot of wisdom and a lot of craziness going on there.

Crazy wisdom in relation to logic and mathematics.

Q: Earlier, when you were talking about crazy wisdom, I was thinking about science and mathematics and logic, and they seemed poles apart. But when you talked about the Coke bottle on the shrine, I thought maybe they could come together. I wonder if there is room, if a coming together of crazy wisdom and logic is possible.

CTR: Absolutely. Crazy wisdom is very logical, very accommodating, in a very crazy way—absolutely. That's good thinking, actually.

Confusion and sanity in the charnel ground as grandmother's soup.

Q: Would it be dualistic to regard some things in the charnel ground as confused and others as not confused? You don't particularly say, "This is confused and that is not confused."

CTR: Everything is both. Grandmother's soup. The whole thing is a big soup. It's like the soup that we usually brew on New Year's Eve in Tibet. Grandmother's soup is supposed to have nine ingredients, which represent everything you could throw in: sweet and sour, bones and fats and vegetables—everything put together.

Relationship of faith and doubt.

Q: Rinpoche, with the exception of a few vivid experiences, like falling into the toilet, I find that doubt has a more rocklike quality than experience does. I'm wondering if you would talk about doubt in relationship to faith.

CTR: Doubt is nonyielding, nongiving. What we are talking about is much more than purely intellectual doubt. Doubt has emotional attachment as well, which is not wanting to give, not wanting to open or expand. You feel that you are surrounded by the enemy. Faith is completely the opposite: everybody is your friend, including your enemy. On the other hand, you might become somewhat too love-and-lighty, which could also be problematic. Faith is not love-and-lighty. It can only be achieved through critical judgment of the situation. That is the essence of faith: you are critical, you are not conned, particularly. On the other hand, you are not particularly put off by your criticalness. There is workability and openness within it. It's like driving on a highway: you have to drive on the highway the way it is. You can't hold a grudge against the people who built each curve. You have to go along with it, but you still have doubt about the problems of that particular road.

The recipe for the charnel ground.

Q: I'm curious and a little confused about the recipe of the charnel ground—the soup that you mentioned. Is it a metaphor for samsara? Are the ingredients prefabricated? Do we just stumble on them, or do we create—

CTR: In some sense we create it, and in some sense it is basic shit; it's a mixture of both. There are little highlights coming up, which are sane and pure; there are also little pollutions coming up. That is actually the perfect picture of the world we're living in. There is a lot of sanity and there is a lot of chaos, at the same time. It's a huge soup, an ecological mess, I would say.

The Buddhist approach to faith and prayer.

Q: In the Christian sense of faith, you have faith that maybe your prayer will be answered. But it seems that in the Buddhist tradition, if you pray, you just have faith that you're praying. Is there a change in that as you get into vajrayana? Does faith become something different, more powerful?

CTR: I think that the Buddhist approach to faith, in terms of the help that you get out of having faith, is that you could help yourself, rather than being helped. You don't have to be crucified for the sake of whatever it may be—plum juice or any kind of colorful image. You don't sacrifice yourself for the sake of orange juice, but you develop your own discipline, your own reality. You learn that you can help yourself—completely. That's the idea, because Buddhism is not particularly a centralized philosophy, a pyramid approach. One of the symbols for Buddhism is a wheel. So it's an eternally circular approach, rather than a pyramid approach. So the idea is that faith is meant to help you. It recirculates things. What you put out goes around; it goes around and then it comes back to you.

Faith and making friends with yourself.

Q: Rinpoche, is faith more than just making friends with yourself? Is it more comprehensive than that? Is it making friends with the whole situation as well?

CTR: It is much more than making friends with yourself. It's having the solid ground of real appreciation of things as they are: that fire burns, that water flows. It's that kind of real experience of how things work.

Fear of sanity.

Q: You talked earlier about people being frightened of experiencing their emotions, because they are afraid of being overwhelmed. And I was wondering if the fear of complete sanity is the fear of the intensity of that sanity, a fear of being overwhelmed by it.

CTR: I think that's a problem we have with faith, because of too much hanging on to the sense of feedback and reward.

Q: I was wondering if people hesitate to allow themselves to be completely sane because that situation would be extremely intense. As with emotions, they might feel that their sanity would overwhelm them completely. Why is there that feeling of being overwhelmed?

CTR: In some sense, it is because you would like to stay in your nest. You don't want to be put on the spot, particularly. You would like to indulge in your own particular nest. You don't want to step outside without an overcoat, in just your shirtsleeves on a winter morning, which would be much more challenging. Then your personality would come through, your relationship to the coldness of it.

Q: So there's a cowardliness?

CTR: Yes, there has to be that.

Q: How do you become brave?

CTR and Q [*in unison*]: You just do it.

8. The Crazy-Wisdom Body of All the Buddhas

Devotion and Blessings

Adhishthana . . . means the radiation that takes place between the opening of the student's mind to the teacher and the teachings, and the opening of the teacher's mind to the student. Between those two openings, experience becomes not only naked but radiant. The two burn each other completely. The teacher begins to understand the student's desire, his devotion. The student begins to feel the teacher's desire and openness.

Before we discuss the visual structure of the mandala in detail, I would like to talk further about the implications behind that setup. On the lotus seat in the center of the mandala sits the crazy-wisdom body of all the buddhas of the past, present, and future. He is the embodiment of basic sanity who actually controls and directs the universe, who controls all apparent phenomena and the whole of existence. That figure is connected with the sense of devotion. It's somebody's rough guess, so to speak, about enlightenment, basic sanity, surrendering, and openness—all that is embodied in this central figure.

However, this figure, this symbol, is not regarded as unreasonably divine or sacred. There is no solidity here in the notion of divinity and sacredness. On a superficial level, the notion of divinity is that it shouldn't be tampered with or touched by dirty hands. That isn't the point here. Sanity and devotion both exist within us. Along with our experience of faith and trust, our sanity and serenity are still very intact. Something that exists within us and something that exists outside of us are combined together in this figure.

MÖGÜ: THE EXPRESSION OF DEVOTION

Möpa: Admiration and Longing

There are several levels of devotion. The Tibetan term for devotion is *mögü*, which is divided into two parts. The first one is *möpa*, which means "admiration" or "longing"; we will talk about *güpa* a little later.

Admiration as spiritual materialism.

Such admiration could be purely looking for an object of worship, a fanclub approach. We would like to worship a hero who possesses a great deal of grace, a great deal of talent. But often we find that looking at an art object or listening to a composition produced by a master artist only makes us jealous and depressed. We say to ourselves, "How come I can't do those things? I would like to be one of those people who can produce fantastic works of art." We have a sense of pain and longing because we are trying to compete with somebody who has actually accomplished tremendous discipline. We feel lonesome because we are unable to execute such a beautiful, brilliant work of art. We feel inadequate and completely stupid, which only makes us depressed.

At the other extreme, all these fantastic things seem like an insult to us. We become tremendously resentful about anything presented to us that is beautiful. We would like to steal works of art from museums; we would even like to burn down the museums themselves. We might feel like going to those extremes, or we might just feel like insulting those people who have actually achieved something—who are in a position to achieve something or who have some appreciation of art. We get completely pissed off at those people.

Another approach is that we feel an immense distance between works of art and our own ability; we feel that those works of art are fine, but they have nothing to do with us. If we want to relax, we would like to put on a record. If we're rich enough, we would like to buy such-and-such painting, or if we're not all that rich, we might be able to buy a postcard from a museum. But that painting or that music has nothing to do with us. We're completely cut off. Our psychological blockage makes us feel humble and resentful and inadequate. It's too painful to look into, so we decide just to cut it off completely.

Sometimes, admiring something means that you want to suck it in. And sometimes admiration is a sense of awe and fear; we don't even want to touch the stuff. Our mind is completely closed off to the possibility of appreciation.

So there are a number of neurotic styles of relating to objects of our admiration based on passion, aggression, and ignorance or indifference. In general, we relate to our guru in the same three neurotic styles. If we meet a crazy-wisdom person—if we could even dare to discuss such a topic at this point—if we even touch on the verge of the possibility of that meeting, we react with passion, aggression, or indifference. We may be completely terrified and threatened, which is an expression of aggression. We don't want to have anything to do with that person—not at all. Or else we would like to suck and chew and gnaw and swallow and digest the guru completely, so that he or she becomes a part of us. Then there would be nobody to threaten us from the outside.

A third possibility of relating with a crazy-wisdom person is to regard that person as purely an icon. We hang his or her picture on the wall; we worship them. We think that if we are on the good side of such a great person and such great concepts, it will be safe for us. We make them into an altarpiece.

Many people in this country have plastered their walls with all kinds of guys and girls: Indonesians, Japanese, Inuit, Native Americans, or whatever you have. Their walls are completely covered with heroes, pinups, personalities. Admiration is very dangerous from that point of view. Here, you want to suck in the object of your admiration. You want to pour your passionate maple syrup, your passionate honey, all over the place until you make the whole thing completely gooey. Then you can eat it up completely. That trip seems to be slightly outdated these days, but it is still going on. It is purely a trip and it is based on spiritual materialism, which this sadhana is meant to cut through. But at the same time you would like to worship. Before you cut through, you want to make sure that you will be on the right side of such people. When you confront Dorje Trolö or Karma Pakshi in person, you would like them to be on your side, to fit your particular perspective. If they happen to show up, you could tell them, "Look! There's a painting of you, an altar I created for you. I'm on your side, see? Don't destroy my ego. I'm on your side."

This approach to devotion is largely based on spiritual materialism: we would like to win those people over. This approach is somewhat theistic, even somewhat Christian. The idea is like having God on our side. As long as we have a Bible and a cross, and quite possibly a sword, we could place the cross on our chest and carry the Bible in one hand and the sword in the other. We are entitled to destroy any nonbelievers completely. We could kill our enemies, who are regarded as nonbelievers: they are anti-God, nonbelievers in the Bible.

Admiration could also become somewhat secularized. You could worship only the highest principles, which are embodied in a certain person of immense accomplishment, immense understanding of reality, and immense richness. You regard the object of your worship as king. As long as you are on the right side of Don Corleone, everything's okay. Otherwise you might be shot down or screwed or ripped off in your business ventures, or whatever the consequences might be. So much for admiration!

When we say, "I admire you so much," your hero might answer, "Yeah? Why? What is it all about? Where does your admiration come from? What do you do with it? Do you just want to tell me that? Or maybe you would like to do something embarrassing about the whole thing."

Admiration as celebration and devotion.

The examples of admiration are somewhat negative from that point of view, but at the same time it can be very positive. Admiring something is not necessarily wanting to be sucked in or wanting to be eaten up or wanting to be part of that particular gang, part of that particular army. Admiration can also inspire a sense of heroism and tremendous dignity. Admiring someone doesn't have to mean competing with that person; you could simply share their immense vision. That could be a glorious, fantastic celebration—with fireworks. Such an attitude can only exist when you have no personal investment in the "cause." Your role is simply to develop complete devotion so that you have no personal investment. You are no longer expecting a certain cut of the deal. Absolutely not! Instead, you really have a complete deal, as a matter of fact. You become part of a fantastic crescendo.

That kind of admiration is heroism in the true sense because you don't regard the whole situation purely as a business deal. You simply regard the whole thing as a journey, and you are not expecting any kind of profit from that journey. So your admiration is complete and clear.

The only analogy I can come up with for this positive sense of admiration is that of a person who can breathe the mountain air without any sinus problems. You can breathe the cool, fresh mountain air completely. You can say, "Ahhh! Look at the mountains." You feel like you are part of the mountains, part of the highlands. That is admiration: it is some kind of sharing. You don't just go back to your bedroom for your duffel jacket, in case you catch cold. "This mountain air is fantastic, but suspicious." You don't do that; you simply breathe your mountain air, which is a source of strength and life. It's fantastic!

Güpa: Absence of Arrogance

The second kind of devotion is güpa, which literally means "absence of arrogance." It goes along with what we've already discussed. If you have a real sense of longing and admiration, that automatically means that absence of arrogance as well.

Levels of arrogance.

There are several levels of arrogance. Sometimes there's a lot of passion, too much wantingness. You so want to be the object of someone's passion that you cease to see the rest of your world properly. You're so passionately involved with your own arrogance, your own passion. Even in relating with a guru, you are primarily involved with your own passion. Such sensual, passionate problems are created around you, which is the definition of what we call a trip. Tripping out on something is a mixture of passion and arrogance.

I had a monumental experience of that when I visited Esalen a few months ago. It was a fantastic demonstration of passion and arrogance. Everybody was appreciating the ocean, the sunset, and the sunrise. Everybody was holding on to each other, shoulder to shoulder, arm in arm. Everybody was drunk with the beauty of whatever it might be. It's an unbelievable place! It's such a decadent place that it even ceases to be decadent; it becomes a horrifying world. Can you imagine such a thing? Even corpses would get up and put on their makeup and begin to dance and make love to you. It's very deadly, but fantastically sensuous. It's a great place—more than you can imagine. I didn't realize that the sunset means all that much to people. It's some kind of demonstration of visual orgasm: everybody loves to watch. And the sunrise is giving birth to your own personal child on the spot. Fantastic place, but let's forget about that place!

There are such moments of neurosis all over the place. Compared to Esalen, even Disneyland is a world of enlightenment. It's just fine. You go and see those things, and it's fine. It's supposed to be some kind of statement of American existence, and Mr. Disney is the perfect analogy of the American businessman. There are all kinds of trips at Disneyland, but it's a very kind and very enlightened place compared with Esalen. There is a lot of sanity there compared with the other place.

So in connection with the notion of the absence of arrogance, it is a question of how much we could indulge ourselves in our collections of information, in all those techniques and stories and quotations and little words of wisdom—how much we could indulge in those things for our own benefit. We could even beat our old teacher to death and get our revenge by saying, "When you used to be my teacher, you treated me badly. You gave me a hard time. But now it's my turn to give you a hard time." That seems to be the wrong end of the stick, that immense arrogance.

Absence of arrogance: offering your neurosis as a gift.

Absence of arrogance is a sense of being less resentful about the world in general, as well as our relationship to our own particular world—our bank, our business deals, our money situation, our landlord, our landlady. We have to make a relationship with all those situations, and that provides us with a way of reducing our arrogance.

Particularly with the notion of guru at the crazy-wisdom level, absence of arrogance is very much required—absolutely so. You have to give in on the spot: unless you are without arrogance, you are not accepted as a good student. You might have your pride in your poetry, your woodcarving, your photography. You might have all kinds of talents, but you can't regard them as a passport to sanity. In fact, when you present them, they are regarded as neurotic garbage. Your visa might be rejected several times if you present your little thingies which hang out and which you would like to use as convenient credentials for your application. You might dress them up and write nice little reports about what you have done with them, but that is only arrogance dressed up as something presentable. It is amateurism presented as something professional. You could write a whole book about the fantastic material that has promoted your spiritual growth: you had fights with your mother for twenty years and how much you have learned from that. You could write a whole essay, a whole book about it. You could give it to your crazy-wisdom guru as an application for entering into vajrayana discipline.

We can imagine what you would experience if you approached the crazy-wisdom person with such little things dressed up as professional credentials. Quite possibly you would be beheaded on the spot—if he's even willing to do that. That would be a sign of acceptance, but he might not even do that; he might just give you a big pain in your neck. Your abilities as a great mathematician (you understand the truth, the real truth of mathematics), your genius as a poet (you understand the truth of that), your skill as a carpenter or a cook or a crook—all of those credentials are regarded as phony. A crazy-wisdom person would not accept such things at all. It is out of the question altogether. It is not that the crazy-wisdom person is involved with morality or with how respectable you are in society; it's that you are bending the truth in some sense.

On the other hand, if you simply offer your neurosis as a gift or as an opening gesture, that's fine. There is nothing wrong with that. But if you begin to dress up your neurosis and make it into a course description, as if you have been invited to teach in a university, that stinks. That is what usually happens in universities: you make up your own particular thing, your particular course, out of what you've learned or out of your own neurosis. You put it in technical terms; you try to dress it up and make it respectable, make it seemingly workable. But the whole thing says, "I would like to present this particular pile of shit to my students." You could call it a turd. Aren't we strange people? We have so many good ideas, such brilliant ideas, but we are basically so dumb, so naive at the same time.

Joining Möpa and Güpa

So möpa and güpa—longing and absence of ego—put together create a very constructive foundation for practice. Experiencing möpa, or a sense of longing and heroism, and güpa, or absence of ego-clinging to our own case history, puts us in a completely naked situation, a completely real situation, properly, fully, and thoroughly. Out of that we get some glimpse of crazy-wisdom possibilities. That twofold devotion process is regarded as an eye-opening operation. First, the tissue of our eyes is sliced open, and then whatever was the obstacle in our retina is removed. Finally, we can see the vivid brilliance of things, which is real seeing.

BLESSINGS

Adhishthana

I'm sorry to bore you with more categories, but there are two types of blessings that come with that experience. The Sanskrit term for blessing is adhishthana, which in Tibetan is *chinlap*. It is not quite the same as the Christian idea of grace. Adhishthana literally means that you're over-whelmed by radiation. You begin to realize that your experience has become so radiant that you can't help but relate with it completely. You are utterly opened up. Otherwise, you would just be scorched, baked. It sounds like a microwave oven, doesn't it?

Seeking blessings as spiritual materialism.

Usually when we use the term *blessing*, we actually have no idea what we are saying. A lot of hippies who have been to India come back saying, "I've got blessings from Mr. A, Mr. B, Mr. C, Mr. D, and Mr. E." It becomes a credential. Well, that's good. You got a blessing from all those people. That's fantastic! But rather than actually receiving blessings, those people seem to be hung up on their experience. That is very disappointing. It's as if you woke up in the morning and said to your friend, "I went to a party and had so much to drink." But when you check back with the people who gave the party, you discover that you just drank water. Somehow or other you have managed to get a hangover. That's your problem: that you get hung over from drinking water. That means that nothing actually happened when you were there, but something happened when you woke up the next day.

Nothing really happens to all those people who go to India looking for blessings—nothing, not a little spot. When they come back, they're just as resilient, just as crazy, just as neurotic, and just as spiritually materialistic as they were before they left. But something happens when they leave. They fly over the Indian continent, and as soon as they land in this country, they're very "high." What happened to them? Is that adhishthana, blessing? If that's what it is, they don't even have to go to India. They could get their blessings from being with their parents or from going to school. Lots of people get high from having a difficult relationship with their parents or with their school. People get spaced out very easily. They don't need any blessings to get spaced out—that's what I'm trying to say. You might find this a slightly obnoxious remark, yes indeed. Nevertheless, it's true. It's not me making an obnoxious remark. Things are obnoxious from that point of view, which is very maddening, absolutely maddening. Who's kidding whom? That is the big problem.

That is the heart of spiritual materialism: we would like to cover the whole area completely. When somebody goes to India or drops out of school— which is saying the same thing at this point—when they leave the country, it makes no difference that they meet great people, because they are not at all equipped to understand them. It's colorful; getting out of school is also colorful. And when you awaken from that you are completely blissed out, so-called. That is very strange. The immense vajrayana teachings are completely descending on us all the time, instigating all these freakouts and rejections of sanity—I doubt it. Where is the blessing? Where is grace, even? Nowhere, absolutely nowhere. It's very sad, actually. It's worth laughing about.

Genuine adhishthana: openness between teacher and student.

That is precisely what we call spiritual materialism. The purpose of this sadhana is to overcome such deceptions. Adhishthana, or chinlap, means the radiation that takes place between the opening of the student's mind to the teacher and the teachings, and the opening of the teacher's mind to the student. Between those two openings, experience becomes not only naked but radiant. The two burn each other completely. The teacher begins to understand the student's desire, his devotion. The student begins to feel the teacher's desire and openness.

What we are talking about here is that you can't expect to become pregnant unless you actually make love. You can't actually receive blessings unless you are open to the guru, and the guru is open to you. That is the basic point. We don't believe in the virgin birth, whether it is called an accident or whether there is a scientific whatever-it-may-be. It's still questionable. We don't believe that anybody can become pregnant in that way. But real radiation and real openness can take place. When that begins to happen, there's a sense of something happening properly to us. That is the first level of adhishthana.

Yeshe Phowa

The second level of adhishthana is what is known as the transference of jnana, or *yeshe phowa* in Tibetan. *Yeshe* means "wisdom," and *phowa* means "transference." So yeshe phowa is the "transference of wisdom" into our system. Once some kind of openness has actually taken place, then something begins to be transmitted to us, properly and fully.

In the sadhana this is the level of supplication. We are appreciating a particular aspect of Dorje Trolö Karma Pakshi,[1] and we are appreciating that particular aspect coming to us. We are beginning to acknowledge those things properly. Although our situation is not so good, we are not particularly trying to reject it. We are actually pleased, actually glad to see what's happening. So there is a possibility of workability. Otherwise, if nothing were workable, true devotion and compassion could not come together.

I'd like to end by quoting several stanzas from the supplication in the sadhana that relate to our discussion of devotion here:

> O Karmapa, lord and knower of the three times,
> O Padmakara, father and protector of all beings,
> You transcend all coming and going.
>
> Understanding this, I call upon you—
> Give thought to your only child.
> I am a credulous and helpless animal
> Who has been fooled by the mirage of duality.
> I have been fool enough to think that I possess my own
>   projections,
> So now you, my father, are my only refuge;
> You alone can grasp the buddha state.
> The glorious copper-colored mountain is within my heart.
> Is not this pure and all-pervading naked mind your dwelling
>   place?
> Although I live in the slime and muck of the dark age,
> I still aspire to see it.
> Although I stumble in the thick, black fog of materialism,
> I still aspire to see it.

The joy of spontaneous awareness, which is with me all the time,§
Is not this your smiling face, O Karma Padmakara?§
Although I live in the slime and muck of the dark age,§
I still aspire to see it.§
Although I stumble in the thick, black fog of materialism,§
I still aspire to see it.§

At glorious Taktsang, in the cave§
Which can accommodate everything,§
Samsara and nirvana both,§
The heretics and bandits of hope and fear§
Are subdued and all experiences§
Are transformed into crazy wisdom.§
Is not this your doing, O Dorje Trolö?§
Although I live in the slime and muck of the dark age,§
I still aspire to see your face.§
Although I stumble in the thick, black fog of materialism,§
I still aspire to see your face.§

The corpse, bloated with the eight worldly concerns,§
Is cut into pieces by the knife of detachment§
And served up as the feast of the great bliss.§
Is not this your doing, O Karma Pakshi?§
Although I live in the slime and muck of the dark age,§
I still aspire to see your face.§
Although I stumble in the thick, black fog of materialism,§
I still aspire to see your face.§

Discussion

Practices like *asanas* and vegetarianism as spiritual materialism.

Question: Rinpoche, do you think doing asanas and purifications and being a vegetarian and eating organic food is all part of spiritual materialism?
Chögyam Trungpa Rinpoche: Yes.

Spiritual arrogance and labeling spiritual practices as spiritual materialism.

Q: I wonder if you could explain exactly what arrogance is?

CTR: Maybe you should tell me. What is your rough guess?

Q: Territorial pride.

CTR: Yes, sure, as well as chauvinistic tendencies and some notion of not accepting your own lameness. You don't want to acknowledge that you are lame and helpless. Because you are arrogant, you think you don't need help from anybody else. You never ask for any kind of sympathy or any kind of genuine communication. That's when devotion comes in. When somebody is willing to help you, you won't buy their sympathy. You regard it as an insult rather than as an act of compassion. You say, "I don't need your help, I'm okay." If you are falling down on the icy road and somebody tries to catch you, you say, "Please don't catch me. Get out of my way. I don't want anything." You say that even though falling down is not a reflection on yourself but some unavoidable, disastrous thing happening to you.

Q: Getting back to the question of arrogance, you said to the lady who asked about asanas and purifications, "That's spiritual materialism." But it seems to me that spiritual materialism is how you do a practice rather than the practice itself. It seems to me that there's a tendency for everything that's not strictly part of this particular scene to get a big *SM* stamped on it.

CTR: SM—you mean spiritual materialism? Well, I think what we're trying to do here is to point out that potential spiritual materialism exists in us. We're constantly trying to expose it. Another possibility is to do asanas to improve your body, or to eat healthy food, whatever that might be, to build a great body, in which case there is not even any hint of any spiritual possibilities. That whole approach seems to be based not on any conscious spiritual materialism but on ignorance. Within such ignorance there is no such thing as a problem of spiritual materialism at all.

I have seen a lot of people in Jackson, Wyoming, and in Snowmass and Aspen who are older but still skiing and trying to look good on the ski hill. There are older and younger people who are trying to be extraordinarily hip. They are all extraordinarily arrogant and unapproachable. They don't want to be approached with any kind of challenge to their approach. But still, you know, they're trying their best. The only thing they talk about at dinner parties is how much inheritance they're going to get.

Q: Might it not be useful to illustrate spiritual materialism with examples of how the practices that we're into can be twisted?

CTR: I think it's very hard not to see that; I think it would be spotted. There is so much prajna around that everybody keeps a keen eye on everyone else, so you can't actually get away with twisting anything.

Q: I hope so.

Heroism.

Q: I'm a little confused about your use of the term *heroism*. Sometimes it seems like it has a very negative connotation, that it is associated with arrogance or pride. Other times it seems to be a very positive thing, something like courage or fearlessness.

CTR: It's both. Basically, heroism is a positive word as I use it. It's connected with a sense of dignity and straightforwardness and not being apologetic. But obviously it has its own negative tendencies as well. If you could disconnect the word from any kind of philosophical or sociological jargon, heroism is the same as devotion. It's very positive. It is what the bodhisattva path is made out of. A bodhisattva is simply someone who is proud and diligent enough to follow the path of enlightenment. The paramita practices of generosity, discipline, and so forth are based on that sense of heroism. I'm not saying that bodhisattvas would like to make themselves into heroes, into movie stars. But they are inspired by something. It's like taking pride in your nation, in your world. In this country, everybody seems to have lost that notion of heroism. Maybe too much has been said; maybe there's too much happening; maybe the country is too big. Everybody has lost their American heroism, their American pride. Only a few awkward, uptight people hold on to that particular truth. It is embarrassing and it's terrible, in some sense, but I suppose that's how the wind blows, how the egg boils.

Theistic and nontheistic supplication.

Q: I'm trying to understand the difference between the nontheistic approach and the theistic approach. In the part of the sadhana we are studying tonight, there seems to be a sense of calling to something outside of oneself, and I didn't think that is what we're doing.

CTR: Well, it seems to be saying the same thing. We're not particularly trying to call on something outside of ourselves. There's a very interesting line in the movie *The Ruling Class*. Someone asks the hero, "Why do you think you are God?" And he answers, "Because when I pray, I hear myself talking to myself." That is very cheap logic, but it is precisely what you are doing. When you talk to yourself, you hear yourself. Even though you are supposedly talking to somebody else, you still hear yourself talking to yourself.

Another thing about the sadhana is that all kinds of demands are being made on you, on your own particular understanding. You are not particularly asking forgiveness for committing a gigantic sin. That's the whole approach of Christianity, as opposed to other theistic religions like Hinduism or Islam or Zoroastrianism or whatever. In the Judeo-Christian tradition there's a lot of emphasis on guilt. In the case of the sadhana, however, the commitment between your inspiration, or your higher being, and you is made purely arbitrarily, even bypassing Christ.

You are talking to something bigger than an intermediary. That is the interesting point: there's no particular lead to follow. You are not actually asking to be forgiven, that you have been a bad boy or a bad girl. You don't need to beg, "Please forgive me. From now on I'm going to be good." Instead, everything is pure demand: you are just talking to yourself, but that has a lot of magic to it at the same time. You are not just naively talking to yourself, thinking that one of these days you are going to wake up as a buddha, but you are talking to your fundamental intelligence and to the fundamental electricity that exists within you, which is called magic.

Magic comes from nowhere. It just exists within us and outside of us as well. It has nothing to do with any gift of God. We just wake up. It's like the magic of electricity, which just comes along. When we get a shock from a thunderbolt, we just get it on the spot. That's the kind of magic we're talking about. We're not talking about invoking anybody or being afraid of anybody. We just do it on the spot. This is starting to get very complicated, but it's actually very simple.

Theistic and nontheistic faith.

Q: You've spoken a lot about faith. You seem to have described the theistic approach to faith as some sort of future orientation, the idea of some future reward. Would it be correct to say that we're just trying to have faith in the present moment?

CTR: Yes—precisely, absolutely. We're not asking for a good harvest or inviting the next messiah. We don't even care about that; we just sit and meditate.

Q: Would it be possible just to have faith in the present moment and also have a theistic approach?

CTR: It doesn't sound like it. Somehow that doesn't work. You see, then you would have an investment in both camps. It would be like somebody who could actually let go by himself, but instead asks somebody else to help him let go. It is like having two homes. It's evident that situations reflect your attitude and automatically bounce back on you. So the situation demands you to make up your mind, in some sense. Think about that. Take it home.

How faith and devotion together avoid arrogance.

Q: Am I right to think that devotion to an external person has to go along with faith in order to avoid arrogance?

CTR: In this case, an external person is somebody you can actually relate with personally. It's not an imaginary person. In that case, yes.

9. Surrendering

The giving process is preparing enough room, enough space so that what is known as enlightenment, the awakened state of mind, can be felt. And that can't take place if the receiver is still clinging to conditions and to reference points and to a business mentality. We have to have an absence of business mentality; otherwise, the awakened state cannot take place. In other words, when we begin to receive the teachings, nobody is receiving them. The teachings become part of us, part of our basic being.

In this chapter we are going to talk about the offering section in the sadhana, which reads:

> To the crazy-wisdom form of the buddhas of the three times,⁞
> The unified mandala of all the siddhas, Dorje Trolö Karma Pakshi,
>   I make this supplication.⁞
> Desire, hatred and other hindrances are self-liberated.⁞
> To the boundless rainbow body of wisdom, Padmakara Karma
>   Pakshi,⁞
> The heruka who, untouched by concepts, pervades all existence, I
>   make this supplication.⁞
> Whatever is seen with the eyes is vividly unreal in emptiness, yet
>   there is still form:⁞
> This is the true image of Tüsum Khyenpa, whom now I
>   supplicate.⁞
> Whatever is heard with the ears is the echo of emptiness, yet real:⁞
> It is the clear and distinct utterance of Mikyö Dorje, whom now I
>   supplicate.⁞

Good and bad, happy and sad, all thoughts vanish into emptiness
　　like the imprint of a bird in the sky:

This is the vivid mind of Rangjung Dorje, whom now I
　　supplicate.

The animate and the inanimate are the mandala of the glorious
　　mahasiddha, which no one can change;

It always remains impressive and colorful. This mandala now I
　　supplicate.

The hope of attaining buddhahood and the fear of continuing to
　　wander in samsara,

Doubt that wisdom exists within one and other dualistic
　　thoughts—all these are my feast offering.

Food, wealth, companionship, fame and sensual attachments—

All these I offer for the elaborate arrangement of the mandala.

Wantingness, desire and passion I offer as the great ocean of blood
　　which comes from the killing of samsara.

Thoughts of anger and hatred I offer as the amrita which
　　intoxicates extreme beliefs and renders them inoperative.

All that arises within—wandering thoughts, carelessness and all
　　that is subject to ignorance—

I offer as the great mountain of torma ornamented with the eight
　　kinds of consciousness.

Whatever arises is merely the play of the mind.

All this I offer, filling the whole universe.

I offer knowing that giver and receiver are one;

I offer without expecting anything in return and without hope of
　　gaining merit;

I make these offerings with transcendental generosity in the
　　mahamudra.

Now that I have made these offerings, please grant your blessings
　　so that my mind may be one with the dharma.

Grant your blessings so that dharma may progress along the path.

Grant your blessings so that the path may clarify confusion.

Grant your blessings so that confusion may dawn as wisdom.[1]

The understanding of devotion brings a further sense of what is appropriate
action in connection with devotion. Longingness, möpa, and the absence

of arrogance, güpa, begin to provide a general background of devotion in which we could operate quite freely. The particular activity connected with the expression of devotion is known as offering or surrendering. Having developed devotion, having the inspiration to open, you are no longer simply paying lip service; at this point you begin to put your devotion into action.

THE MOTIVATION FOR GIVING

The Motivation of Ordinary Persons

Surrendering raises a question: do we know how to give? Sometimes we think we know, and sometimes we wonder. The notion of giving is interesting: usually we don't just give for the sake of giving, unless we want to get rid of something. We can't particularly regard what we discard as a gift; it's just throwing something into the garbage pail. Unfortunately, we have special times for giving things: birthdays, Christmas, baby showers, housewarmings, or whatever occasion it might be. We don't just give things freely. We always like to make our gift-giving coincide with a special occasion. When we travel, if we are generous enough, when we return home, we bring gifts to our spouse or our children. But there is an entirely different tradition, in which giving gifts doesn't have to coincide with social norms; gifts can be given at any time. That seems to be the basic idea.

The question we need to look into is what motivation we have when we give. Ordinarily, we tend to express some kind of appreciation: that the other person has given us enough love, education, support, or whatever. We think we should make this person a gift to pay such a person back. Another kind of gift-giving is done in order to win somebody over, which is a kind of subtle blackmail. If we give someone a gift, hopefully that person will be favorable to us. On the whole, we don't give gifts without a purpose of some kind, without some scheme or other. We carefully arrange the time and place, so that the gift can be made properly.

The Motivation of the Bodhisattva

But at the bodhisattva level, generosity is regarded as an act of letting go. The purpose of giving gifts and the practice of the paramita of generosity is to learn from our life and to experience—or to develop the vision, rather—of giving without expecting anything in return. That is very hard for us to do, because we are brought up in a social norm that expects tit for tat. We may be embarrassed if we are put in a situation of having to make a gift to somebody, having to make some kind of statement of generosity. We don't want to do that.

Obstacles to Giving

The idea of giving something purely without expecting anything in return is the expression of the absence of arrogance; it is longing. It doesn't seem to be particularly smart from an ordinary business point of view. From the point of view of the social norm, we are just throwing our money down the drain. Since we already feel the absence of arrogance, since we already feel humble, why don't we just maintain those virtues, hold them close to our heart? Why don't we make the best of those virtues rather than making any further gifts? Making further gifts would be regarded as completely impractical. In fact, we could go as far as to say that, in the ordinary conventional world, it is insane to do such a thing.

However, here the idea of giving is not to prove how wealthy you are, how artistic you are, how visionary you are. You just give everything there is. You give your body, your speech, your mind. You give the giver completely, in other words. So it ceases to become even a gift; it is just letting go.

Unfortunately, you usually would like to watch the receiver of the gift appreciating what he has received. You would like to hear him say, "Thank you very much. It was very sweet of you to give me yourself."

You are simply asking for confirmation. Suppose you give your whole being to somebody. The minute that person thanks you, you haven't actually given yourself away, because you get your gift back.

When you give up your anger, it is not like giving up cigarettes. You have a tremendous sense of giving up the *security* of anger—or the security of passion. It's not that you regard anger as a nuisance and therefore you decide to give it up, like cigarettes, in order to get rid of it. You usually experience some sense of security even in your hang-ups, your so-called problems. You might feel that you are somewhat inadequate: you keep losing your temper at the most inappropriate times, and you feel bad about yourself. But if you analyze the reason why you lose your temper, it is not so much because you are angry at the cause and effect of a certain situation, but because you would like to reaffirm yourself, your existence. You would like to express yourself. You would like to make a statement: "I do exist." It might be painful to lose your temper; it might be discomforting. But at the same time it is part of the game that you play with yourself. You would like to confirm your existence. You are dying to make confirmations here and there, right and left, all the time.

When we hear something that we don't like, we get angry, pissed off. It's not only that we are pissed off at those things that we are told aren't good for us or that we disagree with; it is also that we have to keep affirming ourselves—all the time. Some people go to the extreme of ceremoniously attempting to commit suicide. They hope that somebody will prevent them from doing so, and that in turn they will get more attention, more confirmation. Somebody will feel sorry for them. We often say, "I don't like this. I want to get rid of it. I want to see a therapist. I want to take a downer"—or an upper, depending on the case. "I want to see a guru. If only I could get rid of these problems, I would be happy. I'd be very happy." But we don't actually mean that. We cherish our neurosis so much. We don't want to give; we want to be improved.

We are usually full of schemes. We scheme so much that we finally lose track of who's doing what. We find that we have completely lost track of our successive schemes. We begin to catch the tail end of one scheme before we even begin another one. We are completely caught up in that kind of confusion. But we would like to maintain ourselves; we don't want to give those things up. We might say, "It would be nice if I could give up my anger, give it to you. Here's my anger, you take it. This is my gift." But we don't really mean it. We are probably proud of our anger. We think we have given a fantastic gift, but it was purely a chauvinistic gesture. It wasn't real giving, real surrendering, free from expectations. The realization that giver and receiver are one never takes place.

Giving the Giver

If we have an immense sense of devotion, if we can actually give the background, the giver, then we are ready to receive blessings, adhishthana. Our usual problem is that we don't want to give. We might be willing to pay for something if it comes along with something else that we can get. But we don't really want to just give, not even knowing whether we're going to get a reward out of it, not even knowing whether we will still have ourselves. That's a terrible thought: If we have to give the whole thing and nothing comes back, we can't even watch the process of giving. We can't even take part in that particular ritual. We might say, "This is asking too much." It is definitely asking too much. That is why it is a very special kind of giving process which asks a lot, which demands absolutely everything, including the giving of the giver, which is very hard for us to do.

The giving process is preparing enough room, enough space so that what is known as enlightenment, the awakened state of mind, can be felt. And that can't take place if the receiver is still clinging to conditions and to reference points and to a business mentality. We have to have an absence of business mentality; otherwise, the awakened state cannot take place. In other words, when we begin to receive the teachings, nobody is receiving them. The teachings become part of us, part of our basic being.

We don't receive the teachings as a gift, as a package deal which makes us the possessor of the dharma, the teachings. We can't insure the dharma. We can't put it in the safe or deposit it in the bank. So receiving the teachings is not regarded as an adornment which can become part of our spiritual materialism.

You might say, "I went to such-and-such teacher, to such-and-such guru, to such-and-such lama. I received millions of initiations, and I was ordained in trillions of sanghas. I am fully ordained and fully initiated. I'm completely soaked in blessings." That is the most decadent way of relating to the teachings. You are merely collecting teachings, which could be regarded as committing a sin, actually. In order to develop your ego's lavish indulgences, you are using teachings and teachers as part of your conspiracy. That will only bring you down and down, rather than opening you up to anything having to do with being awake. Instead of waking up, you are falling deeper and deeper into sleep.

From that point of view, spiritual discipline is obviously quite different from collecting credentials—PhDs, professorial credentials, academic degrees, and all kinds of things that you can receive in the field of education—because you're still trying to become the greatest scholar in the world. But you can't do that with spiritual discipline. The more you collect credentials, that much more you lose your credentials. You become a mystical egomaniac beggar, who keeps on begging, keeps on getting things. You become more and more mystical at the wrong end of the stick, the ego end of the stick. Every minute the whole thing is sinking to a grosser and grosser level, rather than becoming more refined. There is absolutely nothing wakeful about it. There is no prajna whatsoever. The whole thing becomes heavier, dirtier, sloppier. You make more and more collections of credentials, which are based on not giving, not giving the giver.

When you give the giver, you are completely committed. If you feel slightly discomforted with your master, your teacher, you do not run away to find his replacement. You don't use the relationship with your first master as a credential, a passport, before you completely blow up the whole thing; when it's convenient, you take your leave and go on to the next master. Using the previous experience as a passport sounds very unreasonable and very sad, but there are people who do that. In fact, I know quite a lot of them. They are very sweet and nice and rugged and homey, but there are definitely problems with them in spite of their exterior.

The whole point of giving or surrendering seems to be the idea of giving the giver. This is not particularly supposed to be a fund-raising pitch, but the notion of giving the giver is the key point. That seems to be the only way the teacher can relate with you, the only way that you can open up and that the meeting of two minds can take place.

We could quite safely say that, to a certain extent, the real teachings can only be received when nobody is at home. As long as somebody's at home, it is very difficult to receive the teachings. You would like to possess the teachings, own them. You would like to be a homeowner; you would like to turn them into merchandise. So the only way to receive the teachings is if you are not actually there. A lot of demands are made on the practitioners of this sadhana. They are high-level demands because they are based on the highest vajrayana teachings. I suppose the sadhana could also be practiced at a lower level, but the philosophy behind the sadhana is based on teachings that are very subtle, that are unreachable by ordinary minds.

Discussion

Dorje Trolö and the landscape of the charnel ground.

Question: Could you review the principle of the charnel ground? I didn't understand how Dorje Trolö Karma Pakshi fits into that landscape.

Chögyam Trungpa Rinpoche: The idea is that there is basic ground that we all believe in and live on, and out of that we create an extraordinary landscape. Out of that comes further extraordinary imagery, which is not just basic sanity alone, but basic wakefulness within sanity. Sanity can be reasonable, but there has to be something very wakeful about the whole thing.

That wakefulness is embodied in the crazy-wisdom principle, embodied in the yidam, which is not necessarily a native of that particular landscape—for that matter, he is not a nonnative either. He is just there. You might feel threatened because the environment is very spooky. You have to give up your arrogance, which we talked about already in connection with devotion. Giving arrogance up is connected with devotion. Having related with longing and with the absence of arrogance, you have to surrender completely. In other words, everything takes place in the charnel ground. It is a place of birth and a place of death. Is there any problem?

Q: No, it will just take me a while to put it together.

CTR: Well, imagine that you are in a charnel ground, a really vivid one. Then you would figure out everything, including the giving.

Giving without confirmation as an ongoing practice.

Q: Rinpoche, would you comment on giving up without any kind of confirmation as an ongoing process, an ongoing practice?

CTR: I wouldn't say it would necessarily be a twenty-four-hour-a-day job, around the clock. I think it comes in a rhythm: whenever there is a stumbling block, it could be surrendered, given up. Even the background of that could be given up. Whenever you have a sense of wanting to hold back, that surrendering can take place.

Q: Sometimes I get a very stubborn feeling, a sort of blind heroism. Because I feel some resistance, I feel heroic. I say, "Let's just jump in." Is that too dualistic?

CTR: Obviously it doesn't work that way. The whole idea is that before you give in, you have to be devoted. Last night we talked about two types of devotion. Both of them are very intelligent. If you feel like you have to be doing something, then sitting practice will bring you down, make you solid. The whole thing is based on the sitting practice of meditation, which plays a very important part, obviously.

Why the sadhana is read on the full and new moon.

Q: Rinpoche, why is the sadhana read on the full moon and the new moon?

CTR: We could say it is because that is the craziest time.

The connection between the charnel ground and devotion.

Q: Could you speak about the connection between the charnel ground and devotion?

CTR: Connect them? Well, the charnel ground seems to be the general environment. It's where you are, on the spot. Devotion is part of that: you are put on the spot and you accept everything that exists in yourself. Because of that, you are willing to give, without trying to sort things out or trying to find a little clean garden. Just being in the charnel ground.

The connection between outrageousness and giving what is not expected to be given.

Q: Rinpoche, I'm wondering about outrageousness and about giving that which is not expected to be given.

CTR: Are you asking if that is outrageous?

Q: Yes.

CTR: I suppose you could say that, but it's not all that outrageous if you know the whole scheme.

Q: In other words, it's not shoving your giving down somebody's throat?

CTR: It's a regular thing. It might hurt you a little bit, but it's not all that painful—if you mean that.

Q: Oh no, I don't mean outrageousness is painful—on the contrary.

CTR: This is an interesting discussion.

Q: Yes. I don't exactly feel satisfied, but maybe I'm looking for confirmation.

CTR: Well, if I say too much, it's going to be painful.

Q: Maybe you should risk it.

CTR: I think I should leave that to your imagination.

Potential for spiritual materialism when you ask for blessings.

Q: The part of the sadhana you just read says, "Now that I have made these offerings, please grant your blessings." That sounds to me a little bit like a bargain, or like spiritual materialism. It has always bothered me. Could you tell me how you intend that?

CTR: It's not so much, "Now that I have made these offerings, therefore please gimme!" But, "Having done one thing already, now I am prepared enough to receive the next thing." There has to be some time-space accuracy somewhere; otherwise, there wouldn't be any language.

Q: Okay, but right after it says, "I offer without expecting anything in return," it immediately says, "Please grant your blessings."

CTR: That's just the inadequacy of language.

The object of giving when you give the giver.

Q: Does this kind of giving necessarily imply a receiver, an object of the gift?

CTR: I think so. There is some kind of vision taking place. The receiver is more a vision, an ideal, rather than a particular person.

Q: It's not just giving up, just plain giving?

CTR: You're not just abandoning yourself. It's like the difference between worshipping the mountains and having some sense of respect for the teachings. If you want to worship the mountains, you jump off a cliff. If you want to show your respect for the teachings, you prostrate to them.

The meaning of symbolic offerings.

Q: What are symbolic offerings about: mandala offerings, rice . . . ?

CTR: It's the same idea as what we're talking about here. You are offering your world. You're giving the globe, the earth, the sun, and the moon.

Q: Don't we have enough to work with in our lives, just giving up our neuroses? Why do we have to mess around with rice?

CTR: It's saying the same thing. We have enough, but not all that much. We are not usually very precise, so we have to find some kind of alphabet.

The problem of expecting something in return when we give up everything.

Q: I don't know if this is a linguistic problem, but it seems that we're talking about giving up everything in order to receive the teachings. I feel that there is a sense of expectation. As I intellectually ponder the idea of giving myself up, it's still in order to receive the teachings.

CTR: That could be a problem. But I think a necessary prerequisite for receiving the teachings is to understand that you can't receive them unless you first give up.

Q: Is the process of giving up achieved just through sitting practice?

CTR: Yes, as well as through all kinds of little pushes that come up—life situations.

Q: Until that point, could we say you haven't received the teachings?

CTR: Yes, that's why the teachings are called self-secret.

Putting oneself in threatening situations in order to work with surrendering.

Q: In terms of surrendering, would you say that it would be helpful to put yourself in threatening situations—though not necessarily foolish situations—in order to surrender yourself?

CTR: We can't just have a staged situation. If you like, we could organize that. But you might freak out.

Q: I feel a bit like I already am.

CTR: That's it!

Q: Thank you very much.

10. Historical Commentary: Part Two[1]

The Kagyü tradition and the Nyingma tradition are brought together very powerfully at Taktsang; the influence of the practice lineage is very strong there. There is a feeling at Taktsang of austerity and pride, and some sense of wildness, which goes beyond the practice lineage alone. When I started to feel that, the sadhana just came through without any problems. I definitely felt the immense presence of Dorje Trolö Karma Pakshi, and I told myself, "You must be joking. Nothing is happening here." But still, something was coming from behind the whole thing; there was immense energy and power.

This is the final chapter in our discussion of "The Sadhana of Mahamudra." The subjects that we have gone through are connected with our general attitude toward the major principles in the sadhana. We have stayed somewhat on the safe side: the sadhana can be discussed at a much deeper level, but I feel hesitation to get into unnecessary problems. If people don't have enough understanding of these principles, they could become more confused than anything else. Interestingly enough, nevertheless, I have managed to say everything. The subjects that we covered contain many things which have connections at a deeper level, so I suppose you will have to wait and think and read over the material.

Sadhanas are traditionally written in a certain environment by someone who has a feeling about the subject. This sadhana was written in a traditional style.

Spiritual Materialism and Corruption in Tibet

To make a long story short, there was tremendous corruption, confusion, lack of faith, and lack of practice in Tibet. Many teachers and spiritual leaders worked very hard to try to rectify that problem. But most of their efforts led only to failure, except for a few dedicated students who could relate with some real sense of practice. The degeneration of Buddhism in Tibet was connected with that lack of practice. Performing rituals became people's main occupation. Even if they were doing practice, they thought constantly about protocol. It was like one of us thinking, "Which clothes should I wear today? What shirt should I wear today? What kind of makeup should I wear today? Which tie should I wear today?" Tibetans would think, "What kind of ceremony can I perform today? What would be appropriate?" They never thought about what was actually needed in a given situation.

Jamgön Kongtrül, my root guru, my personal teacher, was constantly talking about that problem. He wasn't happy about the way things were going. He wasn't very inspired to work on a larger scale because he felt that, unless he could create a nucleus of students who practiced intensely and who could work together, unless he could create such a dynamic situation, he couldn't get his message to the rest of the people. You might think that Tibet was the only place in the world where spirituality was practiced quite freely, but that's not the case. We had our own difficulties in keeping up properly with tradition. Before the 1950s, a lot of gorgeous temples were built; a lot of fantastic decorations were made. There was lots of brocade, lots of ceremony, statues, lots of *chötens*, lots of horses, lots of mules. The cooking was fantastic, but there was not much learning, not much sitting. That became a problem.

Sometimes Jamgön Kongtrül got very pissed off. He would lose his temper without any reason, and we thought that he was mad over our misbehaving. But he was angry over something much greater than that. It was terrible what was going on in our country. Many other teachers besides Jamgön Kongtrül began to talk about that: the whole environment was beginning to flip into a lower level of spirituality. The only thing we needed was for American tourists to come along. Fortunately, thanks to Chairman Mao Tse-tung, that didn't happen, which actually saved us.

There are a few sections connected with that situation in the first part of the sadhana, which is about why the sadhana was written. The first reads:

> This is the darkest hour of the dark ages. Disease, famine and warfare are raging like the fierce north wind. The Buddha's teaching has waned in strength. The various schools of the sangha are fighting amongst themselves with sectarian bitterness; and

although the Buddha's teaching was perfectly expounded and there have been many reliable teachings since then from other great gurus, yet they pursue intellectual speculations.⁷ The sacred mantra has strayed into Bön and the yogis of tantra are losing the insight of meditation.⁷ They spend their whole time going through villages and performing little ceremonies for material gain.⁷

On the whole, no one acts according to the highest code of discipline, meditation and wisdom.⁷ The jewellike teaching of insight is fading day by day.⁷ The Buddha's teaching is used merely for political purposes and to draw people together socially.⁷ As a result, the blessings of spiritual energy are being lost.⁷ Even those with great devotion are beginning to lose heart.⁷ If the buddhas of the three times and the great teachers were to comment, they would surely express their disappointment.⁷ So to enable individuals to ask for their help and to renew spiritual strength, I have written this sadhana of the embodiment of all the siddhas.⁷

There were a lot of problems, obviously. Tibetan Buddhism was turning out to be a dying culture, a dying discipline, a dying wisdom—except for a few of us, I can quite proudly say, who managed to feed the burning lamp with the few remaining drops of oil.

Suddenly there was an invasion from the insect-eater barbarians called the Chinese. They presented their doctrine called communism, and they tried to use a word similar to *sangha* in order to hold together some kind of communal living situation, in order to raise the morale of the masses. But what they had in mind turned out to be not quite the same as the concept of sangha. There was no practice, no discipline, and no spirituality. When the communists finally realized that they couldn't actually indoctrinate anybody, they decided to use greater pressure. They invaded the monasteries and arrested the spiritual and political leaders. They put those leaders in prison. Asking the communists to do something about the treatment of the Tibetan leaders further intensified their antagonism. Rather than letting these political and spiritual leaders come out, the Chinese just told the stories of what happened to these prisoners. That created further problems.

I don't want to make this a political pep talk as such, but you would be very interested to know that in the history of communism, Tibet was the first place where workers have rebelled against the regime. The Tibetan peasants were not all that aggravated or pissed off by their situation before the communists; they were well off in their own way. They had lots of space for farming. Maybe they were hard up in terms of comfort and things like that, but our people are very tough. They can handle the hard winters; they appreciate the snow and the rain. They appreciate simple ways of traveling; they don't need helicopters or motorcars to journey back and forth with. They are very strong and sturdy; they have huge lungs in order to breathe at a high altitude. We're tough people! The peasants took pride in those things, obviously. Their faith and their security and their pride was based on some kind of trust in the teachings and in the church, which was slightly crumbling but which still remained. So for about nine months new energy was kindled, and the peasants rose up against the communists. That was the first time in the history of communism that such a thing took place.

After I was forced to leave my country, people from my monastery sent me a message: "Come back. We would like to establish an underground monastery." I wrote to them, saying, "Give up. It would be suicidal. I'm going to leave for India in order to do my work elsewhere." So that was that. Hopefully they received my message; hopefully they left my country.

My journey out of Tibet, my walk across the country, is described in *Born in Tibet*. I appreciated enormously the beauty of that country, although we saw only mountain range after mountain range after mountain range. We could not go down to the villages because there might be communist spies there to capture anybody who was trying to escape. So we saw fantastic mountain ranges in the middle of winter, fantastic lakes on top of plateaus. There was a good deal of snow, and it was biting cold, which was very refreshing—fantastic!

TIME IN INDIA AND ENGLAND

I finally crossed the border into India and took my first plane trip, in a cargo plane provided for us by the Indian army. I was excited to fly for the first time, and it was a good trip. A lot of my colleagues got sick; a few were very nauseated. But I was very interested in getting to a new world. We arrived in the refugee camp, where I spent about three months. I could talk on and on about that life, which was very interesting to me because I was having a chance to explore what it was like outside of our world.

India was very exciting to me: in Tibet we had read all about India in our books. We studied all about it, particularly about the brahmins and the cotton cloth that they wrap around themselves. We talked about brahministic ceremonies and all kinds of things. It was very interesting that finally history was coming to life for me. It was good to be in India, fantastic to be in India.

Then one day I was invited to go to Europe, and I managed to do so. I traveled by ship, on what is called the Oriental Lines, or something like that.[2] It was interesting to be with people who were mostly Occidentals. They had a fancy dancing party, and they had a race on board. In fact, they had lots of parties; every night there was entertainment of some kind, which was interesting. That was the first time I actually tasted English beer, which is bitter. I thought it was a terrible taste; I couldn't imagine why people liked the stuff.

At Oxford University

When we got to England, there was a certain amount of hassle with customs, but everything turned out to be okay. My stay at Oxford University was also interesting, because there was a lot of chance to communicate and work with people from Christendom. They were soaked in Christianity and in Englishness to the marrow of their bones, and yet they were still wise, which is a very mind-blowing experience. Such dignified people! Very good people there. But at the same time, you can't ruffle their sharp edges. If you make the wrong move, you're afraid that you are going to freeze to death or else that they're going to strike you dead.

At Oxford, I heard lectures on comparative religion, Christian contemplation, philosophy, and psychology. I had to struggle to understand those lectures. I had to study the English language: I was constantly going to evening classes organized by the city for foreign students. I was trying to study their language at the same time that I was trying to understand those talks on philosophy, which was very difficult, very challenging. The lectures were highly specialized; they didn't build from the basic ground of anything, particularly. They presumed that you already knew the basic ground, so they just talked about certain highlights. It was very interesting and very confusing. If I was lucky, I might be able to pick up one or two points at each lecture.

Teaching in Scotland

I was continuing with that situation, nevertheless, but I was looking for some way to work with potential students of Buddhism. I made contact with the London Buddhist Society, which is an elderly organization more concerned with its form than with its function as Buddhists. Quite a lovable setup! Then I was invited to visit a group of people who had a community in Scotland. They asked me to teach and to give meditation instruction. It was very nice there, a fantastic place! Rolling hills, somewhat damp and cold, but beautiful. It was acceptable. I spent a long time with them, commuting back and forth between Oxford and Scotland. Finally they asked me to take over the trusteeship of their place, and offered their place to me to work with. The whole environment there was completely alien, completely untapped as far as I was concerned. But at the same time, there was some kind of potential for enlightenment in that world. It was very strange, a mixture of sweet and sour.

I stayed there and worked there for several years; I said goodbye to my friends and tutors in Oxford. Great people there! But I was glad to leave Oxford for a while. When I visited Oxford again, it looked much better than it had, for the very reason that I didn't have to live there. The situation in Scotland turned out to be somewhat stagnant and stuffy. There was no room for expansion except for my once-a-month visits to the Buddhist Society, which was filled with old ladies and old gentlemen. They weren't interested in discussion, and the longest they could sit was twenty minutes. They thought that they were very heroic if they could sit for twenty minutes. We wouldn't be able to mention anything about *nyinthüns* to them; they'd completely freak out. From their point of view, being good Buddhists was like being good Anglicans in the Church of England. That problem still continues, up to the present.

RETREAT AT TAKTSANG AND COMPOSING THE SADHANA

At some point, I planned to make a visit to India. I thought it would be appropriate to check it out again, so to speak. I also wanted to visit His Holiness the Sixteenth Karmapa at Rumtek. I was also invited by the queen of Bhutan, Ashi Kesang, to visit her country. She was very gracious, and also somewhat frustrated that she couldn't speak proper Tibetan. She was hoping that her English was much better than her Tibetan, so that I could teach her in English about Buddhist practice. I tried to do so, but she was a rather lazy student and didn't want to sit too long. But she had good intentions. She is now the royal grandmother of the king of Bhutan.

I took my retreat at Taktsang, which is outside of Paro, the second capital of Bhutan. Taktsang is the place where Padmasambhava meditated and manifested as Dorje Trolö. Being at Taktsang was very ordinary at first. Nothing happened; it looked just like any other mountain range. It was not particularly impressive at all, at the beginning. I didn't get any sudden feedback, any sudden jerk at all. It was very basic and very ordinary. It was simply another part of Bhutan. Since we were guests of the queen, our needs were provided for by the local people. They brought us eggs and firewood and meat as part of their tax payment; they were very happy to give their tax payment to a holy lama. They liked to fulfill their function that way rather than give it to the administration. They were very kind and very nice, and we were provided with servants and with everything we needed.

The first few days were rather disappointing. "What is this place?" I wondered. "It's supposed to be great; what's happening here? Maybe this is the wrong place; maybe there is another Taktsang somewhere else, the real Taktsang." But as I spent more time in that area—something like a week or ten days—things began to come up. The place had a very powerful nature; you had a feeling of empty-heartedness once you began to click into the atmosphere. It wasn't a particularly full or confirming experience; you just felt very empty-hearted, as if there was nothing inside your body, as if you didn't exist. You felt completely vacant, without feeling. As that feeling continued, you began to pick up little sharp points: the blade of the phurba, the rough edges of the vajra. You began to pick all that up. You felt that behind the whole thing there was a huge conspiracy: something was very alive.

The gekö and the kunyer, or temple keeper, asked me every morning, "Did you have a nice dream? Did you have any revelatory dreams? What do you think of this place? Did we do anything terrible to this place?" "Well," I said, "it seems like everything is okay, thank you."

The Kagyü tradition and the Nyingma tradition are brought together very powerfully at Taktsang; the influence of the practice lineage is very strong there. There is a feeling at Taktsang of austerity and pride, and some sense of wildness, which goes beyond the practice lineage alone. When I started to feel that, the sadhana just came through without any problems. I definitely felt the immense presence of Dorje Trolö Karma Pakshi, and I told myself, "You must be joking. Nothing is happening here." But still, something was coming from behind the whole thing; there was immense energy and power.

The first line of the sadhana came into my head about five days before I wrote the sadhana itself. The taking of refuge at the beginning kept coming back to my mind with a ringing sound: "Earth, water, fire and all the elements...." That passage began to come through. I decided to write it down; it took me altogether about five hours to write the whole text. During the writing of the sadhana, I didn't particularly have to think of the next line or what to say about the whole thing; everything just came through very simply and very naturally. I felt as if I had already memorized the whole thing. If you are in such a situation, you can't manufacture something, but if the inspiration comes to you, you can record it.

That difference between spontaneous creation and something manufactured is demonstrated by a little poem that I composed after the sadhana was already written. The spontaneousness was gone, but I thought that I had to say thank you. Somehow I had to write a poem for the end, so I wrote it deliberately. You can feel the difference between the rhythm and feeling of the sadhana and that of the poem, which was very deliberate. The poem is something of a platitude, but the rest of the sadhana was a spontaneous inspiration that came through me. Here is what I wrote:

> *In the copper-mountain cave of Taktsang,*
> *The mandala created by the guru,*
> *Padma's blessing entered in my heart.*
> *I am the happy young man from Tibet!*
> *I see the dawn of mahamudra*
> *And awaken into true devotion:*
> *The guru's smiling face is ever-present.*
> *On the pregnant dakini-tigress*
> *Takes place the crazy-wisdom dance*
> *Of Karma Pakshi Padmakara,*
> *Uttering the sacred sound of* HUM.
> *His flow of thunder-energy is impressive.*
> *The dorje and phurba are the weapons of self-liberation:*
> *With penetrating accuracy they pierce*
> *Through the heart of spiritual pride.*
> *One's faults are so skillfully exposed*
> *That no mask can hide the ego*

And one can no longer conceal
The antidharma which pretends to be dharma.
Through all my lives may I continue
To be the messenger of dharma
And listen to the song of the king of yanas.
May I lead the life of a bodhisattva.

I feel that this poem has a lot of platitudes because it was just some personal acknowledgment of my own stuff.

I think that in the future people will relate with this sadhana as a source of inspiration as well as a potential way of continuing their journey. Inspiration from that point of view means awakening yourself from the deepest of deepest confusion and chaos and self-punishment; it means being able to get into a higher level and being able to celebrate within that.

DISCUSSION

Relationship of pain and insight.

Question: It seems that insight could come from some kind of pain, but I was under the impression that it's born of some sort of discipline.

Chögyam Trungpa Rinpoche: What do you mean?

Q: It could be dangerous unless there's some kind of opening up. Could insight also be born of pain?

CTR: Sure. Don't we know that?

Chanting the sadhana on the full- and new-moon days.

Q: Rinpoche, why is the sadhana chanted at the full moon and the new moon?

CTR: The full moon is regarded as the fruition of a particular cycle in one's state of mind. It's like a cosmic docking, like a spaceship landing. It is very conveniently worked out: that day is regarded as sacred. Most of the full-moon and new-moon days are also related with things the Buddha did. So the sadhana is read on that particular day because of our potential openness: we can open ourselves; we can take advantage of the gap that is taking place. It could be a freaky gap or a very sane gap.

Significance of observing monthly ceremonies.

Q: Do you think that the traditional observances of ceremonies on various days of the month—I don't mean just the full moon and the new moon, but a whole month full and a whole year full and a whole calendar full of liturgies—is an expression of decadence? Or do you think there is something to it?

CTR: Well, originally it was not an expression of decadence. Of course, it could *become* decadent, just like the Christian notion of Sunday, which has become just a day off. But at this point, I don't think it's possible. The sadhana is simply an expression of tradition, and it should be conducted properly; it depends on how you take part in it. You have two choices. For instance, you could regard the day that you get married as a sacred day or as just a social formality. It's up to you.

Relationship between tradition and impermanence.

Q: I guess I'm bothered by the relationship between tradition and impermanence. It seems to me that institutions and rigid traditions are the public analogies of ego-clinging at an individual level. It seems like they provide the illusion of security, but that they lead in the long run to the same disastrous consequences for the public that we find at the level of the individual, at the level of ego.

CTR: Well, that's an interesting question. You seem to be speaking from the point of view of revolutionaries, socialists—

Q: Anarchists?

CTR: Anarchists, yes. I think one of the problems with that approach is that if there isn't any format, there's no freedom. Freedom has to come from structure, not necessarily in order to avoid freedom. Freedom itself exists within structure. And the practices that we do in our own discipline are very light-handed practices. They have nothing to do with a particular dogma. We're not particularly making a monument of our practice; we're simply doing it. If we have too much freedom, that is neurotic: we could freak out much more easily. We could get confused much more easily because we have every freedom to do what we want. After that, there's nothing left.

Q: Might that freakout be crazy wisdom?

CTR: Absolutely not! That's just crazy.

Mahakali principle as an expression of the charnel ground.

Q: Would you talk about the *mahakali* principle in the sadhana?

CTR: The mahakali principle is simply an expression of the charnel ground. If you don't relate with reality properly, there are going to be messages coming back to you, very simply.

Q: So the mahakali principle is just that innate energy we have all the time, which gives us messages?

CTR: Yes.

Who can write a sadhana?

Q: You said that there are certain people who can write sadhanas, and I was wondering what you meant by that.

CTR: Well, not just anybody—not just any old hat—can write a sadhana for his girlfriend or for his boyfriend or for his teacher or for his Mercedes or for his Rolls-Royce. You have to have some feeling of connection with the lineage—simply that. That's the basic criterion. You have to be trained in the vajrayana discipline already; you have to have some understanding of jnanasattva and samayasattva working together. You have to understand devotion.

Meaning of Padmasambhava manifesting as Dorje Trolö.

Q: What does it mean that Padmasambhava manifested as Dorje Trolö at Taktsang?

CTR: Well, you could say that you manifest as a mother when you become pregnant or when you bear a child. You have a different kind of role to play.

Discussion of business mentality.

Q: I've been wanting to ask you about the topic of business mentality that keeps popping up. First of all, do you see a problem with it in the business world per se?

CTR: I don't see a problem. The whole point is to have a vision of the totality. Then there's no problem. If you don't have a vision of the totality, obviously you will have problems.

Q: Usually when you talk about business mentality, it seems to be in opposition to a spirit of giving or openness. Does that create a problem if you're involved with businesses in the outside world?

CTR: I don't think so. That's simply part of the adornment. You have to relate with your parents and your background and your culture in any case, which is all outside of the Buddhist tradition. Doing that is very new to most of you. So you have to relate with those situations in any case. I don't see any particular problems; those things are regarded as reference points, as the stuff we have to work with.

Q: I wonder if you think that in terms of this community and the businesses happening within it, if there might be a need for a more straightforward approach to business?

CTR: Sure, on the basis of the same logic that we are involved in already.

This discussion of the sadhana has been an unusual one: it is the first time that I have talked about the sadhana in depth. I'm glad that, in reading and studying this material, you have had a chance to learn more about the sadhana, and I hope you will be able to work on this material in the future. We have seen that there are different levels of development within the sadhana, such as the charnel-ground principle, devotion, surrendering, and generosity. All those subjects are very compact and very definite, so hopefully you will be able to work on those things. In relationship to this material, please try to sit and practice. That's the only way to understand the sadhana better.

I would like to close by sharing this section from the end of the sadhana, which is dedicated to all of you.

> The wisdom flame sends out a brilliant light—
> May the goodness of Dorje Trolö be present!
> Karma Pakshi, lord of mantra, king of insight—
> May his goodness, too, be present!
> Tüsum Khyenpa, the primeval buddha—
> Beyond all partiality—may his goodness be present!
> Mikyö Dorje, lord of boundless speech—
> May his goodness be present here!
> Rangjung Dorje, faultless single eye of wisdom—
> May his goodness be present!

The Kagyü gurus, the light of whose wisdom is a torch:
For all beings—may their goodness be present!:
The ocean of wish-fulfilling yidams who accomplish all actions—:
May their goodness be present!:
The protectors who plant firm the victorious banner:
Of dharma—may their goodness be present!:
May the goodness of the great mind mandala of mahamudra be
    present!:

Afterword from the
Nalanda Translation Committee

———

After escaping from Tibet to India in 1959, the Vidyadhara[1] Chögyam Trungpa Rinpoche made his way to England in 1963 in order to attend Oxford University. In 1967, he cofounded Samye Ling meditation center in Scotland with Akong Tulku. During his time in England, the Vidyadhara came to realize that the clash between Tibetan Buddhism and Western culture was creating as much confusion as wisdom. To most students, his monastic robes were more fascinating than his teaching. At the same time, Tibetan teachers were suspicious of Western students. So Chögyam Trungpa had reached an impasse: caught between the Westerners' fascination with Tibetan culture and Tibetans' mistrust of Westerners. In order to present the teachings of dharma authentically, something had to change.

At that point, he was invited to Bhutan, where he discovered "The Sadhana of Mahamudra" text. He recounts his visit in *Born in Tibet*:[2]

> In 1968 I was invited by the royal family of Bhutan to pay a visit—I had been providing tutoring in Buddhism to the young crown prince, Jigme Wangchuk, now the king of Bhutan....
>
> Of tremendous significance to my future activity were the ten days of this visit which I spent in retreat at Tagtsang. Tagtsang is the place in Bhutan where, over a thousand years ago, Guru Rinpoche (Padmasambhava) first manifested himself in the wrathful form of Dorje Trolö and subjugated evil forces before entering Tibet. Since I had never been to Central Tibet or seen the great holy places of Guru Rinpoche or of the Kagyü forefathers, this visit to Tagtsang was very moving for me. The place is spacious and awe-inspiring, and one can still feel the presence of

Guru Rinpoche. During my retreat there I was able to reflect on my life and particularly on how to propagate the dharma in the West. I invoked Guru Rinpoche and the Kagyü forefathers to provide vision for the future. For a few days nothing happened. Then there came a jolting experience of the need to develop more openness and greater energy. At the same time there arose a feeling of deep devotion to Karma Pakshi, the second Karmapa, and to Guru Rinpoche. I realized that in fact these two were one in the unified tradition of mahamudra and ati. Filled with the vivid recognition of them and their oneness, I composed in two days "The Sadhana of Mahamudra," of twenty-four pages. Its purpose was to bring together the two great traditions of the vajrayana, as well as to exorcise the materialism which seemed to pervade spiritual disciplines in the modern world. The message that I had received from my supplication was that one must try to expose spiritual materialism and all its trappings, otherwise true spirituality could not develop. I began to realize that I would have to take daring steps in my life.

Another account of the visit is provided in an appendix of this book.[3] It was written by Künga Dawa (a.k.a. Richard Arthure), who accompanied Trungpa Rinpoche to Bhutan.

Soon after completing his retreat and translating the text, Chögyam Trungpa gave a formal *abhisheka*, or empowerment, for it to a small group in New Delhi, mostly consisting of Western dharma students. Only a few Tibetans, including Ringu Tulku, were among the participants. Later that year, Chögyam Trungpa conferred the abhisheka again in Scotland. In both cases, it was a formal empowerment ceremony, somewhat extensive and elaborate, which Trungpa Rinpoche composed extemporaneously. He was well equipped for the task, having conferred, at the age of fourteen, the over eight hundred abhishekas of the *Rinchen Terdzö*, an important collection of texts gathered by Jamgön Kongtrül the Great.

Trungpa Rinpoche returned to Scotland from Asia in 1968. It was there that he first invited students to join in the group practice of this text, performed twice a month, on new-moon and full-moon days. No empowerment, reading transmission (Tib. *lung*), or prior training was required.

Beginning in 1970, practice centers were created by Chögyam Trungpa and his students in the U.S. and Canada. After Vajradhatu, the national umbrella organization for his work in the West, was established in 1973, the Vidyadhara encouraged city centers and contemplative centers to offer the group practice of "The Sadhana of Mahamudra" on a semimonthly basis, as long as the center was established enough to do protector chants regularly. At that time, the text of the sadhana was available to centers but not generally to individuals.

Until 1976, the translation had existed only as a typewritten manuscript on legal-sized paper. That year, Samuel Bercholz, founder of Shambhala Publications and one of Trungpa Rinpoche's first students in the United States, produced a beautiful, two-color letterpress edition of the text for Vajradhatu, which was designed like a Tibetan-style book (Tib. *pecha*). He also commissioned line drawings of Dorje Trolö, Karma Pakshi, and Ekajati—important figures in the sadhana—from master artist Glen Eddy to enhance the publication. Sam offered this edition to Rinpoche as a gift. Copies were distributed to meditation centers established by Trungpa Rinpoche; however, the texts were not sold or made easily available to individuals. For the first time, the text included a statement that the sadhana could "not be practiced without formal permission from the Vajracharya[4] Chögyam Trungpa Rinpoche or persons authorized by him to give such permission." As Sam recalls, Rinpoche preferred that people practice the sadhana as a group and generally discouraged them from using the text at home.

Around the time of Trungpa Rinpoche's final illness in 1986–87, Lama Ugyen Shenpen calligraphed a beautiful two-color manuscript of the Tibetan as a devotional offering, which was published by the Nalanda Translation Committee in 1988. The Vidyadhara's original Tibetan text had been lost before he arrived in North America, and the only surviving version of the Tibetan text was a very poor photocopy of a version handwritten by Sherab Palden Beru, many times removed from the original. Lama Ugyen's calligraphed version of the Tibetan text has been used chiefly by students and centers as a shrine object. Some of the words in the text are printed in red—seed syllables, proper names, places where the chanting resumes, and a few other words and phrases—and these were chosen by Lama Ugyen.

In the early 1980s, when several members of the Translation Committee began to study "The Sadhana of Mahamudra" in its original Tibetan, they discovered that some information contained in the Tibetan was not conveyed in the original English translation. We asked Trungpa Rinpoche to read the Tibetan text with us with the intention of retranslating the sadhana, and he agreed. Having prepared a first draft of a new translation of the sadhana with the aid of Lama Ugyen Shenpen, we had one meeting with the Vidyadhara on the text at the 1983 Vajradhatu Seminary, during which we retranslated the first few pages. No further meetings were held.

Previously, over the years, Sherab Chödzin, a senior student of Chögyam Trungpa's and a longtime member of the Nalanda Translation Committee, had asked Rinpoche if it would be permissible to call the sadhana a terma: a hidden treasure teaching that is discovered by a tertön, or treasure revealer, rather than being written by an author in the conventional sense.[5] Rinpoche always answered in the negative. At the 1983 Seminary, Sherab again asked Rinpoche if the text could be called a terma. For the first time, he said it would be fine. During a translation meeting around that time, he explained that his having received abhisheka from Karma Pakshi Dorje Trolö—a direct transmission from the deity himself—indicated that this text was a *gongter*, or "mind terma." Consequently, he agreed that it would be fine to add terma marks (༔) throughout the text, except for the poem and the colophon at the end, which he said he had indeed written himself. As a result, terma marks were added at the end of each line of the sadhana, beginning with the 1990 edition.[6] He also considered his own English translation to be special, even "terma-like."

During Dilgo Khyentse Rinpoche's second visit to North America in 1982, he requested Trungpa Rinpoche to write down the abhisheka text for "The Sadhana of Mahamudra." He was honored by this request, but when asked when he might write it, he answered, "Probably not for a while." After Rinpoche's *parinirvana*, or death, in 1987, we requested Khyentse Rinpoche to compose the abhisheka. He accepted the request and explained that because of their special relationship, he would finish whatever Trungpa Rinpoche had not been able to complete. After composing the abhisheka in 1988, Khyentse Rinpoche bestowed it upon Trungpa Rinpoche's eldest son, Sawang Ösel Rangdröl Mukpo (now Sakyong Mipham Rinpoche), and authorized him to confer it upon others after two years and after completing a retreat on it. The Sakyong first conferred it upon vajrayana students in 1993.

In 1990, Khyentse Rinpoche also wrote a feast offering, *Bestowing the Supreme Wisdom of Great Bliss*, for the sadhana. This is primarily practiced by vajrayana students. However, at a parinirvana commemoration, an annual observance of Chögyam Trungpa's death, all students are permitted to practice the sadhana along with this feast offering.

In 1988, the translators spoke with Khyentse Rinpoche about reprinting the English translation of the sadhana, which was out of print. He agreed with our suggestion that Trungpa Rinpoche's original translation be reprinted without change and that we make our more literal translation separately available as a source for study to senior students. This new edition of the sadhana, an eight-inch-square format, newly typeset, was printed in 1990 and made available for individual students to purchase for the first time. Though first restricted to vajrayana students, it later became available to all students who have taken a course on the sadhana. When it was reprinted in 2006, a few changes were made to the text in order to eliminate gender-biased language in the sadhana.

The Translation Committee's more literal rendering of "The Sadhana of Mahamudra," originally titled the "Annotated Translation,"[7] was also first published in 1990. In order to enhance one's understanding of the practice, it should be read alongside Trungpa Rinpoche's translation. As mentioned earlier, many details present in the Tibetan text do not appear in the original translation. On the other hand, the Vidyadhara's translation conveys many points of understanding that are not apparent simply by reading the original in Tibetan. As both the terma revealer and translator of the text, Chögyam Trungpa Rinpoche presented the dharma in a brilliantly unique way.

In 2023, Shechen Rabjam Rinpoche, the grandson of Dilgo Khyentse Rinpoche, conferred the abhisheka for "The Sadhana of Mahamudra" at a gathering of over five hundred students in Boulder, Colorado. Today in 2024, nearly forty years after Trungpa Rinpoche's death, students still continue to practice this powerful sadhana twice a month in centers around the world, online, and in various retreat settings.

Nalanda Translation Committee
Halifax, Nova Scotia
June 2024

EDITOR'S AFTERWORD AND ACKNOWLEDGMENTS

The Sadhana of Mahamudra: Teachings on Devotion and Crazy Wisdom presents ten talks given in two public seminars conducted in 1975 by Chö- gyam Trungpa Rinpoche. For many years, the material in this book was available within the Buddhist community founded by Chögyam Trungpa as *"The Sadhana of Mahamudra" Sourcebook*. In 2012, in preparation for the twenty-fifth anniversary of the parinirvana, or the death, of the Vidyadhara, Vajradhatu Publications[1] was inspired to rework and reformat the original sourcebook as a book. This seemed fitting for the twenty-fifth anniversary, and indeed it felt long overdue to present these teachings in a more digni- fied format, one more in keeping with the importance of the text and the profundity of Trungpa Rinpoche's commentary.

The newly formatted edition was published in 2015, several years after the actual twenty-fifth anniversary. Several levels of headings were added to the commentary, to facilitate study and link the material in the seminars to the various sections of the sadhana itself. Gender references were updated, a further light edit was undertaken, and as the editor of that version, I also listened to the original recordings and made editorial corrections, where warranted.

As in so many of his presentations, the Vidyadhara did not often repeat himself in these two seminars. His approach was always fresh, evocative, and of the moment, yet it was also intricately structured and comprehensive. He commented on almost every section of the sadhana in one or the other seminar, and the two explications are linked yet distinct. The more I read these talks, the more I find them a brilliant exposition of key principles of vajrayana Buddhism as well as a helpful and in-depth commentary on the sadhana itself.

Now, in 2025, *The Sadhana of Mahamudra* is being published for the first time as a trade paperback for a general audience. It is hoped that the inclusion of the full text of the sadhana along with the commentary will make the material more available and useful in understanding the content and in practicing the sadhana itself. The original language, style, and grammar in the sadhana section have been preserved to match the original rendering of the sadhana.

For those who have been practicing the sadhana for decades, the text remains as potent as the first time it was read. And like so much of Rinpoche's teaching, it was meant not just for then and for those, but as a teaching for now and for the future.

The extensive commentary in this volume stands on its own as a thorough explication of devotion, crazy wisdom, and other themes in the sadhana. It also brings further context and depth to the sadhana itself, which is remarkable given how profound the original text itself is.

ACKNOWLEDGMENTS

Many people have contributed to the translation, editing, and publication of the material in this book. Thanks are due to those who recorded, transcribed, and edited these teachings originally, as well as to students in the audience at the original seminars, who inspired Rinpoche to give these talks.

Particular thanks go to the following: Künga Dawa, a.k.a. Richard Arthure, who attended the original retreat in 1968 and worked with the Vidyadhara on the original translation. He passed away several years ago. We also thank the original editors of the sourcebook, who are not known to us, and Ellen Kearney, who in the early days of the twenty-first century reviewed the original editing for a new edition of the sourcebook, which informed later editions. Immense gratitude is offered to Tingdzin Ötro, who copyedited the edition published by Vajradhatu Publications some years ago. For this new edition, he reviewed the diacritics as well as many other parts of the manuscript, worked extensively on the "Afterword from the Nalanda Translation Committee," revised the glossary for both editions, and helped in other significant ways. Thank you, Ting! We also thank the earlier publisher, Vajradhatu Publications, especially the executive editor, Emily Sell, and the designer, Chris Gibson. We offer thanks as well to the photographers who have allowed us to include their work here, and the amazing artists whose work appears in the book. The renowned thangka painter Sherab Palden Beru, who was a companion and friend of Chögyam Trungpa's, is no longer with us, nor is Glen Eddy, whose line drawings and thangkas are also exceptional. Glen contributed a number of original drawings for the original publication of "The Sadhana of Mahamudra," and they are an integral part of this text.

Special thanks are extended to Larry Mermelstein and the Nalanda Translation Committee and its able translators, who have watched over "The Sadhana of Mahamudra" for many years: translating it, publishing it, offering live and online programs for students interested in these teachings, updating the translation to avoid gender-biased language, providing detailed instructions for its practice, sponsoring commentaries by other teachers, and making many other contributions to its preservation and propagation.

Gratitude is offered as well to the Shambhala Archives, for their work over many decades to preserve the audio and video teachings of the Vidyadhara.

We also thank the Chögyam Trungpa Digital Library, a project of the Chögyam Trungpa Institute at Naropa University, for making the audio and video recordings of the seminars available for streaming online.

We offer heartfelt thanks to Shambhala Publications for their publication of the current edition. Special thanks is offered to Nikko Odiseos, Sara Bercholz, Liz Shaw, Breanna Locke, Anna Wolcott Johnson, and Tracy Davis. We also thank Sam Bercholz for his foreword, as well as for all the efforts he has made over the last half-century to protect and make this precious material available. We also thank Barry Boyce, longtime practitioner of the sadhana and a true student and teacher of these teachings, for updating his introduction. We offer special thanks to Diana Mukpo for her foreword and for her support of all this work over many decades.

Carolyn Rose Gimian
Halifax, Nova Scotia
April 2024

Appendices

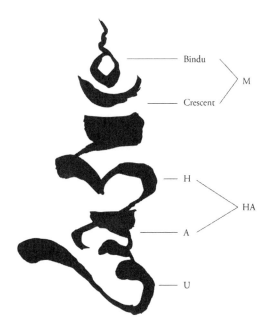

Sanskrit letter HUM, with individual parts labeled. *Calligraphy by Chögyam Trungpa; used by permission.*

HUM: AN APPROACH TO MANTRA

Homage to the guru, yidams, and dakinis! When I hear the
    profound music of HUM
It inspires the dance of direct vision of insight.
At the same time my guru presents the weapon which cuts the life
    of ego,
Just like the performance of a miracle.
I pay homage to the Incomparable One!

One must understand the basic usage of mantra in the teachings of Buddha.
Whether it is in the form of mantra, *dharani*, or a single syllable, it is not at
all a magical spell used in order to gain psychic powers for selfish purposes,
such as accumulation of wealth, power over others, and destruction of enemies. According to the Buddhist tantra, all mantras and other practices,
such as visualization, hatha yoga, or any other yogic practices, must be based
on the fundamental teaching of Buddha, which is the understanding of the
four marks of existence: impermanence (*anitya*), suffering (duhkha), void
(shunyata), and egolessness (*anatman*).

In this connection, it should be pointed out that in contrast to Hindu
tantra, Buddhist tantra is based on shunyata and anatman. The concept of
shunyata is quite easy to relate to the whole content of tantra, as in mahamudra experience, and that of anatman is most essential. Some Western
scholars mistakenly identify the preparation of mandalas and the countless
divinities with the Hindu tradition, as if it were an umbrella under which
all other Indian religions might be found. Although some Vedantic mystics
might claim their experiences to be the same as mahamudra, there is an
essential difference, for the herukas and all the other divinities in Buddhism
are not external. In other words, they are aspects of the awakened state of

mind, such as Avalokiteshvara representing the compassionate aspect of buddha nature.

There are various mantras connected with these bodhisattvas and herukas which help to achieve, for example, the essence of compassion, wisdom, or energy. In this essay we are discussing the single syllable HUM. HUM is the sound connected with energy, and is most profound and penetrating. This mantra was used by Guru Padmasambhava in his wrathful aspect in order to subdue the force of the negative environment created by minds poisoned with passion, aggression, and ignorance. HUM is often the ending of certain mantras used to arouse the life energy.

Before chanting the sacred music of HUM, it is necessary to consider the relationship of teacher and pupil. There must be oral transmission. The pupil should not choose a teacher at random, for unless the teacher belongs to a spiritual lineage, he may be able to give a mantra but he will not be able to transmit its power. With a strong karmic bond between teacher and pupil, the pupil should be inspired with an unwavering conviction of trust in the teacher's spiritual quality. Whatever difficulties the pupil might continually have to undergo and whatever sacrifices he might have to make, his devotion must remain constant until he is able to surrender his ego. If he fails to do this, he will not be able to experience the sacred music of HUM, he will not be able to develop understanding of its profound meaning, and he will not be able to develop the transcendental siddhi.

When a beginner chants the sacred music of HUM, he might find some temporary benefits; for example, his mind might become quiet and irritating thoughts might be eased. This is because HUM is composed of HA, U, and M. HA expels the impure air from the lungs, U releases the most irritating thoughts through the mouth, and M clears the remaining thoughts through the nose.

As mentioned in yogic texts, *prana* (breath) is like a horse, the *nadis* (channels) are like roads, and the mind is the rider. In this way, using prana, tension is released and any psychological disturbance may be relieved, but only as a temporary measure.

For advanced meditators, the syllable HUM is a means of developing the five wisdoms. H is the mirrorlike wisdom, clear and continuous. A is the wisdom of equanimity, panoramic awareness. U is the wisdom of discriminating awareness, awareness of details. The bindu is all-accomplishing wisdom, effortless accomplishment of all actions. The crescent is the wisdom of all-encompassing space (*dharmadhatu*), the ground from which all things originate and to which they return.

The meditator will not find these wisdoms in an external source but, rather like the spark which bursts into flame when fanned by the wind, he discovers them within himself.

HUM is the seed syllable of all herukas in the four orders of tantra (kriya, upa, yoga, and anuttara, which includes ati). The herukas originated with the subjugation and transformation of the Rudra, the personification of ego. The absence of ego is shunyata; in the vajrayana, shunyata, or voidness, is expressed in terms of fullness, as in the line of the *Heart Sutra* that says "form is emptiness, and the very emptiness is form." Therefore this form has tremendous energy which is simply what the five wisdoms are.

HUM is referred to in many texts as the sonorous sound of silence. HUM represents that state of meditation when awareness breaks out of the limits of ego. It was by that force of HUM that the fortress of Rudra was reduced to dust. HUM may be regarded as the fearless utterance of a warrior shooting his arrow in the battlefield. HUM is sometimes referred to as the mantra of the Vajrakilaya mandala of the high tantra school. First, it is the dagger (Skt. kila; Tib. *purba*; *phur ba*) of beyond-thought, which stabs with deadly accuracy into the heart of dualistic thoughts. Second, it is the dagger of luminous transcendental insight, which pierces the heart of confused darkness. Third, it is the dagger of the state of nonmeditation, which pierces the heart of thought-formed meditation, so that the meditator is delivered from subject matter. Fourth, it is the dagger of complete devotion to the all-pervading guru, which stabs to the heart of hopes and fears so that the teacher and pupil become inseparable. These four penetrations of HUM are described in the text of the *anuyogatantra*.

Guru Padmasambhava said that when you sing the crescendo music of HUM and let go of all thoughts, the ultimate meditation experiences are the echo of this music. Also, HUM is referred to as the concentration of all blessings and energy. Etymologically speaking, the Sanskrit word *hum* means "gathering together." HUM is not a magic spell to increase the power of ego, but it is concentrated power devoid of ego. HUM combined with complete devotion is like an arrow piercing the heart—it takes the form of the memory of the guru. Also the abrupt experience of cutting through all thoughts is the action of HUM. Therefore HUM is the energy of universal force which transcends the limitations of ego, or rather, pierces through the wall of ego.

I hope that the people who practice "The Sadhana of the Embodiment of All the Siddhas" ["The Sadhana of Mahamudra"] will study this essay very closely. May we all unite in the crescendo of HUM and liberate all sentient beings into the oneness of HUM.

From *Garuda II: Working with Negativity*. Barnet, Vt.: Tail of the Tiger, 1972, 9–11. © 1972 by Diana J. Mukpo. Also published in *The Collected Works of Chögyam Trungpa*, vol. 5. Boston: Shambhala Publications, 2004, 317–20. © 2004 by Diana J. Mukpo.

COMMENTS ON THE CIRCUMSTANCES
SURROUNDING THE DISCOVERY OF
"THE SADHANA OF MAHAMUDRA"

These comments have been excerpted from a letter written in 2001 by Richard Arthure, a.k.a. Künga Dawa, to Carolyn Rose Gimian, in preparation for the publication of *The Collected Works of Chögyam Trungpa*. Richard was a very early student of Chögyam Trungpa's and he accompanied Rinpoche to Bhutan in 1968. Working side by side with Trungpa Rinpoche, he translated the sadhana into English while they were both still in Bhutan. Richard was the editor of *Meditation in Action* and remained a student of Chögyam Trungpa's until Richard's death in 2018.

Along with the Shambhala teachings, "The Sadhana of Mahamudra" seems to be the quintessential expression of his [Trungpa Rinpoche's] enlightened mind and was openly recognized as such by both Tulku Urgyen Rinpoche and H. H. Dilgo Khyentse. The Vidyadhara [Chögyam Trungpa] himself wanted it to be propagated and practiced widely and without restriction, and he gladly shared it even with acquaintances, such as Thomas Merton, who were not Buddhist.[1]

Before going into retreat at Taktsang, Trungpa Rinpoche and I traveled with Khyentse Rinpoche by jeep from Bhutan to Sikkim in order to spend some time with H. H. the Sixteenth Karmapa. At [Trungpa] Rinpoche's request, the Karmapa performed the Karma Pakshi empowerment for us. Immediately, the Vidyadhara, with my assistance, set to work to prepare an English language translation of the Karma Pakshi sadhana.[2] (There exists a photograph—tactfully suppressed for general purposes—of the two of us sitting side by side in the guest house at Rumtek smoking cigarettes and working on this translation.) It was to be my daily practice at Taktsang. It is unlikely that this translation has survived.

On our return to Bhutan, we received the Dorje Trolö [the wrathful aspect of Guru Rinpoche, in which he manifested at Taktsang before entering Tibet] empowerment from Dilgo Khyentse in a very informal setting, with just a handful of people present in Khyentse Rinpoche's tiny bedroom. Then we went up to Taktsang, traveling on horseback and then on foot up the steep trail, to begin our retreat. Once there, my morning practice was the Karma Pakshi sadhana. At noon I would go to Trungpa Rinpoche's room and we would have lunch together. In the afternoon I would sit with Rinpoche in the main shrine room while he performed a Dorje Trolö feast practice, tormas and butter lamps having been prepared by a Bhutanese monk and a Tibetan yogi who were students of Dilgo Khyentse. We would share a light meal in the early evening and generally stay up late talking. A principal topic of our wide-ranging discussions was how to create an enlightened society, what form it would take, etc., Rinpoche favoring a combination of democracy and enlightened monarchy. The idea of the delek[3] system was first proposed during these discussions. A young Australian woman traveler, Lorraine, showed up with a copy of Erich Fromm's *The Sane Society* in her backpack. We devoured it. Rinpoche had me write a synopsis of the main ideas in it to add fuel to our discussions.

Toward the end of our retreat, "The Sadhana of Mahamudra" arose in Rinpoche's mind, and the main part of it was written down very quickly, in one or two days. Several more days were spent in refining and polishing. We began translating it into English almost immediately, although most of the work was done after we had come down the mountain from Taktsang and were staying in a guest house belonging to the queen's mother on the outskirts of Thimphu. Here's how the process worked, more or less (and you should understand that I don't speak or read Tibetan): Word by word and phrase by phrase Rinpoche would explain the meaning to me, as far as his vocabulary allowed. From those basic building blocks of meaning, it became possible to construct the English language version of the sadhana. I tried to create something that would transmit the dharma in a powerful and poetic way, utilizing the natural cadences and rhythms of spoken English. For example, Rinpoche would say something like: "All ... *namthok* is thoughts ... disappear. . . . Shunyata ... like a bird in the sky, doesn't make, how would you say, footprints?—not like a horse or man walking in snow, but same idea." And this, after a few tries, would give rise to: "All thoughts vanish into emptiness, like the imprint of a bird in the sky." Later, I saw that same simile translated as "like the traceless path of a bird in the sky," which I think is pretty good. I chose the word *imprint* because it gives the echo or faint suggestion of *footprint*, so carries the resonance of that image into the dimension of space.

Perhaps the Dakinis inspired our work together. Rinpoche seemed to think they were taking an active interest, at least. While we were staying in that guest house, tremendous rainstorms and floods caused landslides and destroyed roads and bridges so that we were unable to travel. Rinpoche commented: "This is the action of the Dakinis, making sure we don't leave until the translation is finished."

From a letter from Richard Arthure to Carolyn Rose Gimian, December 2001.

Resources

Relevant publications of the Nalanda/Vajravairochana Translation Committee are available at https://www.nalandatranslation.org/product-category/sadhana-of -mahamudra/.

The Chögyam Trungpa Digital Library (https://library.chögyamtrungpa.com/) presents Chögyam Trungpa's original teachings in captioned audio and video digital recordings available for streaming, along with interactive transcripts. The talks given by Chögyam Trungpa on "The Sadhana of Mahamudra" are available in the library. Also available are the digital recordings and a transcript of a seminar on the "Four Dharmas of Gampopa." The Four Dharmas are quoted in "The Sadhana of Maha-mudra" and discussed by Trungpa Rinpoche in the commentary.

Primary Sources

Chögyam Trungpa. *The Sadhana of Mahamudra*. Halifax: Nalanda Translation Com-mittee, 1990. (This is the original translation by Chögyam Trungpa himself.)
———. *The Sadhana of Mahamudra with Funeral Liturgy*. Halifax: Nalanda Transla-tion Committee, 2012. (This edition includes a fire offering written by Chögyam Trungpa Rinpoche for funerals.)

Additional Sources

Chögyam Trungpa. *Crazy Wisdom*. Boston: Shambhala, 1991. (This focuses on the life and teachings of Padmakara, including a chapter on Dorje Trolö.)
———. *The Tantric Path of Indestructible Wakefulness*. The Profound Treasury of the Ocean of Dharma, vol. 3. Boston: Shambhala, 2013.
———. "The Way of Maha Ati." In *The Collected Works of Chögyam Trungpa*, vol. 1, 461–65. Boston: Shambhala, 2003.
Karma Thinley. *The History of the Sixteen Karmapas of Tibet*. Boston: Shambhala,

2001. (This includes biographies of the four Karmapas who appear in the sadhana: Tüsum Khyenpa, Karma Pakshi, Rangjung Dorje, and Mikyö Dorje.)

Nalanda Translation Committee. *The Rain of Wisdom*. Boston: Shambhala, 1980. (This is a beautiful English rendition of many great realization songs by teachers of the Kagyü lineage, including those of Karmapa Mikyö Dorje, "Lord Gampopa's Song of Response to the Three Men of Kham," and Chögyam Trungpa's own songs of realization. Chögyam Trungpa inspired the Nalanda Translation Committee to undertake this translation and worked closely with them. He also provided an introduction and a colophon. The extensive afterword offers useful background on the Kagyü lineage. The glossary is also an excellent resource.)

Vajravairochana Translation Committee. *The Sadhana of Mahamudra: Resources for Study*. Halifax: Vajravairochana Translation Committee, 2012. (This includes the annotated translation of the sadhana, practice instructions, historical background, pertinent selected writings of Chögyam Trungpa Rinpoche, notes to the original typescript of the sadhana, and a glossary of terms found in the sadhana. Also available at the link given above for Nalanda/Vajravairochana Translation Committee publications.)

GLOSSARY

This glossary includes terms in English, Tibetan (Tib), Sanskrit (Skt), Pali, Chinese, and Japanese (Jpn). In general, Tibetan terms are first spelled phonetically and then transliterated. Definitions provided in this glossary are particular to their usage in this book; they are not intended to offer the sole, or even the most common, meaning of a specific term.

For further information about Kagyü lineage holders, see the afterword in *The Rain of Wisdom* (Shambhala Publications, 1989). See also the glossary and the "Original Notes to the Sadhana," which is found in *The Sadhana of Mahamudra: Resources for Study* (Vajravairochana Translation Committee, 2012), which is available from the Nalanda Translation Committee website (www.nalandatranslation.org).

———

abhisheka (Skt: "anointing"; Tib: *wang*; *dbang*; "power"). Empowerment. A ceremony in which a student is ritually introduced into a mandala of a particular tantric deity by a tantric master and is thus empowered to visualize and to invoke that particular deity. The essential element of abhisheka is a meeting of minds between master and student. In anuttarayoga tantra, there are four principal abhishekas: vase abhisheka, secret abhisheka, prajna-jnana abhisheka, and fourth abhisheka. These four abhishekas are referred to in the sadhana.

acharya (Skt: "teacher," "master"). The teacher in the hinayana, or early stages of the path. The acharya is an example to the student and also presents the practice of meditation and the basic teachings of Buddhism, such as the four noble truths.

adhishthana (Skt; Tib: *chinlap*; *byin rlabs*; "splendor wave"). Blessings. Chögyam Trungpa describes adhishthana as the "radiation which takes place between the opening of the student's mind to the teacher and the teachings and the opening of the teacher's mind to the student. Between those two openings, experience becomes not only naked but radiant." Adhishthana is the result of the development of devotion. It is a nontheistic form of blessings, in which the practitioner recognizes innate qualities of his or her own mind and being, rather than receiving something from the outside.

alaya (Skt: *alaya*; Tib: *künshi*; *kun gzhi*; "ground of all"). Alaya often refers to the ground of both samsara and nirvana, of both pure and impure phenomena. Used in that sense, it is a synonym of dharmata, the primordial basis of samsara and nirvana. In the sadhana, however, it is used as an abbreviation of alaya-vijnana, or eighth consciousness, and is translated as "universal unconscious" or the "universal ground of everything."

Amitabha (Skt: "Infinite Light"). A sambhogakaya buddha of the padma family, red in color, associated with the wisdom of discriminating awareness. He is the buddha of the pure land Sukhavati.

amrita (Skt; Tib: *dütsi*; *bdud rtsi*; "deathless"). Blessed liquor, used in vajrayana meditation practices; more generally, spiritual intoxication.

anuttarayoga (Skt: "none higher yoga"). The highest of the four tantric yanas, according to the New Translation School of Marpa and his contemporaries. The first three tantric yanas are kriya, charya (upa), and yoga. *See also* yana.

anuyoga (Skt). One of the tantric yanas in the Nyingma system. Anuyoga is connected with the expression of passion at a cosmic level, with leanings toward atiyoga, the final yana. *See also* yana.

Ashi Kesang Choden Wangchuck, Her Majesty (b. 1930). The queen grandmother of Bhutan, who invited Chögyam Trungpa Rinpoche to do a retreat at Taktsang. She was the queen of Bhutan at that time. He stayed in touch with her throughout his years of teaching in North America. A major patron of the late Dilgo Khyentse Rinpoche, she has sponsored hundreds of monks and helped to build and renovate monasteries in Bhutan.

ati (Skt; a.k.a. *atiyoga* or *maha ati*; Tib: *dzokchen*; *rdzogs chen*; "great perfection" or "great completion"). According to the Nyingma lineage, the highest of the six tantric yanas: kriya, upa, yoga, mahayoga, anu, and ati. Ati teachings are considered the final statement of the fruition path of vajrayana. In this book, Chögyam Trungpa Rinpoche talks about the six tantric yanas as a progression in one's practice and realization, with ati being the pinnacle of realization. *See also* yana.

bindu (Skt; Tib: *tigle*; *thig le*; "dot," "sphere"). In general, bindu refers to the white element of the subtle body, which is received from the father. But it may also refer to a circle or dot, often seen above a Tibetan syllable, such as in the seed syllable HUM.

black crown. The crown worn by the Karmapa, signifying his power to benefit all sentient beings. It is a replica of the crown given to the fifth Karmapa, Teshin Shekpa (1384–1415), by the Chinese emperor Yung-lo. After receiving the crown, Teshin Shekpa initiated the tradition of the Vajra Crown Ceremony, which has been performed by successive incarnations. In the ceremony, the Karmapa identifies with Avalokiteshvara, the bodhisattva of compassion, then places the crown on his head and blesses students.

bodhisattva (Skt: "awake being"). One who has made a commitment to the mahayana path of practicing compassion and the paramitas. Chögyam Trungpa Rinpoche has said that bodhisattvas are "brave people who can actually tread on the notion of enlightenment, who can dance with it, who are also treading on the charnel ground. They realize that the world they are treading on and working in is filled with intense neurosis, intense chaos, intense ugliness and unpleasantness—all the time. Bodhisattvas are actually inspired to work with such chaos, to tidy up a little bit, without disrupting the generally inspiring qualities of those untidy areas. They just work with what is there." *See also* paramita.

Bön (Tib: *bon*). The religion of pre-Buddhist Tibet. Chögyam Trungpa Rinpoche had great respect for the Bön religion as practiced by some Bön masters. As used in the sadhana, Bön refers to the many spiritual problems widespread in Tibet prior to the Chinese Communist takeover. Buddhism was being practiced in a shamanistic, theistic way. There were similar problems of theism and corruption in Padmasambhava's time, which led him to manifest in a wrathful form as Dorje Trolö.

Buber, Martin (1878–1965). Austrian-born Judaic scholar and philosopher, a prolific essayist, translator, and editor, his work is dedicated mainly to three areas: the philosophical articulation of the dialogic principle, the revival of religious consciousness among the Jews, and the realization of this consciousness through the Zionist movement. His most popular work is *I and Thou*.

buddha (Skt: "awakened one"). Buddha may refer specifically to the historical Buddha Shakyamuni; more generally, it may refer to enlightened beings on the sambhogakaya level, who represent different aspects of enlightened energy.

Buddha Lochana (Skt: "eye"). One of the five female buddhas, consorts of the five tathagatas, who represent the qualities of the five elements. The consort of Ratnasambhava, she is associated with the element of earth.

Buddha Mamaki (Skt: "my"). One of the five female buddhas, consorts of the five tathagatas, who represent the qualities of the five elements. The consort of Akshobhya, she is associated with the element of water.

buddha nature. The intrinsic state of wakefulness inherent in all sentient beings; a synonym of tathagatagarbha.

chakra (Skt: "wheel"). A primary energy center in the body. The major chakras are located within the avadhuti, or central channel. There are different enumerations of chakras, but generally five are named: at the forehead, throat, heart, navel, and secret place. In this sadhana, three Karmapas (Tüsum Khyenpa, Mikyö Dorje, and Rangjung Dorje) are visualized in the forehead, throat, and heart chakras, respectively.

charnel ground. An open field filled with corpses and beasts of prey. In the vajrayana teachings, it represents the original ground from which all phenomena are born and die; it is the basis of both samsara and nirvana.

chinlap (Tib: *byin rlabs*; "splendor wave"). *See* adhishthana.

chöten (Tib: *mchod rten*; Skt: *stupa*). Reliquary; a monument containing the body relics of a great teacher. Circumambulating a chöten is a common Buddhist practice.

In the sadhana, Chögyam Trungpa Rinpoche speaks of great yogic practitioners living in chötens, or stupas, in the charnel ground.

consciousness, eight kinds of. These eight include the six types of consciousness associated with the six sense organs: eye, ear, nose, tongue, body, and mind. In addition, according to the Yogachara school, the seventh consciousness is the klesha consciousness, which conceives the thought "I am," and the eighth consciousness is the storehouse consciousness (Skt: alaya-vijnana), which contains all the karmic seeds that give rise to our experience of the world.

crazy wisdom (Tib: *yeshe chölwa*; *ye shes 'chol ba*; "wisdom gone wild"). The compassion arising from wisdom, which expresses itself without hesitation or reference to conventional standards. Thus, the behavior of a crazy-wisdom teacher may appear very unconventional or "crazy" according to social norms. In Tibet, Trungpa Rinpoche studied with a great crazy-wisdom master, Khenpo Gangshar, and he himself was one. Chögyam Trungpa is widely credited with having come up with the term "crazy wisdom" in English, and he was the first person to use this term in connection with the discussion of the vajrayana teachings. There have been many oversimplifications of the concept, and others have sometimes used the term to refer to bizarre and abhorrent behavior that would not be considered to be the activity of crazy wisdom.

dakini (Skt; Tib: *khandroma, mkha' 'gro ma*; "sky-goer"). A wrathful or semiwrathful female deity, signifying compassion, emptiness, and prajna; a messenger or protector. In this sadhana, the charnel ground is described as the "heavenly realm of the dakinis."

Dalai Lama. The spiritual head of the Gelukpa school of Tibetan Buddhism and the head of state of the Tibetan government in exile. Tenzin Gyatso, the fourteenth Dalai Lama (b. 1935), received the Nobel Peace Prize in 1989.

dharani (Skt). A type of mantra, usually quite long.

dharma (Skt: "law," "norm," "truth"). Specifically, the teachings of the Buddha, also known as the *buddhadharma*. The plural, *dharmas*, refers to phenomena in general.

dharmachakra (Skt: "dharma wheel"). An eight-spoked wheel representing the Buddha's turning of the wheel of dharma, i.e., his propagation of the teachings.

dharmadhatu (Skt: "realm of dharmas"). All-encompassing space; the unconditional totality, unoriginated and unchanging, in which all phenomena arise, dwell, and cease.

dharmakaya (Skt; Tib: *chöku*; *chos sku*; "dharma body"). *See* trikaya.

dharmapala (Skt; "dharma protector"). A deity who protects the teachings of dharma and its practitioners. Oath-bound to the dharma and not bound to the six realms of samsara, dharmapalas fulfill the four karmas, or enlightened actions—pacifying, enriching, magnetizing, and destroying—in order to protect the integrity of the teachings and practice.

dharmaraja (Skt: "dharma king"). An epithet applied to a great ruler who has realized and fulfilled the vision of the Buddha's teaching; it may also be applied to great teachers.

Dilgo Khyentse Rinpoche (1910–1991). A great Nyingma scholar and a teacher of Chögyam Trungpa. Dilgo was his family name; Khyentse means "wisdom" (and) "love." Trungpa Rinpoche, whose first meeting with Khyentse Rinpoche is described in *Born in Tibet*, sponsored several visits by Khyentse Rinpoche to America. Khyentse Rinpoche conducted the funeral rites for Trungpa Rinpoche in 1987 and then traveled to major centers established by Trungpa Rinpoche, where he gave many empowerments and teachings to Chögyam Trungpa's students.

dorje (Tib: *rdo rje*). *See* vajra.

Dorje Sogdrubma (Tib: "vajra owner of life"). A mahakali, dark blue in color, holding a water dagger in the right hand and a skull cup of blood in the left, depicted as leaping with one leg raised. *See also* mahakali.

Dorje Trolö (Tib). A wild and wrathful form of Padmasambhava, he is the embodiment of crazy wisdom and symbolizes self-existing equanimity. Dorje Trolö Karma Pakshi is described in the sadhana as the "crazy wisdom form of the buddhas of the three times, the unified mandala of all the siddhas." *See also* the "Original Notes to the Sadhana" in *The Sadhana of Mahamudra: Resources for Study*.

duhkha (Skt). Suffering, anxiety; the first of the four noble truths.

dzokchen (Tib: *rdzogs chen*). *See* ati.

eight worldly concerns. Eight types of hope and fear that bind sentient beings to suffering in samsara: gain and loss, fame and disgrace, praise and blame, and pleasure and pain.

Ekajati (Skt: "one lock of hair"). A mahakali of the Nyingma lineage, she is an important protector of the ati teachings. She is the protector of the Karmê Chöling Meditation Retreat Center in Vermont. Chögyam Trungpa received terma teachings from Ekajati before departing from Tibet. He painted a thangka of her, which now hangs at Karmê Chöling.

See also the glossary entry for "mahakali" and the "Original Notes to the Sadhana" in *The Sadhana of Mahamudra: Resources for Study*.

equanimity (Skt: *samata*; Tib: *nyam-nyi*; *mnyam nyid*). Understanding the equality of samsara and nirvana; also, freedom from any kind of bias, such as likes and dislikes, attraction and rejection, or hope and fear.

five buddhas. *See* five families.

five families (Tib: *rik nga*; *rigs lnga*). The mandala of the five buddhas, who embody the five types of wisdom. Each family is associated with a particular buddha, wisdom, and energy. Related to the buddha family are buddha Vairochana, the wisdom of dharmadhatu, and the energy of spaciousness. Associated with the vajra family are Akshobhya, mirrorlike wisdom, and the energy of precision. Correlated with the ratna (Skt: "jewel") family are Ratnasambhava, the wisdom of equanimity, and the energy of richness. Connected with the padma (Skt: "lotus") family are Amitabha, the wisdom of discriminating awareness, and the energy of seduction. Related to the karma (Skt: "activity") family are Amoghasiddhi, all-accomplishing wisdom, and the energy of activity.

five poisons (Tib: *dug-nga*; *dug lnga*). Poison is synonymous with klesha, or confused emotion. The five poisons are passion, aggression, delusion, pride, and envy.

five wisdoms. *See* five families.

four noble truths. The first teaching of the Buddha after he attained enlightenment; it is the foundation of the hinayana and of the Buddhist path altogether. The four truths are (1) suffering, (2) the origin of suffering, (3) the cessation of suffering, and (4) the path of liberation.

fourth abhisheka (Tib: *shipé wang*; *bzhi pa'i dbang*). An empowerment in which the vajra master bestows upon the student the wisdom of the deity—the essence of mind, beyond words or concepts. *See also* abhisheka.

Gampopa (Tib: "man from Gampo"; 1079–1153). A great scholar and philosopher, he was the dharma heir of Milarepa and the teacher of Tüsum Khyenpa, the first Karmapa. He established the monastic tradition within the Kagyü lineage and authored many important texts, including *The Jewel Ornament of Liberation*.

garuda (Skt). A bird of Indian mythology, often depicted with a large owl-like beak, holding a snake, and with large wings. As the garuda is said to hatch full-grown and soar into space beyond all limits, it is a symbol of buddha nature, or the awakened state of mind—vast mind that cannot be measured.

gekö (Tib: *dge skos*). A senior monk in charge of discipline at a Tibetan monastery; he may also be the head of the monastery's administrative body. Traditionally, the gekö receives visitors and keeps lists of the monks and novices. As the head of discipline, the gekö may control access to the meditation hall during practice sessions.

Geluk (Tib: *dge lugs*). One of the four major lineages of Tibetan Buddhism. Founded by Tsongkhapa (1357–1419) as a reformation of Atisha's Kadampa tradition, it emphasizes the thorough study of authoritative texts. The Dalai Lama, widely regarded as the overarching head of all Tibetan Buddhist lineages, is most prominently associated with the Geluk lineage. A follower of the Geluk school or lineage is called a *Gelukpa*.

glorious copper-colored mountain. The name of the pure land of Padmakara, which is located in the middle of the southeastern subcontinent of Chamara. It is inhabited by demons called rakshasas.

Great Wrathful One (Tib: *trowo chölwa*; "Wrathful Crazy One"). The principal deity of "The Sadhana of Mahamudra," Dorje Trolö Karma Pakshi, who embodies crazy wisdom.

Guenther, Herbert (1917–2006). A German-born professor of Tibetan and Indian studies, Guenther headed the Department of Far Eastern Studies at the University of Saskatchewan from 1964 until his death. A pioneer in approaching contemporary philosophical issues from a learned Buddhist perspective, he produced some of the earliest translations of important works of Tibetan Buddhism, including *The Jewel*

Ornament of Liberation. Chögyam Trungpa admired Guenther, and they gave a seminar together, which was edited and published as *The Dawn of Tantra*.

güpa (Tib: *gus pa*). Humbleness, or being without arrogance. An essential aspect of devotion. *See also* mögü.

guru (Skt: "heavy"; Tib: *lama*; *bla ma*). A teacher, in particular, a spiritual master; often used synonymously with vajra master.

heruka (Skt). A wrathful male yidam, the masculine principle of energy and skillful means. The Tibetan term (*traktung*) means "blood drinker," one who drinks the blood of ego-clinging, doubt, and dualistic confusion. In this sadhana, Karma Pakshi is known as the "heruka who, untouched by concepts, pervades all existence."

hinayana (Skt; Tib: *thegmen*; *theg dman*; "lesser vehicle"). The first of the three yanas of Tibetan Buddhism, which includes the shravakayana ("vehicle of hearers") and the pratyekabuddhayana ("vehicle of solitary buddhas). Chögyam Trungpa Rinpoche does not use the term hinayana, meaning literally "lesser vehicle," in a pejorative sense. He speaks of the hinayana as the necessary starting point of the path of dharma and as the narrow discipline and simplicity necessary to travel it. To understand the spaciousness of the mahayana and vajrayana, "you are expected to do a lot of sitting practice; a lot of training is needed." *See also* yana.

Jamgön Kongtrül of Shechen (a.k.a. Pema Trimé; 1901–1960). One of the five incarnations of Jamgön Kongtrül the Great, he was Chögyam Trungpa's root guru.

Jamgön Kongtrül the Great (a.k.a. Lodrö Thayé; 1813–1899). One of the most important scholars of the Nyingma and Kagyü schools of the nineteenth century and one of the founders of the Rimé school. He collected teachings of all the schools of Tibetan Buddhism and instructed students in accordance with their own background. He is widely revered as the embodiment of the esoteric and intellectual tradition of Tibetan Buddhism. His collected works, comprising 101 volumes, contain many teachings that would otherwise have been lost. *See also* Rimé.

Jigme Lingpa (1730–1798). One of the most important teachers of atiyoga. In three visions of Longchen Rabjam, he received transmissions that became famous throughout Tibet under the name of Longchen Nyingtik.

jnana (Skt; Tib: *yeshe; ye shes*; "primordial knowing"). The wisdom of enlightenment, transcending all dualistic conceptualization. Jnana is the wisdom that manifests when the obscurations of mind are eliminated. It is an inner quality that one uncovers, rather than something one receives from the outside.

jnanasattva (Skt: "wisdom being"). In contrast to the samayasattva, or the visualization created by a practitioner, jnanasattva refers to the actual deity beyond conceptualization. In many sadhanas, the samayasattva is first visualized, and then the jnanasattva descends and merges with it. The jnanasattva represents the wisdom of the lineage entering one's visualization and blessing it, giving it power and wisdom. This process is understood in a nontheistic way. Although one visualizes that the jnanasattva descends and merges with the samayasattva, one does not take it to be an independent entity. In fact, the union of samayasattva and jnanasattva represents the fundamental unity of experience, beyond this and that. In "The Sadhana of Mahamudra," the two sattvas are inseparable from the beginning. *See also* samayasattva.

Kagyü (Tib: *bka' brgyud*; "command lineage"; *ka* refers to the oral instructions of the guru, which often includes the connotation of command). One of the four main lineages of Tibetan Buddhism, stemming in Tibet from Marpa, who traveled to India to receive the Kagyü teachings from Naropa. In "The Sadhana of Mahamudra," the Kagyü lineage is represented by the Karmapas.

kalyanamitra (Skt). Spiritual friend; a term used for the teacher in the mahayana relationship between teacher and student.

Karma Dzong (Tib: "fortress of action"). The meditation center in Boulder, Colorado, founded by Chögyam Trungpa in 1970, now known as the Boulder Shambhala Center. Trungpa Rinpoche also gave the name "Karma Dzong" to the center in Halifax, Nova Scotia, the seat of his work in Canada, and to the center in Marburg, Germany, the seat of his organization in Europe.

Karma Pakshi (1206–1283). The second Karmapa, who is the central deity of the sadhana, inseparably united with Dorje Trolö. *See also* the "Original Notes to the Sadhana" in *The Sadhana of Mahamudra: Resources for Study*.

Karmapa (Tib: *kar ma pa*; "one [who performs] activity"). Head of the Karma Kagyü lineage, often called "Gyalwa Karmapa" (Tib: *rgyal ba*; "victorious one"). He is considered to be an emanation of the tenth-level bodhisattva Maitreya manifesting as Avalokiteshvara, the bodhisattva of compassion. Until the tenth incarnation, all Karmapas were invited to be Chinese imperial teachers. The image of the Karmapa is prominent in "The Sadhana of Mahamudra," since the principal figure and the figures in his three centers are visualized as Karmapas.

Karmapa, Sixteenth Gyalwa (a.k.a. Rangjung Rigpe Dorje; "Self-Born Awareness Vajra"; 1924–1981). The spiritual head of the Kagyü lineage until his death in 1981. Chögyam Trungpa, who was enthroned as the eleventh Trungpa Tulku by the Sixteenth Karmapa, sponsored three of his teaching visits to North America.

Karmê Chöling (Tib: "Dharma Land of the Karma [Kagyü]"). The meditation center in Barnet, Vermont, founded by Chögyam Trungpa in 1970. It was originally known as "Tail of the Tiger."

Khenpo Gangshar Wangpo (1925–1961). A *khenpo*, or scholar, of Shechen Monastery before the Chinese invasion of Tibet, he was an important teacher of both Chögyam Trungpa Rinpoche and Venerable Thrangu Rinpoche. While teaching at Surmang Dütsi Tel, he became ill and seemed to have died. After reviving, his personality changed dramatically. Once a respected scholar and model of a proper monastic, he began to manifest the activity of crazy wisdom. After the Chinese takeover, he died in prison.

kriyayoga (Skt). The first of the tantric yanas, stressing purity and purification. *See also* yana.

Künga Dawa (a.k.a. Richard Arthure). A close student of Chögyam Trungpa who accompanied him on the trip to Taktsang and helped him to translate the sadhana into English. He was also the editor of *Meditation in Action*.

Künga Gyaltsen (fifteenth century). The first Trungpa, a disciple of Trungmasé. For more information, consult *The Mishap Lineage: Transforming Confusion into Wisdom* (Shambhala Publications, 2009).

lama. *See* guru.

Longchen Rabjam (a.k.a. Longchenpa; 1308–1364). A great scholar of the Nyingma lineage, he systematized the Nyingma teachings in his *Seven Treasures* and wrote extensively about dzokchen.

maha ati (Skt). *See* ati.

mahakala (Skt: "great black one"). Wrathful dharmapalas, or protectors of the dharma. Of the three roots—gurus, yidams, and dharmapalas—they are the root of action, fulfilling the four karmas of pacifying, enriching, magnetizing, and destroying. They are depicted as fierce, black or dark blue, and wearing the charnel-ground ornaments made of bone.

mahakali (Skt: "great black female"). A female guardian protector of the dharma. In this sadhana they are called the "terrifying trees": Rangjung Gyalmo, Dorje Sogdrubma, Tüsölma, and Ekajati. *See also* the "Original Notes to the Sadhana" in *The Sadhana of Mahamudra: Resources for Study*.

mahamudra (Skt: "great seal"). The inherent clarity and wakefulness of mind, vivid and yet empty. It is the main meditative transmission within the Kagyü tradition, handed down from Vajradhara to Tilopa up to the present. The Karmapas are the primary lineage holders of this tradition. The mahamudra teachings, as well as special transmissions connected with Vajrayogini and Chakrasamvara, are held by the Trungpa tülkus. The fourth Trungpa, Künga Namgyal (1567–1629), who was a scholar and great practitioner of mahamudra, wrote a famous text on the practice, which has not yet been translated into English. Needless to say, "The Sadhana of Mahamudra" has a strong basis in the teachings of mahamudra.

mahayana (Skt). The great vehicle; the second of the three yanas. Going beyond individual liberation, the mahayana teachings are based on the union of shunyata (emptiness) and compassion, and working for the benefit of others. Chögyam Trungpa describes the mahayana as "dedicating oneself to a much wider level of practice." *See also* yana.

mahayoga (Skt: "great yoga"). The yoga of great union; the fourth of the six tantric yogas. *See also* yana.

mandala (Skt: "circle"; Tib: *kyilkhor*; "center and periphery"). A vision that unifies the seeming complexity and chaos of experience into a simple pattern with a natural hierarchy. The outer mandala of external phenomena, represented in either two or three dimensions, is commonly depicted as a four-sided palace, inhabited by a central deity and surrounded by charnel grounds and a protection circle. The inner mandala of one's own body, considered to be the living palace of the deity, is visualized with various energetic centers, or chakras, in the forehead, throat, and heart. Chögyam Trungpa's teachings on mandala principle are published as *Orderly Chaos: The Mandala Principle*.

Manjushri (Skt). The bodhisattva of wisdom, commonly depicted holding a book and a sword, the sword representing prajna. In "The Sadhana of Mahamudra," Mikyö Dorje is considered an emanation of Manjushri.

mantra (Skt: "mind protection"). Words or syllables, generally in Sanskrit, that express the essence of various energies. The HUM chanted in "The Sadhana of Mahamudra" is a seed syllable connected with the essence and power of the deity.

Marpa (1012–1097). The chief disciple of Naropa, who brought the Kagyü teachings from India to Tibet in the eleventh century. Often referred to as "Marpa the Translator," he was the first Tibetan lineage holder of the New Translation School. A farmer with a large family, he was known not only for his meditative realization of mahamudra, but also for his attainment of spiritual realization within a secular lifestyle. His most famous student was the great yogin Milarepa.

Meister Eckhart (1260–c. 1327). A thirteenth-century German theologian and philosopher. His works are remarkable for their depth of mystical teaching. His themes include the relationship of being and intellect and the relationship of absolute being in its identity with God.

Mikyö Dorje (1507–1554). The eighth Karmapa. A scholar, grammarian, and artist, he was one of the greatest teachers of his time, a completely accomplished tantric master. In the sadhana, Mikyö Dorje is considered an emanation of Manjushri. He resides in the throat center of Karma Pakshi as the "lord of speech, the unceasing voice of Amitabha," thus representing the proclamation of the teachings. *See also* Manjushri.

Milarepa (1040–1123). The chief disciple of Marpa and the teacher of Gampopa. A great ascetic and poet, he is renowned as a wandering, solitary practitioner who meditated in the caves and wild places of Tibet.

mögü (Tib: *mos gus*). Devotion. Mögü is composed of two Tibetan terms: *möpa*, or longing, and *güpa*, or humility. Both longing and humility are necessary qualities of devotion. *See also* möpa *and* güpa.

Mongol emperor. Kublai Khan (1215–1294), the founder and first emperor of the Chinese Yuan dynasty. At the invitation of Kublai Khan, Karma Pakshi spent three years traveling in China. While there, he is said to have performed many miracles and played an important role as peacemaker.

möpa (Tib: *mos pa*). Interest or admiration; connected with longing for the teacher and the development of devotion.

mudra (Skt: "seal," "gesture"). A symbolic hand gesture that accompanies vajrayana Buddhist practice. More generally, mudra refers to the basic sign or symbolism of reality. Mahamudra is the "great seal," or the symbol of reality as itself. The three marks of existence—suffering, impermanence, and egolessness—are sometimes also called the three mudras.

nadi (Skt). A subtle channel in the body through which prana, or energy, flows.

Naropa (1016–1100). Along with his teacher Tilopa, Naropa is one of the best-known Indian mahasiddhas and an important holder of the transmission of the mahamudra teachings. Naropa's chief disciple, Marpa, was the founder of the Kagyü lineage in Tibet.

nidana (Skt; Pali: "link"). One of the twelve links of interdependent origination, the samsaric cycle of cause and effect: ignorance, karmic formations, consciousness, name and form, the six senses, contact, feeling, craving, grasping, becoming, birth, and old age and death. In the wheel of life, a symbolic representation of samsara, the twelve nidanas are depicted as the outer ring of the wheel. The innermost ring contains the primary kleshas: passion, aggression, and ignorance. Around those, the six realms of conditioned existence revolve: gods, jealous gods, humans, animals, hungry ghosts, and hell beings.

nirvana (Skt: "extinguished"; Tib: *nya-ngen ledepa*; "gone beyond suffering"). Freedom from the sufferings of samsara, or confused cyclic existence; thus, a synonym of enlightenment.

Nyingma (Tib: *rnying ma*; "old ones"). One of the four principal lineages of Tibetan Buddhism, focusing on the Buddhist teachings and practices brought to Tibet from India in the eighth century by masters such as Padmasambhava, Vimalamitra, and Vairochana. It is especially associated with the ati teachings.

nyingtik (Tib: *snying thig*; "heart essence"). The name of several cycles of teachings in the Nyingma lineage, which are considered to be the inner secret teachings of dzokchen. The Longchen Nyingtik is a well-known example. *See also* Jigme Lingpa.

Padma Thötreng (Tib: *pad ma thod phreng*; pronounced "Tö-treng"; "Lotus Skull Garland"). A wrathful manifestation of Padmakara, who is depicted as wearing bone ornaments.

Padmakara (Skt; Tib: *Pema Jungne*; *pad ma 'byung gnas*; "Lotus Born"). Indian ati master who brought vajrayana Buddhism to Tibet in the eighth century, founding the Nyingma lineage. He is also referred to as Padmasambhava or Guru Rinpoche ("Precious Teacher"). A principal figure in the sadhana, he manifests in his crazy-wisdom aspect as Dorje Trolö, who is inseparable from Karma Pakshi.

paramita (Skt; Tib: *pharol tu chinpa*; "gone to the far shore"). One of the six or ten transcendent perfections of the mahayana. The six paramitas are generosity, discipline, patience, exertion, meditation, and prajna (knowledge).

phurba (Tib: *phur ba*, pronounced "pur-ba"; Skt: *kila*). A three-bladed ritual dagger, a symbol of wrathful action that suddenly penetrates through the three kleshas or conflicting emotions of passion, aggression, and ignorance all at once, thus liberating them into their wisdom aspect. Dorje Trolö Karma Pakshi holds a phurba in his left hand.

practice lineage (Tib: *drub gyü*; *sgrub brgyud*). A title applied to the Kagyü and Nyingma lineages, emphasizing their strong allegiance to the practice of meditation. It is also referred to as the "practicing lineage."

prana (Skt; Tib: *lung*; *rlung*). Wind, breath, or energy. Prana is the energy, or "wind," that circulates through the nadis, or channels, of the body.

pratyekabuddha (Skt: "solitary awakened one"). A hinayana practitioner who, without relying on a teacher, realizes one-and-a-half-fold egolessness through insight into the working of the twelve nidanas.

psychological materialism. The use of concepts and ideas—comparing oneself to others, looking for external sources of praise, and so on—to reinforce one's solid sense of existence.

Rangjung Dorje (Tib: "Self-Born Vajra"; 1284–1339). The third Karmapa, the incarnation of Karma Pakshi, who brought together the two traditions of the mahamudra teaching of devotion and the ati teaching of crazy wisdom. He wrote a number of important commentaries. In the sadhana, he resides in the heart center of Karma Pakshi as the "king of the tathagatas . . . the Vajrasattva nature of never-ending awareness." *See also* the "Original Notes to the Sadhana" in *The Sadhana of Mahamudra: Resources for Study.*

Rangjung Gyalmo (Tib: "Self-Born Queen). The queen of the mahakalis, she is dark blue and rides on a mule. In her left hand is a snake lasso, in the right a mirror. *See also* mahakali and the "Original Notes to the Sadhana" in *The Sadhana of Mahamudra: Resources for Study.*

Rimé (Tib: *ris med*; "unbiased"). The Rimé school was started by Jamgön Kongtrül the Great and Khyentse the Great, together with several other teachers of their era. Jamgön Kongtrül collected teachings from many major and minor lineages in Tibet, both to ensure their preservation and to overcome sectarian bias. Chögyam Trungpa Rinpoche studied with Shechen Kongtrül, an incarnation of Kongtrül the Great and an important Rimé master in his own right. "The Sadhana of Mahamudra" may be viewed as an important text within the Rimé movement, as it brings together the highest views of the Kagyü and Nyingma lineages.

rinpoche (Tib: *rin po che*). An honorific term that means "precious one." Many of the great Tibetan teachers are addressed as Rinpoche.

rishi (Skt; Tib: *trangsong*; "straightforward one"). An ascetic Indian saint or sage; an advanced practitioner.

Rölpe Dorje (a.k.a. Trimé Öser). The fifth incarnation of the tertön Rölpe Dorje and regent abbot of Surmang Dütsi Tel. The first Rölpe Dorje was a contemporary of the fifth Trungpa, Tenpa Namgyal, and the teacher of Tai Situ Chökyi Jungne (1700–1774). Before training extensively with Jamgön Kongtrül and Khenpo Gangshar, Chögyam Trungpa Rinpoche received much training from Rölpe Dorje, whom he considered one of his spiritual fathers.

roshi (Jpn: "old [venerable] master"). Title of a Zen master.

rudra (Skt). A personification of ego, the opposite of buddhahood. In the sadhana, rudra is synonymous with ego-clinging and "fighting for your territory."

sadhana (Skt). A vajrayana liturgy incorporating visualization practice, formless meditation, mantras, and mudras. Sadhana can refer to a particular text, such as "The Sadhana of Mahamudra," or to the practice itself.

Sakya (Tib). One of the four major schools of Tibetan Buddhism, founded by Khön Könchok Gyalpo (1034–1102). Known for systematizing the tantric teachings, it wielded political influence in the thirteenth and fourteenth centuries.

Samantabhadra (Skt; Tib: *Küntu Sangpo*; *kun tu bzang po*; "All-Good"). The primordial dharmakaya buddha in the Nyingma lineage. He is depicted naked and blue in color.

samaya (Skt). Binding vow or commitment. Samaya is an essential principle in the vajrayana. One has samayas with one's teacher, one's yidam, the practice, and the sangha of fellow vajrayana practitioners. More generally, the tantric practitioner maintains a samaya with life and experience itself. During an abhisheka, one affirms one's samayas in connection with a particular practice.

samayasattva (Skt: "commitment being"). In vajrayana practice, the deity that one creates through one's own power of visualization, which expresses one's commitment with the teacher and the teachings. It is contrasted with the jnanasattva, or "wisdom being," which one invites to empower the samayasattva. In "The Sadhana of Mahamudra," the samayasattva and jnanasattva are indivisible from the very beginning. *See also* jnanasattva.

samsara (Skt; Tib: *khorwa*; *'khor ba*; "circling"). Cyclic existence; the repetitive cycle of births and deaths that arises from ignorance and is characterized by suffering and confusion. Samsara is generally contrasted with nirvana, which is the liberation from suffering. However, from the higher perspective of vajrayana, samsara and nirvana are understood to be inseparable.

sangha (Skt). The community of practitioners, companions on the path of dharma; as one of the three jewels, an object of refuge.

Sarvastivada (Skt: "doctrine that all exists"). An early Buddhist school that affirmed the existence of the dharmas of the three times—past, present, and future. Like all other Buddhists, Sarvastivadins considered everything empirical to be impermanent. However, they held that there are discrete entities, called "dharmas," that exist eternally and give rise to the conditioned phenomena of the world. They are renowned for their abhidharma texts, such as the *Abhidharmakosha* of Vasubandhu.

satori (Jpn). A Zen term for the experience of awakening.

Sengge Samdrup (Tib).The guardian deity of the cave of Padmasambhava. *See also* Taktsang Sengge Samdrup.

Shamarpa (Tib: *zhwa dmar pa*; "One [i.e., holder] of the Red Hat"). A principal lineage holder of the Karma Kagyü lineage, considered to be the mind manifestation of Amitabha, the buddha of limitless light.

Shambhala (Skt). A legendary kingdom, said to have been located in Central Asia, which represents the ideal of an enlightened society. It is closely associated with the *Kalachakra Tantra*, which Shakyamuni Buddha is said to have taught to the Shambhala King Dawa Sangpo. The Tibetan for Shambhala is *dejung* (*bde 'byung*), which means "source of happiness."

Shechen (Tib: *zhe chen*). One of the six main Nyingma monasteries in Tibet; the seat of Jamgön Kongtrül of Shechen, Chögyam Trungpa Rinpoche's root guru. The monastery was destroyed by the Chinese, but was rebuilt in 1985 by Dilgo Khyentse Rinpoche. In 1980, another Shechen Monastery was built in Nepal near the great stupa of Boudhanath.

shravakayana (Skt: "vehicle of hearers"). A stage of the hinayana path. It is the first yana of the nine-yana system, where the practitioner concentrates on meditation practice and understanding fundamental Buddhist teachings, such as the four noble truths. *See also* yana.

shunyata (Skt: "emptiness"). A completely open and unbounded clarity of mind, characterized by groundlessness and freedom from all concepts. In the second turning of the wheel of dharma, such as in the *Heart Sutra*, the Buddha taught that external phenomena and the self, or ego, have no inherent existence and are therefore "empty." However, emptiness does not refer to a void or blankness; rather, it is an openness inseparable from compassion and all other awakened qualities.

siddha (Skt: "accomplished one"). One who is accomplished or has powers over the phenomenal world. Best known are the group of eighty-four mahasiddhas (Skt: "great siddhas"), said to have lived in India from the eighth to the twelfth century. Chögyam Trungpa Rinpoche described siddhas as crazy-wisdom masters distinguished by their ability to transform unconventional circumstances into the path of realization. Chögyam Trungpa Rinpoche himself is often considered to be a mahasiddha.

siddhi (Skt: "accomplishment"). Yogic accomplishment, which is of two types: relative and ultimate. Each of the eight relative siddhis (called "supernormal powers" in the sadhana) involves a particular kind of mastery over the phenomenal world. Ultimate siddhi is enlightenment itself.

single circle (Tib: *tigle nyak chik*; *thig le nyag gcig*). A dzokchen term referring to original wakefulness. "Single" means that it is beyond any type of duality. "Circle" suggests that it is complete and all-encompassing.

skandha (Skt; Tib: *pungpo*; *phung po*; "heap"). Aggregate. The five skandhas are five aggregates or collections of phenomena that we take to be a self: form, feeling, perception, formation, and consciousness.

spiritual materialism. Using spirituality for personal gain or in order to bolster ego; a fundamental perversion of the spiritual path. One of Chögyam Trungpa's best-known books is entitled *Cutting Through Spiritual Materialism.*

suchness (Skt: *tathata*; Tib: *teshin-nyi; de bzhin nyid*). Things as they are; the true nature of reality.

supernormal powers. *See* siddhi.

Surmang (Tib: *zur mang*; "many cornered," referring to the irregularly shaped huts of the first monastics in the area). A monastery complex in Eastern Tibet, which has been the seat of the Trungpa lineage for twelve generations. It includes, among others, the monasteries of Namgyal Tse, Dütsi Tel, and Kyere Gompa. It traces its roots back 550 years to the mahasiddha Trungmasé.

Suzuki Roshi, Shunryu (1904–1971). A master of the Soto Zen lineage, who founded the San Francisco Zen Center and Tassajara Monastery. He was a close colleague and friend of Trungpa Rinpoche, who called him the father of the practice lineage in America. Chögyam Trungpa Rinpoche adopted a number of aesthetic and practice elements from the Zen tradition for the Shambhala community, based on his admiration of Roshi's style of presenting them.

svatantrika (Skt). One division of the madhyamaka ("middle way") school, the other of which is the prasangika. The madhyamaka school, established by Nagarjuna (ca. 150–250), is based on undercutting any attempt to establish a solid logical position. The key distinction between the two divisions is whether one works with assertions about the ultimate nature of reality (svatantrika) or refrains completely from doing so (prasangika).

Taktsang Sengge Samdrup (Tib: "Tiger's Den Wish-Fulfilling Lion"). The cave in Bhutan where Padmasambhava manifested as Dorje Trolö and where "The Sadhana of Mahamudra" was discovered by Chögyam Trungpa.

tantra (Skt; Tib: *gyu; rgyud;* "continuity"). A synonym of vajrayana. Tantra may refer both to the root texts of the vajrayana and to the systems of meditation they describe. *See also* vajrayana.

Tarthang Tülku (b. 1934). A Nyingma meditation master and scholar who came to North America in the 1970s, at about the same time that Chögyam Trungpa arrived in America. He and Chögyam Trungpa Rinpoche had a number of meetings and encounters in the United States.

tathagata (Skt; Tib: *teshin shekpa; de bzhin gshegs pa;* "thus come" or "thus gone"): Epithet of a buddha, one who has "gone to the other shore in this way." One who has traveled the path of the enlightened ones and reached the final goal of complete awakening.

terma (Tib: *gter ma;* "treasure"). Hidden teaching. Termas are the teachings hidden by Padmasambhava, either physically—for example, in rocks or lakes—or in the space of mind. They are meant to be revealed later at an auspicious time by tertöns, or treasure revealers. "The Sadhana of Mahamudra" is a terma teaching, the first terma discovered by Chögyam Trungpa after he left Tibet. In Western terms, terma teachings, especially mind terma, might be considered akin to prophecy. *See also* tertön *and* terma mark.

terma mark (Tib: *tertsek*; *gter tshegs*). A symbol (⸝) placed at the end of a word or line of text in order to indicate that it comes from a terma.

tertön (Tib: *gter ston*; "treasure revealer"). A revealer of terma teachings. Tertöns are regarded as incarnations of the chief disciples of Padmasambhava, who in their subsequent lives are able to reveal teachings hidden by him. Chögyam Trungpa was a tertön, discovering his first terma at the age of nine in Tibet. He revealed several cycles of terma before he left Tibet. Although many of these were lost, some were preserved and are now being transmitted to students in the West. "The Sadhana of Mahamudra" was the first terma discovered by Trungpa Rinpoche after his escape from Tibet. *See also* terma.

three lords of materialism (Tib: *lalo sum*; *kla klo gsum*; "three barbarians"). Three ways of solidifying and securing experience by means of body, speech, and mind. The lord of form, or body, refers to the neurotic pursuit of physical comfort, security, and pleasure. The lord of speech refers to the use of intellect in relating to the world; concepts are used as tools to solidify our world and ourselves. The lord of mind refers to using spiritual and psychological disciplines in order to maintain a sense of self.

three times (Tib: *tüsum*; *dus gsum*). The past, the present, and the future.

Tilopa (988–1069). A great Indian siddha and forefather of the Kagyü lineage. Tilopa unified various tantric systems and transmitted them to his student Naropa. He is said to have received the highest teachings of mahamudra directly from the dharmakaya buddha Vajradhara.

torma (Tib: *gtor ma*; Skt: *bali*). A sculpted form made from barley flour and molded butter, which may be used as an offering or as a representation of deities. In the sadhana, it refers to offering "all that arises within—wandering thoughts, carelessness and all that is subject to ignorance."

trikaya (Skt; Tib: *kusum*; *sku gsum*; "three bodies"). The three bodies of a buddha: dharmakaya, sambhogakaya, and nirmanakaya. The dharmakaya is the mind of a buddha, which is enlightenment itself. The sambhogakaya is the speech of a buddha, represented iconographically in the form of the five buddhas and the yidams. The nirmanakaya is the physical form of a buddha.

Trungmasé (a.k.a. Lodrö Rinchen). A great siddha, he was a student of Karmapa Teshin Shekpa (1384–1415); the teacher of Künga Gyaltsen, the first Trungpa; and the founder of Surmang Monastery. For further information, consult *The Mishap Lineage: Transforming Confusion into Wisdom* (Boston: Shambhala Publications, 2009).

Tsurphu (pronounced "Tsur-pu"). The principal monastery of the Karma Kagyü lineage in Tibet, traditionally the main seat of the Karmapas, founded by Tüsum Khyenpa in 1159.

Tsurphupa. *See* Tüsum Khyenpa.

tülku (Tib: *sprul sku*; "emanation body"). A person who is recognized as the reincarnation of a previously deceased and usually renowned teacher. Also a reference to the nirmanakaya, one of the three kayas, or bodies of enlightenment, in the Buddhist teachings.

Tüsölma. One of the mahakalis described in the charnel ground in the sadhana. The creator of illness as well as its cure, she is dark blue and rides on a donkey with a white star. She holds a mirror in the right hand and a phurba in the left. *See also* mahakali and the "Original Notes to the Sadhana" in *The Sadhana of Mahamudra: Resources for Study*.

Tüsum Khyenpa (Tib: "knower of the three times"; 1110–1193). The first Karmapa, one of the principal students of Gampopa, who founded the Kagyü monastery of Tsurphu in 1159. As depicted in the sadhana, he resides in the forehead center of Karma Pakshi as the "unchanging form of Vairochana . . . the dharmaraja of the three worlds." In the sadhana, he is also referred to as Tsurphupa, or "the one from Tsurphu."

Ugyen (Tib; Skt: *Uddiyana*). Name of the birthplace of Padmakara, which is said to be located in the area between Afghanistan and Kashmir. The name may also refer to Padmakara himself.

universal unconscious / universal ground of everything. *See* alaya.

upayoga (Skt). One of the tantric yanas. *See also* yana.

Vairochana (Skt: "radiant"). The sambhogakaya buddha of the buddha family, white in color, associated with the wisdom of dharmadhatu. In the sadhana, Vairochana is understood to be the essential nature of Tüsum Khyenpa, the first Karmapa, who abides in the forehead center of Dorje Trolö Karma Pakshi.

vajra (Skt; Tib: *dorje*; *rdo rjee*, "adamantine," "indestructible," "diamondlike"). In Hindu mythology, the vajra is Indra's thunderbolt, a magical weapon that can destroy anything but cannot itself be destroyed. In Buddhism, it is a quality of tantric realization and of the true nature of reality, or emptiness. Vajra also refers to a ritual scepter used in tantric practice. In the mandala of the five buddha families, vajra is the family of pristine clarity, associated with the east, the buddha Akshobhya or Vajrasattva, the klesha of anger, and mirrorlike wisdom.

vajra master (Skt: *vajracharya*; Tib: *dorje loppön*). A tantric teacher; one who is accomplished in the vajrayana teachings and is capable of transmitting them to others. In general, Chögyam Trungpa Rinpoche emphasized the paramount importance of the relationship between vajra master and student for entering and treading the vajrayana path. In this book, he equates the vajra master with the guru, the teacher who introduces the student to reality.

vajracharya. *See* vajra master.

Vajrakilaya (Skt; Tib: *dorje phurba*; *rdo rje phur ba*). One of the principal yidams of the Nyingma tradition, belonging to the karma family. His form is dark blue or black and very wrathful. He wields a three-bladed kila, or phurba, which penetrates and destroys the kleshas with a single blow.

Vajrasattva (Skt: "vajra being"). A buddha of the vajra family, Vajrasattva is depicted as white and is associated with purification. Sometimes he is considered a sambhoga-kaya buddha who embodies all the five buddha families. Meditation on the form of Vajrasattva and the recitation of his hundred-syllable mantra is one of the four extraordinary preliminaries practices (Tib: *ngöndro*) of vajrayana.

vajrayana (Skt: "indestructible vehicle"). The highest of the three yanas in the Tibetan Buddhist tradition; also referred to as tantra, tantrayana, mantrayana, and secret mantra. Although based on the discipline of hinayana and the view and motivation of mahayana, vajrayana excels both by virtue of its many upayas, or skillful means, for actualizing realization. *See also* yana.

Vedantic. Pertaining to Vedanta, a major Hindu philosophy based on the Upanishads, which deals with the doctrine of the identity of brahman (ultimate reality) and atman (the true self).

vidyadhara (Skt; Tib: *rigdzin*; *rig 'dzin*; "knowledge holder"). An accomplished tantric practitioner, usually a lineage holder. An honorific title for Chögyam Trungpa, who in the latter years of his teaching was referred to as "the Vidyadhara." In earlier years, he was referred to as "the Vajracharya," or vajra master.

yana (Skt; Tib: *thekpa*; *theg pa*). Vehicle or way; what carries the practitioner on the path to liberation. In the general Tibetan Buddhist tradition, there are three principal yanas: (1) hinayana, which includes shravakayana and pratyekabuddhayana, (2) mahayana, also known as bodhisattvayana, and (3) vajrayana. In the Sarma tradition (the Kagyü, Geluk, and Sakya lineages), vajrayana is divided into four tantric yanas: kriya, upa (or charya), yoga, and anuttara. Anuttara itself has three further divisions: father tantra, mother tantra, and nondual tantra. In the Nyingma tradition, vajrayana is divided into six tantric yanas: kriya, upa, yoga, mahayoga, anu, and ati. Sometimes it is said that the last three yanas of the Nyingma tradition correspond to the anuttara in the Sarma tradition. Chögyam Trungpa Rinpoche discusses the six tantric yanas as a progression in one's practice and realization, ati being the pinnacle of realization. See also his description of the yanas in the discussion at the end of chapter 2, under the heading "Mahamudra and ati in the nine yanas."

yeshe (Tib). *See* jnana.

yeshe chölwa. *See* crazy wisdom.

yeshe phowa (Tib: *ye shes 'pho ba*; prounounced "po-wa"). Transference of wisdom. Adhishthana, or blessings, can be transmitted from teacher to student only when there is a complete openness between them. Yeshe phowa is mind transmission, or the merging of the minds of the teacher and the disciple, which can only occur as a result of the student's devotion and complete surrender.

yidam (Tib: *yi dam*). In the vajrayana, one's personal meditation deity, which represents one's own awakened nature. In practice, one visualizes the deity, repeats its mantra, and identifies completely with its wisdom. The term *yidam* is said to derive from *yikyi tamtsik*, "samaya of mind," which refers to binding one's mind to wisdom. Dorje Trolö Karma Pakshi is the principal yidam in "The Sadhana of Mahamudra."

yoga (Skt: "yoke," "union"). In the Buddhist tantric tradition, yoga is a means of synchronizing body and mind to discover reality or truth. Here, it is synonymous with the practices and disciplines of the tantric yanas. Yogayana is one of the nine tantric yanas. *See also* yana.

Yungtön Dorje Pel (b. 1284). Nyingma master who brought together the traditions of the Kagyü and Nyingma. He was a student of Karmapa Rangjung Dorje.

zabuton (Jpn). A flat, rectangular cushion used for meditation in the Zen tradition.

zafu (Jpn). A round cushion used for meditation in the Zen tradition.

Zen (Jpn; Chinese: *Chan*; Skt: *dhyana*; "meditation"). A school of mahayana Buddhism which stresses the prime importance of the enlightenment experience. Zen teaches the practice of zazen, sitting meditation, as the shortest way to awakening. Zen was introduced to North America in the twentieth century. Shunryu Suzuki Roshi was an important pioneer in bringing Zen to America. Chögyam Trungpa admired the Zen tradition greatly, and a book of his teachings on the relationship between tantra and Zen, is published as *The Teacup and the Skullcup: Where Zen and Tantra Meet. See also* Suzuki Roshi, Shunryu.

About Chögyam Trungpa Rinpoche

Born in Kham, East Tibet, in 1940, Chögyam Trungpa Rinpoche was discovered at the age of fourteen months to be the eleventh incarnation of the Trungpa tülku. From the time of his discovery he was raised to become the abbot of the Surmang Monasteries in Eastern Tibet. He was fully ordained by the sixteenth Gyalwa Karmapa, head of the Kagyü lineage, and received intensive training under Rölpe Dorje, a Kagyü master, and Karma Tendzin, a disciple of the tenth Trungpa tülku.

When Rinpoche was nine years old, Jamgön Kongtrül of Shechen was invited to visit the Surmang Monasteries. Upon meeting Jamgön Kongtrül, Rinpoche recognized him immediately as his meditation teacher and experienced an overwhelming urge to be with him. He often spoke of Jamgön Kongtrül as his "root guru." From the first time Trunpga Rinpoche met Kongtrül Rinpoche, he alternated the study of philosophy with Khenpo Gangshar and meditation with Jamgön Kongtrül, spending extensive periods of time at the Shechen Monastery, finally completing the study and practice of the nine yanas, or vehicles, on the Buddhist path, as well as receiving initiations into the highest of them. Part of his study was the 101 volumes of the works of Jamgön Kongtrül the Great, which broadened his understanding to include all the schools of Buddhism in Tibet. In his late teens, Rinpoche completed his training as a meditation teacher under Jamgön Kongtrül of Shechen and received the Khenpo degree (equivalent of Doctor of Divinity in the West).

Shortly afterward, when the Chinese Communists took control much more aggressively in Tibet, Rinpoche found himself cut off from his gurus. At this point, the situation forced him to act independently, relying upon the teachings of his gurus rather than their personal guidance. Realizing that Buddhism and his personal safety were severely threatened in his country, he fled to India. There he served by appointment of His Holiness the Dalai Lama as spiritual advisor to the Young Lamas' Home School founded by Freda Bedi.

After four years of living in India and experiencing its culture, he accepted a scholarship from the Spalding Trust which allowed him to pursue studies at St. Antony's College at Oxford University in England. At Oxford he studied philosophy, psychology, politics, economics, and Western history, literature, and culture. He also pursued his study of the English language while in Oxford, and privately studied Ikebana and Japanese calligraphy. While at Oxford, he gave lectures at the Buddhist Society in London and at other locations. After five years of living and studying in Oxford, he founded the Samye Ling meditation center in Scotland, along with his close companion Akong Tulku. At Samye Ling he began to connect with many Western dharma students and also continued to travel and teach within England. During his years in England and Scotland, he wrote his first two books in English: his autobiography, *Born in Tibet*, and a collection of talks entitled *Meditation in Action*. This was the first title ever published by Shambhala Publications, who acquired the rights for the US edition.

In 1968, Chögyam Trungpa returned for the first time to Asia since his departure for England six years before. It was during this trip that he uncovered "The Sadhana of Mahamudra" while practicing in retreat in Bhutan. After this retreat, his teaching style changed dramatically, and he became a lay teacher and married Diana Judith Mukpo. In May 1970, in response to increased interest in North America in his teachings, Chögyam Trungpa arrived in the United States, after a brief stay in Canada. He opened the Tail of the Tiger Meditation Center in Vermont (later renamed Karmê Chöling) and founded the Karma Dzong Meditation Center (now known as the Shambhala Center) in Boulder, Colorado. The establishment of the Rocky Mountain Dharma Center (now renamed Drala Mountain Center), a rural retreat center, followed shortly thereafter. Naropa Institute, the first Buddhist-inspired school of its kind in North America (now the fully accredited Naropa University), opened in the summer of 1974. Around that same time he founded Vajradhatu, the international association of his meditation centers, which has since become Shambhala International.

He established many meditation centers in North America and Europe in the years that followed, and in 1977, Rinpoche introduced the Shambhala Training program. Until his death in 1987, he continued to explore, master, and teach a wide variety of disciplines from both Eastern and Western traditions. "The Sadhana of Mahamudra" was an important first jewel in the crown of his teachings and is practiced today by students throughout the world.

NOTES

INTRODUCTION BY BARRY CAMPBELL BOYCE

1. The material in this and the next two paragraphs first appeared in very similar form in "Ocean of Dharma," an article by Barry Boyce for the commemoration of the twenty-fifth anniversary of the parinirvana of Trungpa Rinpoche in the January 2012 issue of the *Shambhala Sun*.
2. See, for example, Chögyam Trungpa, *Shambhala: The Sacred Path of the Warrior* (Boston: Shambhala, 1984), 154.
3. Vajradhatu refers to the name Trungpa Rinpoche gave to his organization of meditation centers. Shambhala became one of the primary terms describing his work after he introduced Shambhala Training in the late 1970s.
4. From the Nalanda Translation Committee annual newsletter, 2012.

EDITOR'S INTRODUCTION BY CAROLYN ROSE GIMIAN

1. *Collected Kalapa Assemblies: 1978–1984* (Halifax: Vajradhatu, 2006), 274.
2. *Great Eastern Sun: The Wisdom of Shambhala* (Boston: Shambhala, 2001), 35.
3. Ashi Kesang Choden Wangchuck was the queen of Bhutan when she invited Chögyam Trungpa to Bhutan. She is now the queen grandmother.
4. *Crazy Wisdom* (Boston: Shambhala, 2001), 177.
5. Lightly edited from the verbatim transcript in the Chögyam Trungpa Digital Library "Community Talk: Introduction to the Sadhana of Mahamudra," from February 18, 1975. https://cti.aviaryplatform.com/collections/2233/collection _resources/104795.
6. See pp. 26–27.
7. See p. 156.
8. OG is defined by dictionary.com as "a person or thing that is respected as genuine and classic (often used attributively)." One example in the sources I accessed mentioned Julia Child as the OG of gourmet American cuisine. https://www .dictionary.com/browse/og. Accessed Feb 26, 2024.
9. Some of those who have played a major role in translating, publishing, and propagating the sadhana and these teachings have contributed a foreword,

introduction, or comments in the back matter of this book. Please also see the editor's afterword and acknowledgments at the back for further information.

1. Historical Commentary: Part One

1. Although Chögyam Trungpa Rinpoche was a tertön, at the time that he gave the two seminars in this book, he described himself as the author of the sadhana. The sadhana was later acknowledged to be a terma text. For more on this, see the editor's introduction. See also the glossary entries for *terma* and *tertön*.
2. These were practice sessions of other sadhanas, not of "The Sadhana of Mahamudra."

2. Devotion and Crazy Wisdom

1. The next three yanas, sometimes called the lower tantras, are *kriyayoga, upayoga,* and *yogayana.*
2. For a further explanation of these yanas, see the glossary entry for *yana.*

3. The Mandala of the Siddhas

1. The sadhana now contains the current translation of the "Four Dharmas of Gampopa," rather than Chögyam Trungpa Rinpoche's original translation, which he made shortly after discovering the terma text in 1968. At his own insistence, the Nalanda Translation Committee revised the translation of the Four Dharmas in 1979, publishing the new version for the first time in 1980. The original translation is as follows:
   Grant your blessings so that my mind may follow the dharma;
   Grant your blessings so that my practice may win success on the path;
   Grant your blessings so that, following the path, confusion may be clarified;
   Grant your blessings so that confusion may be transformed into wisdom.
2. The discussion of abhisheka in this chapter is about the abhisheka section of the original sadhana. Following Chögyam Trungpa Rinpoche's death, a separate abhisheka for the sadhana was composed by His Holiness Dilgo Khyentse Rinpoche at the request of Sakyong Mipham Rinpoche. For more information about this abhisheka, see "Afterword from the Nalanda Translation Committee," pp. 163–67.
3. Chögyam Trungpa Rinpoche discusses all eight aspects of Padmasambhava in *Crazy Wisdom* (Boston: Shambhala, 1991).
4. Teachings discovered in the way Chögyam Trungpa Rinpoche describes the process in this section are called terma teachings. See the glossary entries for *terma* and *tertön.*
5. A time capsule containing the Vidyadhara's terma and his vast treasury of precious teachings was completed by Steve Roth in 2012, the Year of the Water

Dragon, and concealed within the Great Stupa of Dharmakaya Which Liberates Upon Seeing. In 1974 His Holiness the Sixteenth Gyalwa Karmapa chose and blessed this site for a future stupa to be built. It was later built to hold a body relic of Chögyam Trungpa, who died in 1987. The monument is located at Drala Mountain Center in Colorado, USA. In many Buddhist traditions it is common to build a stupa to honor a respected teacher after their death. Due to the Vidyadhara's encouragement in 1975, decades later this capsule and its contents were constructed from leading-edge technology, designed to last five thousand years.

6. See "Lord Gampopa's Song of Response to the Three Men of Kham" in *The Rain of Wisdom* (Boston: Shambhala, 1980), pp. 275–82. This is the English translation of the *Kagyü Gurtso*.

7. Chögyam Trungpa Rinpoche refers to the Sixteenth Karmapa, who passed away in 1981. He was the head of the Kagyü lineage at the time of the talk.

8. This refers, of course, to the destruction of many Buddhist texts, religious items, and entire monasteries during the Chinese takeover of Tibet.

4. Joining Insight and Devotion in the Rimé Tradition

1. Originally, this line was "the spontaneously-existing rishi."

2. Earlier edits of this material had "falutin" instead of "floating." To this editor's ears, it sounds more like "floating," although that is slightly more eccentric.

3. The questioner here is referring to an earlier version of the sadhana, in which it says that Karma Pakshi exists independent of people's belief. In the current edition of the sadhana, this line reads: "To the boundless rainbow body of wisdom, Padmakara Karma Pakshi, / The heruka who, untouched by concepts, pervades all existence."

5. The Guru Principle

1. In order to wake us up.

2. I.e., the teacher.

6. Crazy Wisdom

1. Literally, "with the charge."

2. For discussion of the blue pancake, see "Maha Ati" in *Journey without Goal: The Tantric Wisdom of the Buddha* (Boston: Shambhala, 1981), especially pp. 136–38.

3. At the time of this talk, the Vajradhatu Buddhist community in Boulder, Colorado, was fundraising to buy the building in which the talks in this seminar were being held. In the end, this plan was unsuccessful.

4. The questioner is Chinese.

5. At the time of the talk, the Sixteenth Karmapa had recently visited the West for

the first time. His successor, Karmapa Ogyen Trinley Dorje, is currently the head of the Karma Kagyü lineage.

7. THE CHARNEL GROUND

1. Presumably this is related to Christ's saying, in reference to his disciple Peter: "On this rock I will build my church." It is believed that Saint Peter's Basilica is actually built above the tomb of Peter.

8. THE CRAZY-WISDOM BODY OF ALL THE BUDDHAS

1. In an earlier chapter it was explained that Karma Pakshi and Padmasambhava in his aspect of Dorje Trolö are both embodied in the central figure of the sadhana.

9. SURRENDERING

1. For further information on the translation of the "Four Dharmas of Gampopa," see note 1 from chapter 3.

10. HISTORICAL COMMENTARY: PART TWO

1. A discussion of the history of the sadhana was also the starting point of this book. Although the two talks were given only a few months apart, Trungpa Rinpoche's characterization of his retreat at Taktsang has a different emphasis in the second talk; even some of the details are different and seem contradictory. Taken together, the talks provide a rich background for our understanding of the sadhana.

2. In *Born in Tibet*, Chögyam Trungpa Rinpoche says that he traveled from Bombay to Tilbury aboard the P & O line. P & O is an abbreviation for the Peninsular and Oriental Steam Navigation Company, which was established in England in the nineteenth century.

AFTERWORD FROM THE NALANDA TRANSLATION COMMITTEE

1. *Vidyadhara* is an honorific Sanskrit title that means "wisdom holder" and is given to highly realized teachers in the Tibetan Buddhist tradition.

2. *The Collected Works of Chögyam Trungpa* (Boston: Shambhala, 2003), 1:263–64; originally published in *Born in Tibet* (Boston: Shambhala, 2000), 253–54.

3. See appendix, "Comments on the Circumstances Surrounding the Discovery of 'The Sadhana of Mahamudra.'"

4. *Vajracharya* was an earlier title held by Chögyam Trungpa. It means "vajra master."

5. For more information about the meaning of terma and terma revealers, see the glossary.
6. For more information about the meaning of the terma mark, see the glossary.
7. Now published in *The Sadhana of Mahamudra: Resources for Study* (Halifax: Vajravairochana Translation Committee, 2012).

EDITOR'S AFTERWORD AND ACKNOWLEDGMENTS

1. Vajradhatu Publications was the publishing house established within the Vajradhatu Editorial Department, for the presentation of internal publications of interest to the Vajradhatu community, renamed Shambhala International after Chögyam Trungpa's death. Many of these publications were available to the public as well, but they had very limited distribution.

COMMENTS ON THE CIRCUMSTANCES SURROUNDING THE DISCOVERY OF "THE SADHANA OF MAHAMUDRA"

1. It was during the 1968 visit to Asia that Rinpoche met Thomas Merton, shortly before Merton's untimely death.
2. Karma Pakshi (1203–1282) was the second Karmapa. He was invited to China by Prince Kublai Khan and by his rival and older brother, Mongka Khan. When His Holiness the Sixteenth Karmapa made his second visit to the United States in 1976, Trungpa Rinpoche asked him to perform the Karma Pakshi abhisheka as a blessing for all of Rinpoche's students, which he did.
3. *Delek* is a Tibetan word that means "auspicious happiness." Chögyam Trungpa used it to refer to creating a system of governance that fosters peace and good communication within the meditation centers he established. The discussion here is of the genesis of the idea of the delek system in 1968. Trungpa Rinpoche did not actually introduce deleks until 1981. At that time, he suggested that people in the Buddhist communities he worked with should organize themselves into deleks, or groups, consisting of about twenty or thirty families, based on the neighborhoods in which they lived. Each neighborhood or small group was a delek and its members, the delekpas. Each delek would elect a leader, the dekyong—the "protector of happiness"—by a process of consensus for which Rinpoche coined the phrase "spontaneous insight." The dekyongs were then organized into the Dekyong Council, which would meet and make decisions affecting their deleks and make recommendations to the administration of Vajradhatu, the international organization he founded, about larger issues.

INDEX

Ekajati with Samantabhadra above her head. Ekajati is a protectress of the dharma and a guide to the masters of tantric teachings. She is a destroyer of those who pervert the true meaning of the dharma. Samantabhadra is the primordial buddha who represents the final state of wakefulness. *Drawing by Glen Eddy.*